Synthi[...]

I d[...]

Thank you for your[...]
with the adaptation
to the theatre!

DRIVING TO THE
END OF THE
WORLD

By Mark McMahon

Edited by Eric Osborn

Best
Wishes,

PRAISE FOR DRIVING TO THE END OF THE WORLD

"The author repeatedly asks himself the question, why? As in, why are we here? What is the meaning of life? After several months and several thousand miles, he is able to answer that question. Moreover, he inspires the question, why not? Why not live an adventure of our own? Why not live our dreams? Why not live? For those of us without motivation enough to get off the couch and change the watering schedule for our lawns, McMahon gives us hope. An honestly remarkable undertaking."

– Brent Kenton Jordan, Author of, *The Chivalry Code: Discussions on Becoming a Man in a Modern World*

"Mark McMahon is a true adventurer and a magnificent raconteur. Living life to the fullest and immersing himself where many fear to tread, Mark generously shares with his readers tales of peripatetic tribulation and travail told with a tremendous sense of humility, humanity and humor."

– Christopher Baker, Author of *Cuba Classics: A Celebration of Vintage American Automobiles*, *Moon Handbook: Cuba* and *Moon Handbook: Costa Rica*

"McMAHON'S REAL LIFE TALE OF LATIN AMERICAN ADVENTURE HAS SOMETHING FOR EVERYONE... politics, sex, culture clashes, and crime. He even explores eco-tourism! Like a page-turning novel, I wanted to know what would happen next!"

– Larry Fahn, Sierra Club Immediate Past President

"Thanks a lot Mark, you ruined my day. I was up until 6 AM reading your blasted book!"

– Hal Robb, Inventor and International Businessman

"An extraordinary book about a courageous adventure. The wide breadth of experiences, shared so openly, keeps you wondering what will happen next."

– Betty Counseller, Acclaimed Artist and Teacher

Also by
Mark McMahon

The Portable Professional
visit www.portableprofessional.com

On the Streets and Between the Sheets
A novel Coming Soon

Dedication

I dedicate this book to two people who have been an inspiration to me
in life and beyond:

To my father,
William Joseph McMahon,
June 3, 1929- July 5,1998

"Our parents hold us on their shoulders so that we can see into the future.
We should not look down on them for their lack of vision."
– West African Proverb

To my brother-in-law,
Kevin Vincent Teed
May 16,1964 - December 31, 2001

Your fearless, soaring spirit lives on inside me.

Thank you both.

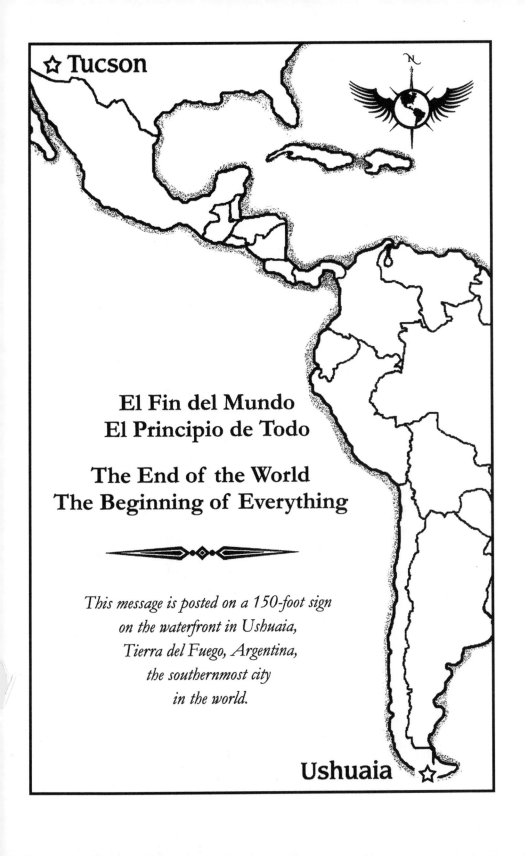

☆ Tucson

El Fin del Mundo
El Principio de Todo

The End of the World
The Beginning of Everything

*This message is posted on a 150-foot sign
on the waterfront in Ushuaia,
Tierra del Fuego, Argentina,
the southernmost city
in the world.*

Ushuaia ☆

First Printing, Feburary 2007

Published by
Live Your Adventure Publishing
Tucson, Arizona
LYAPublishing.com

ISBN 978-09771478-1-6

Acknowledgements

First and foremost I want to thank my editor, Eric Osborn,
for his many roles outside the scope of editing. Namely babysitter,
Professor of English and co-conspirator. Could not have done it
without you-Thanks Dude!
Thanks are also in order for Barbara Counseller, Kelli Lynn Hann
and her mom, Ducky in Buenos Aires, plus Robert Mac and Dr. Farb,
my comedy and cosmic consultants respectively. Thanks guys!

INTRODUCTION

I'm gonna die!

That realization poured into me like rainfall into a reservoir. Something inside me clicked, and the dam burst. That was the beginning of everything. I knew I had to do something about MY LIFE! I wasn't having any fun. I needed a sabbatical. I needed to recharge my batteries and re-focus.

The marketing company I had started was faltering. The original promise it showed had dimmed. There was no joy in Mudville or in my dental practice for that matter. My live-in girlfriend had just packed her bags and moved home to Texas. Basically, life sucked.

The click inside of me was the seed of a commitment being planted; a commitment to take six months off and do what I loved— traveling and taking pictures. I wanted an adventure. I decided to drive from my home in Tucson, Arizona to the southernmost tip of South America. Come Hell or high water, I was going. I committed myself to a date: November 1st, 1999— a date that I will always remember. That commitment led to a shift to living a life beyond my dreams.

> "Until one is committed there is hesitancy, the chance to draw back, always ineffectiveness. Concerning all acts of initiative (and creation), there is one elementary truth, the ignorance of which kills countless ideas and splendid plans: that the moment one definitely commits oneself, then Providence moves too. All sorts of things occur to help one that would never otherwise have occurred. A whole stream of events issues from the decision, raising in one's favor all manner of unforeseen incidents and meetings and material assistance, which no man could have dreamt would come his way.
>
> I have learned a deep respect for one of Goethe's couplets:
>
> 'Whatever you can do, or dream you can, begin it. Boldness has genius, power, and magic in it.'"
>
> From *The Scottish Himalayan Expedition*
> W. H. Murray

My father had passed away just a few weeks earlier and my own mortality had really sunk in. My dad had a good life. He raised an amazing family of seven— four boys and three girls. He pursued his passion for the great outdoors. His dental practice in Tucson spanned an incredible 36 years. That's a lotta teeth. But fate played a cruel joke on my Dad at the end of his career.

I had followed my father's footsteps into dentistry. The molar doesn't fall far from the jaw. I could have joined his practice right out of school. Although my father's partner had planned his retirement around my graduation, I chose another path and decided to stay in the San Francisco Bay Area, where I had studied, to try to make it on my own.

My father and I had never been particularly close. There was always an unspoken competition between us, at least on my part. We had our professional relationship. As dentists we always had something to talk about, albeit superficial, but we did not have the emotional bond that he had with some of my other siblings.

I went my own way, did my own thing, for better or for worse. In his eyes, mostly for worse. Some ten years into my career, he told me, in no uncertain terms, what he thought of my accomplishments. I was sitting across from him in his living room, asking if I could borrow some money to help build my business. He said, "Mark, you're a failure." It hit me like a shotgun blast to my gut. It was a hurtful statement but we both survived that hurdle in our relationship and the wound healed.

At the time he didn't fully appreciate the direction I'd taken with my career. I was focused on cosmetic dentistry and finding ways to market it. A traditional general dental practice simply was not my cup of tea. Perhaps he thought what was good enough for him should have been good enough for me.

Years later circumstances were ripe for me to return to Tucson, purchase the old man's practice, and send him off into his golden years. However, golden they were not. To commemorate his retirement, along with me taking over the practice, we decided to take a vacation together. It was to be a bike tour of Ireland; a combination of two of my father's great loves. That's when the twist of fate turned ever so sharply. In London, on our way to the Emerald Isle, my father fell ill. Some gastrointestinal symptoms that had been misdiagnosed a week earlier returned with a vengeance. British doctors found colon cancer and my father went under the knife in London.

In the very first week of his retirement came the diagnosis of a disease that eventually took his life. The initial treatments were successful at keeping the cancer at bay for several years. This allowed him the gift of time with his family. The quality of the time was heightened light-years beyond our previous emotional threshold.

He also got some quality time on his bike, urgently completing the 500-mile RAGBRAI, the Des Moines Register Annual Great Bicycle Ride Across Iowa, his home state. It had been a goal of his for many years. He completed the event while still recuperating from two surgeries and chemotherapy. "Now or never" took on real significance for him.

For a short time, I had the father I always wanted. He took a genuine interest in my professional pursuits and even told me that I was smarter than those other dentists for my endeavors in cosmetic dentistry and for developing a successful marketing company. It was a hundred and eighty degrees from the "failure" I had been years prior. He also became interested in my spiritual pursuits like personal-growth seminars and meditation. It was a bittersweet time. As my relationship with him grew stronger, his body grew weaker.

The cancer returned and took him four years after the original diagnosis. I still remember the exact stretch of road on Speedway Boulevard in Tucson, early in the evening, heading toward my home, when my own mortality became so very real. I'm gonna die!

That's when I committed myself to the November 1st departure date. I had built up my father's practice by adding new services and bringing on an associate dentist. I told the associate that if he wanted to stay with the office he had to buy a portion of the practice. I wanted to leave with the confidence that he would take care of my practice during my six-month absence. I told him that he could buy a third interest of the business. He said he wanted to buy half. I said no, I didn't want a full partner. Without really thinking I blurted, "You can buy a third or you can buy the whole thing." Much to my surprise, he said he wanted to buy all of it! This was something I had not really considered.

My newly formed dental marketing company had attracted some attention within the profession. People offered to buy the assets of my young company. Specifically, a marketing videotape I had created and the company name, SmileWorks™, which I had wisely trademarked. Keep in mind that this was 1999, the craziest of the dot com craze.

One thing led to another, or shall I say, "Providence moved," and I ended up selling all three items: my dental practice, the videotape, and the trademark. All three different deals were closed and signed on the same day, November 1, 1999 (cue dramatic music here: da da da dahhhhh…).

Just like that, I had earned some cash and my freedom. Before long I was on the road and south of the border. I created a web site to document my journey. Six months turned into four years and a new way of life for me! I pursued my primary passion for photography and nurtured a new one for writing. I wrote and photographed my way through 15 different countries. I posted over 120 journal entries and 1,000 photographs online. It all started with a commitment!

****

The reason I set up a web site with journal entries in the first place was to stay connected to my family and friends. In the writing of this book I did not want to lose the immediacy of the original journal. To achieve this and solve the grammatical dilemma of what tense to use, I have chosen to use some of the actual entries from my web site, inserted directly into the text of the book. I have inserted them "as is" from the web site with as little editing as I could (my striving for immediacy is perhaps but a thin veil for my laziness).

Romantic descriptions have been included here that are not in the online version. I did not include them previously out of respect for the privacy of those involved. Herein I have changed names and identifiable details where needed. I even thought about changing my own name, but thought that it might interrupt the flow if some guy named Fred suddenly showed up in an intimate moment.

My Internet connection grew as my trip progressed. The group of friends and family I started out with expanded and took on a life of its own. I made wonderful friends from all over the world, many of whom I still have not met face-to-face. This is the story of my trip.

Enjoy the adventure!

I'm wanna live!
Author's note: If you didn't read the intro, now would be a good time to do that.

My newfound realization of my own mortality compelled me to take action. At the same time, five words kept ringing through my head, "Why am I doing this?" Even though I was committed to this adventure, I couldn't help but ponder that question in this journal entry:

Location: Tucson, Arizona U.S.A.

Subject: Why Am I Doing This?

Because I'm having a midlife crisis? Because I can? To take pictures? Write a book? Meet people? Learn Spanish? Have fun? Adventure? Yes, adventure! Perhaps all of the above but mostly the adventure. Not knowing exactly where I will be going and for how long. Having a flexible schedule and a fairly open agenda. To explore externally with my lens and internally with my pen.

"I know that something good is gonna happen...just saying it can even make it happen."

Kate Bush

I don't know exactly what will come out of the trip. I'm at a point in my life that I'm able to do this. I have lots of ideas about the direction of my life but it's not exactly clear. THAT'S THE ADVENTURE.

Yes, adventure. I wanted an adventure, not just another trip or extended vacation. I wanted to accomplish something. A mission. My own personal Mt. Everest! Something that offered a real challenge and would push me past my comfort zone.

But why? Why do I need my own Mt. Everest? Why do people climb mountains? The stock answer of course, is because they are there. But not everyone wants to climb mountains. A common goal of world-class mountain climbers is to scale the highest peak on every continent. My friend and high school classmate, Jim Malusa, is an avid cyclist and something of an underachiever. He actually completed his goal of bicycling across the lowest point on each continent. He sets his goals low, and achieves them! He reached his final continental low point, riding from his home in Tucson to Death Valley California, several hundred feet below sea level. Again, you gotta ask "Why?" But you might as well ask why the chicken crossed the road.

An acquaintance of mine, Dave Horning, is another gotta-ask-why-guy who lives in the San Francisco Bay Area. His aspirations and accomplishments started local and then went global. Most of us are content to drive across a bridge. Not Dave, he prefers swimming under it. He started with the Golden Gate Bridge then worked his way to other bridges on the San Francisco Bay. Then, he went international. On the fiftieth birthday of the Golden Gate Bridge, he swam under the London Bridge, the Brooklyn Bridge and the Golden Gate Bridge – all in the same day! If he has a problem in life, he'll swim under that bridge when he comes to it.

You can ask, what is the purpose of swimming under bridges or bicycling the low points? Or, for that matter, why would someone drive to the end of the world? I guess I had many justifications for my own particular adventure, but I think it all got back to "I don't know." When it came down to it, the adventure chose me. The way a grizzly bear chooses a salmon, it just grabbed me.

There were also some logical justifications for the trip. I wanted to learn Spanish. I had studied it in high school and college and dabbled with it in Mexico, but now I really wanted to learn it. The trip would also be an excellent opportunity to explore indigenous cultures and pursue my passion for photography.

I had been inspired in this regard on previous visits to Indonesia and Thailand. On a trek into the hills off Chang Rai, in Northern Thailand, I had an intense "*National Geographic* moment."

The four-day trek into the wilderness was supposed to lead to an encounter with a nomadic tribe. Our guide could not promise we would make contact, but we did. It was a group of five, with two adults and three children. It was unclear how or if they were all related. An older man smiled shyly as he prepared dinner over an open fire, cooking strips of some kind of meat inside a large section of bamboo. Our guide made small talk with the group while my girlfriend combed the kids' hair. She eventually left the comb with them as a parting gift, so to speak.

The apparent matriarch of the group seemed much younger than the man, perhaps his daughter. She was clearly the most leery of our presence, almost completely avoiding eye contact with us. She held the youngest child in a cloth around her neck as she fired up a large carved wooden pipe. High and wide cheekbones made her face very compelling. The blocky, primitive pipe protruding from her lips was an unforgettable sight. Her exotic beauty in this primitive setting was striking.

It felt like a once-in-a-lifetime photo opportunity. I was trying to maintain some rapport with the group and get some natural shots. They didn't seem to mind the camera. I'm not sure they even knew what it was. I was so in awe of the moment, I was trembling. The low light in the jungle compounded the photographic dilemma of my shaking hands but I was still able to get some good shots.

The photos never made it into *National Geographic*, but I was, nonetheless, very proud of them. I will certainly never forget the experience. Without the courage to seek out adventure, deep down I knew I would never have moments like that. I wanted more, I wanted to live!

The question, "Why am I doing this?" stayed with me as I contemplated the size, shape and details of the adventure. I was planning a six-month journey that would ultimately become a four-year odyssey. So much for the value of planning ahead. Have you heard how to make God laugh? Tell him your plans.

I had been on a number of overseas trips, for weeks at a time, carrying nothing but a backpack. But this time I wanted to take more camera equipment than I could easily fit into a backpack. As I contemplated my problem, a buddy who knew of my idea for a Latin American adventure gave me a gift that he thought might be appropriate. It was a book by Jimmy Buffet entitled, *A Pirate Looks At Fifty*. Prior to reading the book, the only thing I knew about Jimmy Buffet was "Margaritaville," both a song and a place I had visited a few times myself.

A Pirate Looks at Fifty is about Jimmy's 50th birthday expedition through Central America, South America and the Caribbean. He did it in a seaplane! I guessed he confused *pirate* with *pilot*. I enjoyed the book immensely, imagining myself in the same exotic locales he describes, getting me more excited about my own adventure and giving me a great idea. Backpack, schmackpack! After reading the book, I decided to take my own vehicle. I'm not Jimmy Buffet, can't afford a plane, nor can I fly one. But hey, I could handle my own beat-up pick-up truck!

I had never been a car person. Nor a computer person. To this day, I have yet to change my own oil and I'll gladly pay a mechanic to rotate my wiper fluid. In my dental offices I certainly had computers, but I never gained the confidence to actually turn one on or off all by myself. Thank God for my highly paid staff. My lack of skills presented a challenge for someone (that would be me) who wanted to drive through numerous under-developed countries while maintaining a web site.

In my research about driving through Latin America, I found the consensus for an auto manufacturer was Toyota, both for availability of parts and durability. It was a choice between a Toyota pick-up and a Toyota Land Cruiser. I also had to choose between gasoline and diesel fuel. Simply out of familiarity I chose the pick-up that ran on regular gas. I figured a small pick-up with a camper shell would provide plenty of space for storing gear. The back would also provide a comfortable place to sleep when needed.

I mail-ordered two manuals on the subject of driving through Latin America from the South American Explorers Club. One of them inspired the following online journal entry:

MARK'S
ADVENTURE ALERT

Location: Tucson, Arizona U.S.A.

Subject: Am I Crazy?

That's the title of the first chapter of a guidebook entitled "Driving through Latin America." That's what many people ask me when I tell them what I'm going to do. The guidebook says, "Don't worry, there are hundreds of travelers driving to Central America every year." But, the State Department says there are hundreds of foreigners kidnapped in Colombia every year. You do the math. Okay, so I'll do what I can to avoid Colombia. But keeping a little perspective, there are cities in the good ol' USA where hundreds of people are murdered each year! No one would ask me if I was crazy for visiting those cities. We live in a very dangerous country. But it's our country. We know it. Fear of the unknown begs the question that I don't quite know how to answer. Sure I'm crazy. My pirate friend who helped inspire this trip said in a song: *"If we weren't all crazy we would go insane."*

Okay, so maybe I am mental. But I'm not stupid. Security was a very real issue for both my vehicle and my person (again that would be me). I was also concerned about maintenance for the vehicle in out-of-the-way-places. Newer vehicles with complex computer systems would be difficult, if not impossible, to fix in remote locations. This necessitated purchasing a vehicle whose vintage was prior to the nineties. I wanted a four-wheel drive truck even though I had almost no off-road experience. I wanted to get off the beaten path.

Shopping the want ads, I found a blue 1985 Toyota HiLux pick-up that fulfilled my requirements. The very low price reflected the fact that the engine and transmission were both shot. I needed to replace the entire drive train plus add desired amenities and security systems. I definitely had my work cut out for me. Thus, began my relationship with "Baby Blue."

I relied on many people to compensate for my lack of expertise in the automotive arena. My pal Dana was especially influential. One might have called Dana homeless at some points in his life, but in this case, his homelessness was a virtue. He was highly qualified for this consulting job, having lived out of his pick-up while he toured the U.S. making a living as a street performer. I valued both his philosophical insights into life on the road, plus the day-to-day details of living out of a pick-up truck. But most of all, I valued our long-term friendship. To this day Dana earns his keep as a performer (www.danasmith.com).

Dana helped me shop for a camper shell, designed and built a bed, and even installed an electrical system for inside the camper. The camper shell was old and beaten up. The rough look of my truck and camper was perfect for blending into the third-world environment. I didn't want to stand out like a shiny target for the *banditos*.

I also needed secure locks and wanted a sophisticated and discreet alarm system, with a carjack kill switch. I had a steel box welded into the bed of the truck for secure storage of my camera and computer equipment. The box doubled as a base for my custom-made bed. I also had cigarette lighter jacks installed in the camper so I could use my computer and satellite phone in the back. Ultimately, my electrical system didn't survive the literal bumps in the road and the satellite phone system did not live up to its promise. I thought the satellite phone might be useful for emergency purposes. Only once did I actually make a connection, and only to ask, "Hey Mom, guess where I am." (After lots of clues and three guesses, she was not even close. I was on a beach in El Salvador. But, back to the story.)

Let's talk about locks. Eighteen of them: door locks, window locks, wheel locks, spare tire locks, hood locks, gas cap locks, a bagel with lox… I had hardware for padlocks welded everywhere! The result of the welding was scorch marks, huge sunbursts of blackness surrounding my shiny new padlocks. Not far into the journey, I realized that all the attention the locks were attracting was defeating the purpose of having a beat-up looking truck. At gas stations people would look in awe at the shiny locks and ask, "Wow, whatcha got in there, man?" On the road, I eventually got some matching blue spray paint and covered the scorch marks and the shiny chrome locks. After that, no one seemed to notice all of the security.

In addition to vehicle and security issues, I had a rather large issue to take care of at home.

MARK'S
ADVENTURE ALERT

Location: Tucson – Arizona U.S.A.

Subject: Who would want such a gift?

Kenny is my pet 200lb. "miniature" potbelly pig. He was given to me as a gift. You're probably wondering, "Who would want such a gift?" That's a very good question, particularly right now since I must arrange for his care while I'm away.

Let me start from the beginning. The summer before last I had a girlfriend who shall remain nameless but not shameless. The girlfriend, her dog Pandora, and her two kids (humans), were all living with me when Father's Day arrived. Being a good part-time step dad, I received a baby pot-bellied pig for Father's Day. I was wondering, "Who would want such a gift?"

Kenny was the size of a small cat, all black and cute as a button. He was fairly easy to potty train and we all lived in a nice state of harmony for a short time.

Kenny's personality and sexuality developed very early. He was not a very discriminating little pig. He would have his way with just about anything, animate or inanimate. He really liked an old dining room chair we had in the back yard. He and Pandora became more than just friends. Pandora tolerated Kenny's advances. She seemed to like the attention but certainly did not get the same fulfillment that he did.

We were not able to tolerate the smell Kenny left with Pandora. It was ghastly. I had to take Kenny to the vet to solve this problem. Upon his return, he was an it.

Fast-forward. The girlfriend moved to Texas to become the ex-girlfriend. She took Pandora but not the pig. I didn't want to keep him initially and considered Easter Sunday brunch or the Humane Society. Neither option seemed humane and I decided I liked him enough to deal with his maintenance.

Fast-forward to the present time. The miniature pig is now the monster pig. The Ex is recently married and living in South Texas (I'm sure my invitation got lost in the mail). I'll be driving through South Texas to get my border crossing. AHA! I can kill three birds with one stone:

1) Kenny gets re-united with Pandora, his first and only love.

2) My pet care hassle is history.

3) The Ex and the new guy get the perfect surprise wedding gift! I know what he will be wondering. "Who would want such a gift?!"

gift seemed like a brilliant idea, but I didn't have the heart to put
journey and made other arrangements to have him cared for at

Preparations dragged on beyond my intended departure date. My car alarm system was still not working. I bought it mail order from a specialty supplier specifically for its carjack kill switch feature. Having thought through numerous possible *bandito* scenarios, I reasoned that I was willing to give up any and all of my worldly possessions— or I should say traveling possessions— if my life were threatened. The worst-case scenario in terms of loss of material goods, but short of bodily harm, would be carjacking. The kill switch feature would allow me to step on a secret button as I agreeably exited my truck. I would cooperate with the banditos in hopes of saving my life and cheerfully let them drive away victorious. However, their victory would be short lived. About a mile down the road the motor would be programmed to cough, sputter and die, not to be restarted without the knowledge of another top-secret switch. Just like James Bond but without the supermodel secret agent at my side.

Sadly, the system was never even functional. I had been getting the runaround by both the factory and the local company doing the installation. Each blamed the other for the malfunction. I was quite certain the local installer was to blame but he got the factory to agree to send a new unit. I was not willing to wait another week and again risk more installer incompetence. I left the shop for the last time with the defunct device under my hood. The kill switch never came to life.

Another thing I had to decide was whether I would carry a weapon with me on the trip. I would not be carrying a gun for legal and personal reasons. They are prohibited at many border crossings anyway. I had read that flare guns were not illegal and that a blast to the chest from a flare gun would most certainly slow down an attacker. I decided not to go that route either. I also chose not to carry mace due to its questionable legality in some jurisdictions. I decided on a hefty Mag-Lite flashlight— for use as a weapon to knock someone's lights out — hidden but easily accessible from the driver's seat.

I was not as ready as I wanted to be, but the road was calling. If I waited to dot every *i* and cross every *t* I might never leave. I was anxious and ready enough!

12

It was really happening. I was actually pulling out of my driveway! I was excited, exhilarated and a little nervous. But there was still another delay in store for me. I headed out a little before 10AM only to encounter traffic as I left town. Traffic? Outside of town? On a Sunday? Eventually it ground to a complete halt. What a way to start my trip. Ready, set, stop! I came to find out that the traffic was being diverted for the El Tour de Tucson Bike Race, which my dear ol' departed Dad had participated in many times. Upon learning the source, it made the hold-up seem infinitely more tolerable, even apropos. It was as if my Dad was waving goodbye to me. I waved back and finally made it past the racers and onto the freeway. I had to smile at the song blaring on my radio, "Life is a highway, I'm gonna ride it all night long!"

Having spent considerable time in Mexico over the course of my life, I decided to get to Central America as quickly and directly as possible to maximize my time there. With that in mind, I headed east out of Tucson, barreling toward the eastern-most Mexican border crossing at Brownsville, Texas. From there I would head straight down the eastern coast of Mexico, avoiding the lengthy curve of the west coast. In addition, traveling on American highways through New Mexico and Texas, I knew I would make much better time than the same distance on Mexican roads.

On this first leg of my journey, roadkill jumped out as the photographic theme. Nothing actually jumped into my path, but I saw more than 40 deer carcasses along one 200-mile stretch of road between New Mexico and Texas (It was like a scene from Wes Craven's version of Bambi). That stretch of road was also home to the Roadkill Café. Went there, did that, and actually got the T-shirt. Not sure if I can adequately explain my fascination with roadside remains, but it's there. It got me into some car trouble, which was ultimately a blessing.

I had pulled over for a photo of a decaying carcass of a cow resting eternally in a field. Its ribs were denuded of flesh and fur, reaching for the sky. The composition (or should I say decomposition) was striking, but the field was overgrown with extraordinarily sharp thorns. Three out of four tires succumbed to the stickers. The leaks were slow so I was never stranded. I had hoped I could get some mileage out of the tires that came with Baby Blue, but I coughed up the cash for four new ones before crossing the border.

I spent two days in Brownsville, taking care of a list of miscellaneous last minute items and getting increasingly frustrated over my lack of computer know-how. E-mailing was a brand new skill for me, if you could call it a skill at all. It was more of a non-skill. A busy Kinko's employee did not feel that guiding me through every click was part of his job description. I was pissed at him and at myself. I don't think even Mr. Kinko himself could have helped me.

It was two days before Thanksgiving and I could have delayed my departure a few more days and spent the holiday with family and friends. It would have been another easy way to delay the start of my adventure. Thus far, the beginning of my trip was not fulfilling my idealized and romantic view of this journey. I was dealing with computer and car problems in a dingy border town. I was alone and struggling with irritating little details, wishing I had stayed with my family for the holidays.

I wanted to get my Mexican paperwork in order before driving across. I stayed in a hotel in Brownsville and walked across the border. To prevent passage of stolen cars into Mexico, there was an $800 deposit necessary to cross over with Baby Blue. I wasn't coming back any time soon and I didn't want to make an $800 donation. I spent an aggravating day talking with government and private agencies with no results. I returned the following day and managed to get a *transmigrante* permit that allowed me to pass through Mexico without paying the deposit.

It's a good thing I could not see into the future. It did not occur to me that I would face similar struggles at many borders to come. If it had, I may well have turned back.

Since I'd had my share of adventures in Mexico, I did not mind passing through it quickly. As I barreled through the countryside memories began storming back of days long since gone.

As a child, I camped on the beaches at Rocky Point in Mexico more times than I can count (even back then I didn't like to do the math). My Dad, younger brother Mike, and I were part of the father-son Indian Guides program. Mike's Indian Guide name was "Flaming Arrow" and I was "Dark Cloud." How did I get that name? They might as well have called me "Little Big Drag" or "Dances With Pessimism." Our contact with Mexican culture and language was only incidental. It was all about fun at the beach. My mind has deleted all of the discomforts and difficulties of the trip, camping in the sand with no facilities, and the inevitable sunburn. The memories that remain are idyllic hours of snorkeling in the sea of Cortez, rolling down sand dunes inside gigantic inner tubes, and pancakes made by Bald Eagle (our breakfast chef who needed no hairnet).

Our fearless leader on the back roads leading to the beach was my dad, whose Indian Guide name was "Turtle Head." We were almost always driving "Big Red," the family Chevy Suburban. It was an Indian Guide icon and my inspiration for the name "Baby Blue." We usually got lost for hours at a time. Looking back on it now, I'm proud that my Dad was a leader, even though he may have been geographically challenged at times. Being lost can be a treat when you are traveling on your own, but when thirty others are depending on your guidance, an unintended side trip will lead to good-hearted but never-ending teasing and taunting. Turtle Head took it all in stride (small little turtle strides). I have since learned that being lost is the same as being on an unguided tour. Another truism I have come to celebrate is that if you're not getting lost every once in awhile, you're not on much of an adventure.

I flashed on other Mexico memories, specifically, my wild and carefree college days. It was then that the travel bug first sunk its teeth in me. It was Christmas break during my sophomore year.

I had met my pal Dave in Spanish class at the University of Arizona. Dave was studying anthropology and had a fascination with Mexican culture and particularly ancient ruins. Dave was a year ahead of me in school and had traveled to Mexico on multiple occasions. This made him an ideal guide. For Dave, this was not just a vacation but truly a mystical and spiritual experience. He was pursuing his twin fascination with Mayan ruins and the author Carlos Castenada, who wrote, The Teachings of Don Juan: A Yaqui Way of Knowledge and many other books on sorcery and shamanism. Still, Dave had yet to visit the Yucatán! Both a peninsula and a state in Mexico, Yucatán was to be the future home of the international resort destination Cancún. It was about as far away from Arizona as you could get and still be in Mexico.

Dave and I had been planning our Christmas escapade for some time. Another college friend drove us and our backpacks the one-hour drive from Tucson to the border town of Nogales. On the Mexican side we caught a bus to Mazatlán. We arrived late the next night. That's when things got interesting.

We never visited the world-class beaches of Mazatlán; instead we headed straight to the train station to catch a midnight train to Mérida, the capital of the state of Yucatán. We paid a bit extra for first-class seats, but ended up with the throngs of locals who piled into a train car with only enough seats for one out of four passengers. It was full, well beyond standing room only; people were actually lying in the luggage racks above the seats. Mind you, this was to be a two-and-a-half day train ride.

The first class tickets may have been only for preferential boarding. Whatever the case was, we were actually among the first to board, allowing us to claim actual seats. As the journey progressed, the sardine can of humanity intermingled and settled.

We chitchatted with our neighbors, exchanging English lessons for Spanish. There was an older woman, apparently alone, standing in the aisle just over my right shoulder. The tiny woman was clutching a brown paper bag. Those around her noticed that she had begun to weave back and forth. I stood up and let her take a seat, wedged between Dave and me. In the brown bag was a bottle of pulque, a product of the agave plant before it is further refined to become tequila. It is a pulpy, fruity brew enjoyed by locals of the region. She had, apparently, enjoyed a little too much. She was relieved to be seated but certainly not cured of her obvious intoxication.

Her chin began to lurch forward and her free hand came up to her face. Yes, you guessed it. Her hand covered her mouth just in time to deliver the spray of pulque puke sideways onto Dave and me. The bathrooms aboard were disgusting, with filthy toilets and no running water. It was a very long ride.

Despite my new aroma I was able to make some friends on the train. I met a couple and their daughter from Coatzacoalcos, an industrial port town on the Gulf coast. They extended an invitation for me to visit them on my return. Little did I know how very hospitable they would be.

Finally, we made it to Mérida, which was an hour drive from Chichén Itzá, home to some of the showcased Mayan pyramids. For Dave, they were the highlight of our itinerary. The steep pyramids were a challenge to climb. Once on top, the majesty of it all was overwhelming. It made me wonder, what were the roots of this civilization? Why did it end so abruptly? Would I ever lose the smell of pulque puke? Off in the distance were green mounds as far as the eye could see. They were said to be pyramids reclaimed by the jungle, awaiting defoliation and restoration.

At the time, I believe it was 1976, Cancún was not even a glimmer of what it was to become. There was not a single high-rise hotel (there are now hundreds lining the beach). We went across the water to Isla Mujeres, the Island of Women. But where were all the *mujeres*? There were only two small *pensiones*, bed-and-breakfasts, on the mostly uninhabited little island that has since become a major tourist stop. Dave and I hitched a ride about seven kilometers to Garrafón, a beach at the east end of the island. I had brought my snorkel and mask and was pleasantly astounded by the tropical colored fish that absolutely surrounded me before I was even waist deep in the water. Some even nibbled curiously at the hairs on my legs.

In my youth, the endless hours I had spent underwater at Rocky Point were comparably drab and desolate to this Caribbean spectacle. Yet, back then I was enthralled to be underwater. I was Jaques Cousteau Jr., exploring with my fins and snorkel. The magnitude of the beauty surrounding Isla Mujeres can't be overstated: the sand, the crystal-blue water, the psychedelic explosion of colored fish!

From Cancún we headed south down the coast of the Yucatán Peninsula en route to the ruins of Tulum. After visiting Chichén Itzá, the ruins here were not impressive. However, the scenery was spectacular. They were located on a cliff over the sea adjacent to a pristine white sand beach. You know what they say, *locacion, locacion, locacion.*

We found lodging a few kilometers south of the ruins. Our deluxe accommodations consisted of a hut in which we hung our hammocks. From there my health had a definite impact on the remainder of the trip. I spent a miserable night shivering inside my rain-dampened sleeping bag in my hammock. I awoke the next morning feeling miserable. Our plan for the morning was to get to the main road and continue hitchhiking south.

To get to the main highway we had two options, hike through the jungle for three kilometers or take our chances hitchhiking a 23-kilometer stretch of deserted road. That's 14 miles for you *gringos*. We chose to fight our way through the overgrown jungle trail. I felt like crap but I thought I could make it.

Hacking our way through the jungle was much harder than anticipated. Halfway into it, I began to feel faint. I was worried I would pass out. The humidity was overwhelming and it was all I could do to drag one foot in front of the other. But I had to get to the road.

When we finally reached the highway I could barely stand. I can't recall how we arrived at the next town, but Dave checked me into a hotel and summoned a doctor for me. Meanwhile, Dave found accommodations for himself outside of town. Up until that point we had only camped out, or found a makeshift shelter under which to hang our hammocks. I appreciated Dave taking care of me. In that state, a real bed felt as if I were lying on clouds. The doctor soon came and prescribed antibiotics for what I understood to be pneumonia.

I spent two nights in the hotel, building enough strength to continue our journey. I would have spent a few more days resting and recuperating had I known what would occur in the coming days. (Cue foreshadowing music here.)

Editor's note: Mark, this is a book, we can't add music.

Author's note: Use your imagination butt-munch; pretend I'm humming the theme from Jaws.

Editor's note: Fine. I'll root for the shark.

Our next anthropological destination was the ruins of Palenque, in the neighboring state of Quintana Roo. The Palenque ruins had some distinct features, including many stelas, which are elaborate drawings carved into large stone walls. Underneath the main pyramid, you could take a stairway about four stories underground to see a particular stela illuminated by a low wattage electric bulb. The main feature was a life-sized carving of a man in a reclined seat with a nosepiece attached to a long cord or tube. To be four stories under an ancient pyramid and see the apparent image of an astronaut boggled my mind.

Palenque was also famous, at least on the Gringo Trail, for something else— a breakfast food with mind-altering effects. *Hongo omelettes!* Breakfast made with magic mushrooms. More adventurous, self-reliant souls could harvest their own mushrooms by simply searching the surrounding fields for cow pies early in the morning. The mushrooms grew right out of the cow shit. The menus in the cafés didn't note this unappetizing source of their ingredients. I harvested a few by myself, but was leery of eating them. Dave didn't hesitate. He didn't even wash them. As I recall, the effects he felt from the mushrooms were rather mild.

After Palenque our paths diverged. As per our original plan, his was to be a longer trip. Dave would continue south and I would head back north toward home. But my adventure was certainly not over, nor was my foray into Mexican health care.

I caught the same train back from Mérida. I took my new friends up on their offer to visit them in Coatzacoalcos. It happened to be New Year's Eve day when I arrived. They were very pleased to see me, just in time for the New Year's Eve festivities. They handed me a brandy and Coke before I could even take off my backpack.

Their custom for the holiday was a big greasy dinner that began at midnight. I switched to rompope, a creamy vanilla liquor. Whether it was the mixture of liquors, or the time that has passed since, the details of the party are hazy for me now.

I awoke the next morning with a hangover that lasted four days. At least I thought it was a hangover, but in reality my pneumonia had returned. I spent the next four days in bed in the home of people I barely knew. They treated me extremely well. Their twenty-something daughter rubbed Vick's VapoRub on my chest daily. Sadly, I was not in any frame of mind to enjoy it.

It wasn't until the third day that I was healthy enough to get to a pay phone to try to call home. I was never able to make a connection, but I was able to get back on the road a day or so later never having caused any worry at home in Tucson.

My health issues in Coatzacoalco could be taken in a couple of ways: an example of the risks of traveling alone, or as a tremendous affirmation of the generosity of my new friends and the goodness of the Latino culture. Back then I didn't give it too much thought. But, I must have assumed the latter.

The travel bug had bitten, and I've yet to recover.

Thirty years later, as I approached the Guatemalan border, I was excited to begin a new adventure. Mexico offered me a chance to relive my past. Now, it was time to live my future. The actual journey through Mexico was not easy, as the following journal entry shows:

MARK'S ADVENTURE ALERT

Location: Mexico

Subject: Memories of Mexico

        I blasted through Mexico very quickly. I heard it would take three to four days and I made it in two. Needless to say I did not stop to smell the roses nor wake up and smell the coffee, I just got in the truck and drove. I met some friendly people, to be fair, but most of the people I encountered wanted my money simply because I had it and they didn't— "La Mordida," the bribe or literally "the bite." I got bitten by the police and the Federales a couple of times. No blood or rabies involved but I was pissed.

The first time was the worst. After that I learned to stand my ground and negotiate — haggling, if you will. If I didn't cave in and instead stared them down, usually there was a little fear in their eyes. Or when I confronted one official he sheepishly admitted he wanted a handout. I felt better knowing that I was making a "donation." Other memorable moments along the road: Pick-up trucks with 25 people standing in the back. Small children playing next to the highway. Courteous truck drivers signaling it was okay to pass regardless of a solid yellow line or blind curve. Numerous speed bumps in every little town and village like trying to drive over four inch steel pipes. Two different maps that seemed to be for two different countries. Plenty of potholes and dozens of detours.

"Dame tus papeles," "Dame tus papeles," "Give me your papers." I pulled up to the border in Tapachula and was immediately swarmed by over twenty people looking to help me handle my paperwork and exchange currency. I hadn't done my homework on the exchange rate in Guatemala, had barely come to grips with the Mexican peso, and it was already time to change over. The tramitadores were people who would, for a fee, help expedite the paperwork needed to get me and Baby Blue across the border.

Yeah, sure, I'll just hand over my passport and the title to Baby Blue to a complete stranger on the street. Not gonna happen. I would maintain control of my documents, thank you very much. Eventually I would come to trust and utilize some of these enterprising youngsters at this and other borders. But not that day.

With my papers in hand I approached the first office and got in line. Forty minutes later, the clerk at the head of the line barked out something in Spanish that I only pretended to understand. He waved me away and pointed to an office across the street. I hadn't a clue what he said but I headed toward the office.

One persistent young *tramitadore* was still lurking about, wanting to be of assistance. *"Tus papeles, señor"*— "Your papers, sir," he pleaded. He seemed very sincere. The rest of the crowd had given up on me, but not him. He was not giving up. The office was a small photocopy booth. I finally realized that the youth had been trying to tell me for an hour that I needed photocopies of my documents. Oh. Maybe this little guy might be of some use after all. Once inside the booth, Diego sorted through my papers and helped me get the right number of copies of the necessary documents. He was building trust, but I still wasn't letting my papers out of my sight.

Once the documents and copies were in order I made my way back across to the first office. They were done for the day. It wasn't even three o'clock but they were already closed. I had already checked out of one country and was unable to check in at the next. That meant I was in no-man's-land, stuck in between, forced to spend the night in the border zone. James Bond never had to put up with this.

I needed a place to stay for the night and, equally important, a safe place to park. My options were slim and nothing seemed terribly secure. The transient nature of the entire scene made me nervous and hesitant to stay anywhere. But I had no choice. The hotel I found was busy, catering to people just like me, wishing they were somewhere else, but making do for the night. I found a place in the parking area where I could back Baby Blue against a wall for added security.

The back of the vehicle, where the camper shell door met the tailgate, was the most vulnerable to attack by *banditos*. The camper shell door was flimsy and the latch mechanism did not interface well with the tailgate. Even with two locks welded on, not much effort would be required to pop the whole thing off.

Diego was probably 14 years old, and was friends with all of the other *tramitadores*. He asked me to meet him and his friend Felix at a little café on the main drag. He said Felix might be able to speed things up for us the next day. I thought it would be okay. Felix would prove to be less trustworthy than his younger protégé.

The three of us enjoyed dinner where I sampled my first Guatemalan beer. I felt relieved that I now had friends to help me with the border crossing. The next day Diego and Felix went with me to the border offices. Felix began telling me that he needed an exorbitant sum of money in order to get anything done. I was being fleeced. I felt betrayed and hurt. They were my buddies that night and they tried to screw me over the next day.

I ended up telling them to get lost and took care of everything myself. It was such a frustrating and helpless feeling. An official would blurt something out to me and the only thing I knew for sure was that he was not interested in helping me. They could just roll over me like a steamroller. I was emotionally immobilized and distraught.

In a moment of dire frustration, I got some guidance and encouragement from a bilingual fellow traveler. He was in the clothing industry and did business between New York and Costa Rica. He had driven between the two places several times and seemed to know the drill. The traveling businessman told me to stand up to the clerks and demand that they do their jobs— this is difficult when you're not sure what their job is! His advice was a big help. In the future I was more assertive with them and made certain that they spoke slowly enough for me to understand. After a day and a half, I finally made it across into Guatemala.

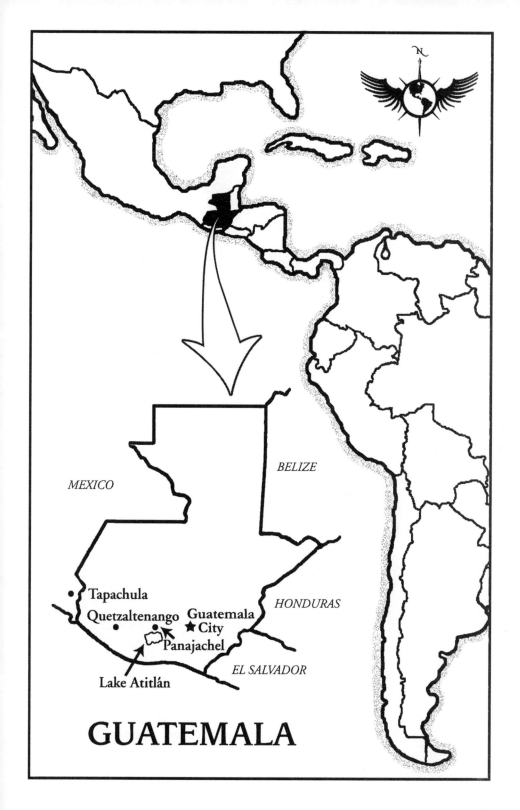

MEXICO

BELIZE

HONDURAS

Tapachula

Quetzaltenango

Guatemala
City

Panajachel

EL SALVADOR

Lake Atitlán

GUATEMALA

My experience with the first two border crossings, and the Mexican police, motivated me to learn Spanish. I planned to complete a two-week program in Guatemala and chose to take the lessons in Quezaltenango (also known as Xela). I had done some research online, or I should say, I had someone do some research online *for me*. I was still a stranger in the digital domain. We located a language program prior to my departure. If I had to do it to over, I would have waited until I arrived to locate a school. It's a competitive business and I could have received a much better deal. Then again, how do you negotiate a deal with a Spanish school if you don't speak any Spanish?

Spanish immersion programs are really an incredible deal. You get to stay with a local family and are thus completely immersed in the language. You simply can't get that from a hotel or tour. Generally, you get four hours of one-on-one instruction in the classroom. That is plenty for one day. After that, there were practical assignments to be done out in the community, plus extracurricular cultural activities. The price for the whole package is less than the cost of a stay at a cheap hotel.

MARK'S ADVENTURE ALERT

Location: Almolonga, Guatemala

Subject: Learning in the AM, Teaching in the PM

The school has an outreach program that teaches Spanish to adults in the little farm village of Almolonga, near Xela. I joined the small group that trekked into the hills for the afternoon session. Each volunteer had several students, outdoors or in a small room with a dirt floor. The ceiling was about 5'10", which is fine for the villagers since they are mostly under 5 foot tall. But they sure got a big kick out of me walking around with my 6'2" head cranked all the way over to one side.

I was blown away by the enthusiasm we encountered. They were absolutely thrilled to have us there. I was inspired by their desire to improve themselves. Their native language is called "Mam." I call it "Twenty-Seven Different Ways to Clear Your Throat." I couldn't come close to differentiating and pronouncing the guttural sounds they tried to teach me. Certainly Spanish and English are just as foreign to them.

MARK'S
ADVENTURE ALERT

Location: Quezaltenango, Guatemala

Subject: One More Thing to Learn

In the last few months I've been forced to learn many new things. Don't get me wrong, I'm not complaining. I asked for it. Prior to preparing for this trip, I literally did not know how to turn on a computer nor change the oil in my car. I knew a little Spanish but now I'm totally immersed in it. Computers, E-mail, the Internet, typing, satellite technology, auto mechanics, Spanish, a new climate, a new diet, a new family... could I possibly take on one more thing? Yes!

Tonight was my first Merengue lesson here in Xela. I was up to the challenge. The fact that I was the only guy with five women made it more than tolerable. It was actually a lot of fun. I already know the Country Swing, which gave me a head start. The Merengue upper body movements are the same. I just had to learn the steps, and, as a French girl kept trying to tell me in English, "Move your butt!" I did my best to oblige.

In addition to the dance classes and opportunities to explore surrounding villages, the director gave informal evening lectures on local culture and politics. He highlighted the conflicts between the Latino and indigenous cultures. The Spaniards controlled Guatemala until 1851, when the country declared independence.

However, the Latino dominance over indigenous groups continues to this day. Language, geography and social differences separate the indigenous groups from each other and the rest of Guatemala. In fact, there are over 23 different indigenous languages. Just like blacks and other minorities in my own country, the indigenous people are often treated like second-class citizens. I found that as Americans we don't have a corner on the market when it comes to racial prejudice.

We learned about the struggles of Rigoberta Menchú, who championed indigenous rights in Guatemala and won the Nobel Peace Prize. I was also horrified to learn about the intervention and impact the U.S. had on the country. In 1954, the CIA helped orchestrate the removal of a democratically elected government by placing its support behind a military regime. The threat of communism was the justification for the acts, which led to over three decades of violence and oppression. More than 450 Mayan villages were decimated – their culture and civilization along with it. In all, over 200,000 Guatemalans were killed. It was a lot for me to take in.

Even though I was very busy and having fun, my first week was brutal. Being high in the mountains, Quezaltenango was much colder than I was prepared for, mentally and physically. I was miserably cold and did not feel at ease in my assigned family setting. They lived in a sprawling dwelling that housed several generations and branches of their clan.

Entering from the street, you had to pass through the family business of aluminum frames and fixtures to get into their home. On a hillside, a maze of stairs led to different wings of the family compound. There was one big kitchen, plus each branch had its own smaller kitchen and dining area. My family unit was a young couple with three small children. Rosa, the mom, was sweet and tried to be accommodating while Pablo, the dad, was surly and generally seemed unhappy. It was obvious he didn't appreciate me being around. In fact, he resented any attention Rosa gave me. For all intents and purposes, the rest of the extended family ignored me.

I didn't understand the meal program. The first night, I was expecting to sit down to a hearty dinner. Instead, I was served only crackers and juice. Oops! I guess I should have been a little more aggressive at that midday meal.

After a couple of days, the director of the school checked to see how I was doing in my assigned home. I told him about feeling less than welcome and by the end of the day he had moved me to a different family. This one actually felt like a family and was almost next door to the school, eliminating the long chilly walk each morning.

I also had a new roommate, a classmate from the school who prompted some early morning expeditions. He was a shutterbug as well and we found lots to do each day before class. We discovered a public bathhouse at a natural hot spring. A long hot soak in the cement tank each morning was heavenly. Following our bath we would get freshly squeezed juice from the street vendors. It was a great way to start each day. The same vendors were selling sea turtle eggs. My heart cried silently inside. Didn't they know? Didn't they care? I felt the urge to do something, but was helpless, not knowing what to do or say.

The second week things got significantly better. I was assigned a new teacher. Doris was nineteen and had to be the cutest girl in all of Guatemala. I spent four hours a day sitting across a tiny table from her. By the end of the week I was fantasizing about changing my plans and spending the next six months in Guatemala. Doris was very fastidious with the specifics of punctuation and the written form of the language. This was not my interest in the least. I wanted to SPEAK the language. Nonetheless, I hung on every word of her detailed explanation of accent mark placement and the difference between *si* and *sí* (One means *if*; the other, *yes*. God knows which is which).

By the end of the week we were spending lots of extracurricular time together. There were romantic cafés where we shared tea or cocoa. One in particular seemed to be a hundred years old with an ageless style. It was a cozy retreat from the cold, where the rest of the world seemed to disappear, as we shared moments lingering over our cocoa. In the evenings, stolen kisses in front of her parents' house made me dream of much more. It was as if I were back in high school where I had certainly never kissed a girl who was so sweet and lovely. Only now, I had more experience and more knowledge. This knowledge was a double-edged sword. I could see into the future of the relationship and saw the problems ahead. It was not meant to be.

I admit, I was smitten. But I was also on a mission. For her to join me on the road was just not realistic. She was very attached to her family and serious about her own education. I knew better than to try to convince her to come with me or to give up my adventure and stay there with her. But the fantasy was rich.

As we exchanged e-mail addresses and said our goodbyes I realized I was really going to miss her. But it was time to go. I loaded up Baby Blue and headed out to explore other parts of Guatemala on my way to El Salvador.

MARK'S ADVENTURE ALERT

Location: Panajachel, Guatemala

Subject: So Romantic But Alas...

...I'm here all by myself! In the charming mountain village of Panajachel on spectacular Lake Atitlán. The lake is surrounded by volcanic mountains and about eight small villages. Absolutely gorgeous!

Panajachel is the main visitor center for the lake and a bit touristy for my taste, and yet I'm captivated by its romantic charm.

Some very stylish restaurants have been here for a long time. I had dinner at the Circus Club that was decorated with antique European circus memorabilia. Sounds corny, but it was warm and cozy and somehow I felt as though I had been transported to another time and place. Live music by a very talented guitar duo added to the ambiance.

MARK'S ADVENTURE ALERT

Location: Lake Atitlán, Guatemala

Subject: The Road Less Traveled...

...could be that way for a reason. A narrow dirt road, on a steep mountain, waaay above the lake is not the best place for a dead end. I got some good pictures and I got to put Baby Blue into four-wheel drive, but it was a little hairy turning around. Yiiikes! Yesterday I took the highway around the lake and today I took a road much closer to the lake. Most tourists take a boat to one or two specific villages. Each boat is greeted by a flock of merchants and local guides hungry for the tourist Quetzales. I was able to visit the smaller villages that don't get any tourist traffic. The brilliant colored outfits that Guatemala is famous for are different in every village. At the time of the Spanish conquest, each village was assigned different colors as a way of keeping tabs on the Natives. The colors are now a source of pride, like school colors, if you will. "We're from the blue village, Rah, Rah, Rah! We grow onions, Sis, Boom, Bah!" OKAY, they're not that excited, but the colors are awesome!

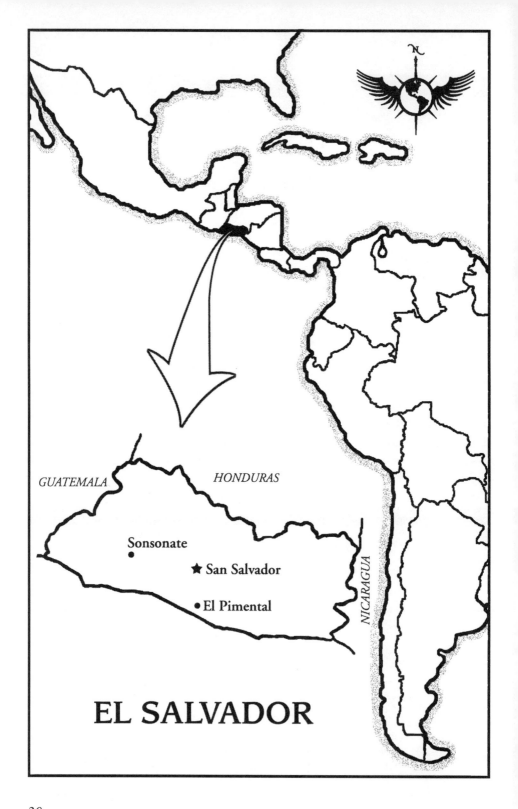

GUATEMALA

HONDURAS

Sonsonate

★ San Salvador

• El Pimental

NICARAGUA

EL SALVADOR

My timeframe of taking six months to finish my goal was not looking realistic at this point. After a whole month in tiny Guatemala there was still so much I wanted to see, and I had more than a dozen countries to go. I could only go so deep if I wanted to go so far. Oh well, next country please.

The border crossing into El Salvador was not a town, but only a couple of buildings on either side of the line. There was almost no traffic. Still, it took me several hours to pass through. Piles of paperwork and plenty of confusion for me. Relatively speaking, however, I made it through unscathed.

I was on the road in another country! Both of my windows were open and the late afternoon sun was streaming into the passenger side as I headed south gliding through rolling green hills. The highway was smooth yet other signs of civilization were few and far between. I felt elated and triumphant to be embarking on a new chapter of my adventure. Little did I know that my first 24 hours in the country would knock all of the triumph right out of me. It began with a very quirky first night.

MARK'S ADVENTURE ALERT

Location: Sonsonate, El Salvador

Subject: Sex Salvadoran Style

The big neon sign clearly said: Auto Hotel. "I just don't get it! Is this just a place to park your auto? Where's the freakin' office?" I drove around the circular interior of the drab cement complex several times and all I could see were small garage spaces with a door inside and a rolling metal garage door outside. "Where's the office?" I asked the security guard with a big shotgun and a nasty German Shepherd. My much improved Spanish was not enough to comprehend the situation. "Are there rooms here?"

   "Yes. You have to use the telephone."

   "But I'm a traveler, I don't have a telephone." I drove out, still mystified, looking for an office somewhere outside the complex.

Nope. Nada. Nothing. I was running out of options. I had already been looking for a place to stay for forty-five minutes and it was way after dark. I had to try again with my heavily armed friend. He told me there was someone in the office who spoke English. "What office? Where is the office?" I said, not hiding my frustration. "On the telephone." He repeated for the fifth time. He finally motioned for me to come with him into a garage and through a door into a small room. It was painted a fleshy pink color and there was a huge mirror on the wall next to the bed. "Omigawd! I'm in a whorehouse!!" I thought, as he handed me the phone.

   The girl on the phone spoke English with some kind of European accent. She told me the room was $13 and that included two beverages and that checkout time was 7:00a.m.. 7:00a.m.?? Hmm. OKAY, I think I'm making progress. Then it got weirder. I was unpacking and I heard a knock on the door. But, there was no one at the door. There was no one at the garage door. Was I hearing things? No. I heard it again, this time with a girl's muffled voice. "Omigawd!" I thought again, "Is there a naked girl somewhere in my room?" No. A box in the corner with a hand! Just like the Addams Family on TV! And it wanted my money!

   After an explanation from Brigitte, the Austrian girl on the phone, it all made perfect sense. This was a place were Salvadoran couples came for discreet sex. You can't bring your girlfriend home to Mom, nor your mistress home to the wife. So you come here. No one sees you, your partner, or your car! Completely anonymous. With a free porno channel! But alas, I'm here all by myself!

A fitful night's sleep and a 7:00 a.m. checkout had me back on the road towards San Salvador, the capital of El Salvador, feeling less than 100%. More like 30% at best. I had not done my homework on El Salvador and I didn't know the exchange rate. I seemed to have been short changed on energy. An hour later I was into urban traffic. I had not done any research on the city, and as much as I wanted to pull over and take a nap, this was not the place for that. It did not look or feel safe.

   The congested highway was flanked by a hodgepodge of businesses and run-down residences. Tattered clothing and stray dogs were everywhere. I had someone to look up in San Salvador. I had known Oscar from the late '80s in San Francisco.

I wanted to get into town and call him. I just had this feeling of tension. The reality of a new country meant a new set of rules of the road. The signage and the system of traffic controls were closing in on me. I had a brief "I wanna go home" moment, but I pushed on into the city, struggling to keep my attention focused on the task of finding my way to a phone. I needed gas so I pulled into a gas station mini-mart. The Tony-the-Tiger motif and color scheme were familiar, but nothing else. Grreeeeeaaat! (I know I am mixing the tiger in your tank with the tiger on your cereal box; but hey, I hadn't got much sleep.)

I found myself struggling with uncertainty. Who do I pay? When do I pay? Do I pump the gas myself? Should I smile at the armed guard drenched in bullets? How do I use the public phone? I had a phone number, but what part was the country code and what part was the city code? Did I even need to dial the city code? Should I put the coins in before or after dialing? I didn't have the answers to these questions, so I gave up.

Reaching Oscar seemed like a bit of a long shot anyway. I had not seen him in more than twelve years. I knew of his presence here in San Salvador from the same person who introduced me to him originally— my ex-wife. She and Oscar were dating at the time. One could imagine that being a rather awkward connection, but no. I had remained friends with my ex, and she'd referred Oscar to my dental practice. Oscar had been trained as a doctor in El Salvador and had met my ex while they were both studying acupuncture in San Francisco. We had our health care careers in common, and though we were not terribly close, we were certainly friendly.

I was feeling quite out of place and unwelcome in what struck me as a hostile environment. I realize that "hostile" is a very harsh word, but it fit — guns, poverty, people struggling to survive. And Baby Blue was about to make an acquaintance in a hostile way.

I consulted my guidebook before I got back into Baby Blue and left the gas station. Baby Blue and I came to a large roundabout, a huge circular intersection that you could enter or leave from six different directions. It struck me as a merry-go-round for cars that you could jump onto or off of at any time. That is, if you knew what you were doing and where you were going. I knew neither.

I approached the circle and wondered about that quaint American notion of right-of-way. As an American I know my rights. The right to remain silent and the right of way. Both are in the Bill of Rights, right?! "When is it my turn?" I thought, just before someone behind me started honking. I took that to mean it was my turn to go. "Beep beep" means "get moving" in any language! I pulled into traffic and WHAM! I collided with a small white sedan. Welcome to El Salvador, señor.

The car resembled a Fiat or a Toyota, but it was actually a regional model that I was not familiar with. The driver was in his early twenties. He was not nearly as upset as I was exasperated. For me this had not been a good day to put it mildly, and it was not even midday. I managed to pull off of the roundabout without another collision. The other driver followed, and we got out to assess the damages and figure out what to do. My front left fender had crunched into his right rear. I could only assume that I was at fault and I apologized as profusely as my Spanish would allow.

I trusted him to tell me what needed to be done. He made a few calls on his cell phone. Then he asked me to follow him to a nearby auto body shop for an estimate. At the body shop the emotional dust from the crash settled and we began to talk. His name was Tomas and he seemed like a decent fellow. He asked what I was doing in El Salvador, while politely straining to understand my Spanish.

The estimate for the damages to his vehicle turned out to be less than $300, a very small fraction of what the stateside price would have been. I followed him to a bank and paid him in cash. Eventually I would return to the same shop for my repairs. Tomas was also kind enough to help me make it through to Oscar. He sorted out Oscar's phone number and actually used his own cell phone to call for me. Thanks to his kindness, by the end of the day I was a houseguest at Oscar's. Phew!

Oscar lived in a residential area close to a main business district. He lived with his 17-year-old son Juan, in an upper-class neighborhood. It was not much more than middle class by American standards, though he did enjoy the benefits of a maid and a driver who worked for his business and ran his personal errands. Oscar had a national radio talk show on natural health that had been running for ten years. He was a big fish in a small pond, probably the most well-known doctor in the country.
Because of Oscar's busy schedule with his practice, I spent a lot of time with Juan. Two years earlier Juan had spent a year in a Salt Lake City high school. He was eager to use his English, which had been getting rusty since his return to San Salvador. Juan drove a gunmetal gray VW Beetle and had posters of Jim Morrison, The Beatles, and Latin-American icon Che Guevara on his bedroom wall.

We had a blast cruising the streets of San Salvador. He was re-living his American experience with me while I got a peek at the urban upper class of El Salvador. He told me about the differences between his social life in the States and here at home. He had been a novelty in Salt Lake City and he liked all the attention he got. Back home in San Salvador he just blended in.

We hit all the tourist-type monuments and sculptures. On one of our tours we passed a large, rather nondescript pinkish-beige building set back securely behind a tall chain-link fence topped with razor wire. The building was three or four stories tall and went on for blocks. "That's the American Embassy," my young guide explained. "It's what?" I asked, not sure if I understood his English. I was certain he was mistaken. How could this monstrous compound be the American Embassy for this tiny country the size of a golf course? "Yeah. For sure, for sure." He said in his best American slang. I still didn't believe it.

That evening I questioned Oscar about the compound we had seen. Indeed it was the American Embassy. Still confused, Oscar responded with a light-hearted mixture of disgust and amusement. "Markie, Markie, Markie!" (a nickname from my ex from way back) "You are such an American!" He continued to chide and chastise me about my ignorance of the foreign affairs of my own country. It was the beginning of my on-the-street education; opening my eyes to things that part of me really didn't want to know. He was very condescending but eventually I began to understand why. I tried not to take it too personally. American intervention in the region often had a profound impact on the lives of residents. Americans in general, (and me in particular) are clueless about the real impact. "Of course it's too big for El Salvador, you lamebrain!" Those were not his exact words, but they might as well have been. He explained that the huge pink complex serviced the entire region and the covert operations in neighboring Guatemala, Honduras and Nicaragua.

Oscar went on to describe aspects of their civil war that had impacted him most directly. Most notably, being stranded in his home overlooking the city with no power, watching as American helicopters crisscrossed the skies. Though the war has been over for more than 12 years, San Salvador still has a feeling of being war-torn, its guts having been ripped out, not yet fully repaired or healed.

I spent a lot of my time writing on Oscar's computer. I slept in the den on a comfortable pullout couch. Best of all, they had cable Internet access. At the time this high-speed net access was just getting a foothold in the U.S. I was impressed and amazed to be enjoying it in El Salvador. It turns out that a large segment of the Salvadoran population was computer crazy, way beyond any of their Central American neighbors and me. Although their development had been stunted in some areas, they excelled in computer technology.

I had been parking Baby Blue on the street in front of the house, directly below the window when I could. It was the best I could do, but still risky according to Oscar and Juan. The risk was taken and the danger realized.

Still badly wounded from the collision at the roundabout, Baby Blue received yet another assault. *Banditos* gained entrance to her cab by breaking the passenger-side wing window. They certainly bungled the job by only getting away with something of absolutely no value, an old radio/cassette player from under the seat. The cassette player didn't work and the radio was iffy at best. It was at least ten years old and totally useless without the in-dash hardware that it plugged into. There was a functional Walkman, cassettes, tools, and my hefty flashlight that didn't get touched. The *banditos* were hindered by not being able to open the padlocked doors once they got inside the windows, so the extra locks evidently served me well. There was an all-night armed guard at the back of a casino a half block away. His presence probably made them more cautious, but didn't stop them.

Two days later, the guard at the same post would have little effect on an even more significant offense. I was home alone, midday, tapping away on the computer when I heard some commotion outside — raised voices in Spanish. I ignored it for a moment, but the intensity escalated, and I was drawn to the window. Right below me was a black BMW sedan with black tinted windows. It was in the middle of the street with both back doors ajar. There were two men in black ski masks and military fatigues confronting a couple in a VW mini-bus stopped behind the BMW. The barrel of a submachine gun was being pressed against the side of the head of the driver. Unlike the bungling burglar who attacked Baby Blue a few nights ago, these guys were pros. The term "military precision" comes to mind, for good reason. No amateurs here. My jaw dropped as the events unfolded. I felt like I was watching a movie.

My first thought was, "What a photo opportunity!" Then, self-preservation kicked in. If they knew I had a picture of them in the act, I'd be a dead man. I ducked below the window and decided I was way too close for comfort and did not look out again.

Besides, what could I do? I knew there was an armed security guard within eyesight and he was doing nothing. He was actually helpless in the face of the heavily armed bandits and he probably would have lost his life in a valiant attempt to intervene, not to mention risking the lives of the couple. In retrospect it was probably the best for all concerned. As it turned out, no shots were fired and no one was hurt.

I found out later that the couple in the van had just come from the bank where they had withdrawn the equivalent of $5,000 U.S. This was not a random attack. It was most likely an inside job as the result of a tip-off from the bank. I flashed back on the withdrawal I had made to pay off the collision damages. It was a smaller sum and I handed it over almost instantaneously, but it certainly made me stop and think.

Oscar had been constantly discouraging me from driving anywhere in town by myself. "Relax!" I tried to tell him, "I'm a big boy! This is not my first time in a city!" But he was insistent, urging me instead to go with Juan. I was beginning to appreciate why.

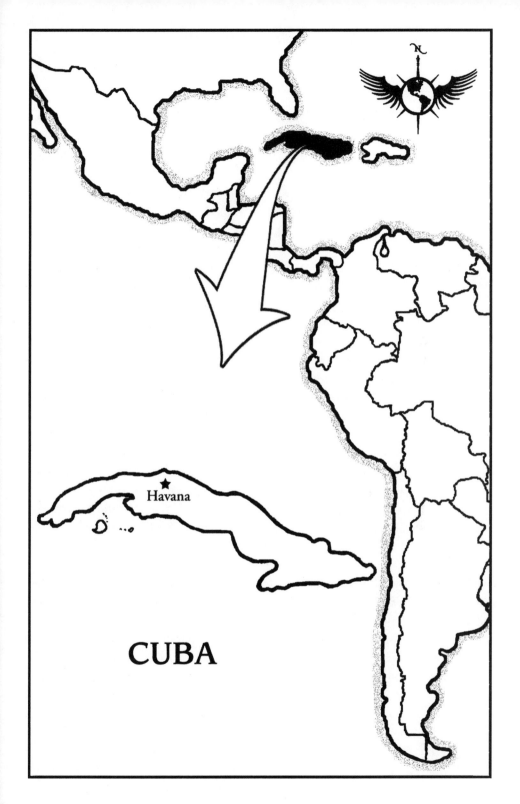

CUBA

Havana

The millennium was approaching quickly which meant it was almost time to party like it was 1999. I wanted to be somewhere exotic and memorable and San Salvador was not exactly party central. I had friends, experienced travelers, who had visited Cuba and absolutely loved it. There were direct flights from San Salvador to Havana. Yes, Havana, now we're talking! A party with the Communist Party!

I arrived at Havana's Jose Marti International Airport to less than a cordial welcome. I thought I had made it through the customs and immigration red tape without a hitch, but no. The open space of the airport's public waiting area was within my view when a khaki-uniformed official waved me out of the flow of travelers. He asked me where I was from and what was the purpose of my visit. I answered in my best Spanish. It wasn't good enough. He had me follow him down a dimly lit hallway isolated from the throngs of travelers. We entered a small room, devoid of windows or décor—just a table and a few chairs. It made me wonder about the purpose of this room and why was I in it. Havana for the Millennium sounded exotic, but New Year's in a Cuban jail did not. This seemed serious. I had no idea what I was in for. Who else even knew I was here besides Oscar and Juan?

Two more khaki-clad officials arrived. They looked through my bags and inspected each and every page of my passport. They opened my laptop and clicked through my files. The youngest official was more proficient in the Windows operating system than I was. I sat anxiously in one of the chairs with all of my luggage spread out on the table. I had no idea what was happening nor why I deserved this special attention. I explained that I was on a long trip taking pictures. The interrogation focused heavily on whether I had been drinking (I hadn't). Apparently I had appeared intoxicated to the first official. Perhaps it was my ruddy complexion or I had staggered under the weight of my luggage. I never found out exactly.

I showed them some of the digital photos I had taken in Guatemala. By then I think they had established that I was neither a drunk nor a threat to the Castro regime. By the end of the session we were joking and laughing. They cordially sent me on my way, but it would not be my last encounter with Cuban authorities.

I had a contact in Havana. It was not a close one. In fact, it was a friend of a friend of a friend (of a friend of a friend of Kevin Bacon). It didn't matter though. I called Fernando from the airport and he happily gave me directions to his house. I chatted with the cabbie as I took in the sights along the highway. Bicycles shared the road, and people waited and hitchhiked from the bus stops. Large billboards carried patriotic messages instead of McDonald's advertisements. It was hard to pinpoint or explain, but the vibe was very different than Mexico or Central America.

Fernando had invited me to his home in *Habana Vieja* (Old Havana), which was a neighborhood in the capital city. The slight awkwardness of our initial meeting gave way to mutual interest in each other's lives. I was in a strange new world, and to him, I was from one.

The address I had was his parents' home, a third-floor flat in a crumbling old building. The inside of their home was a sharp contrast to the exterior. Meticulously neat and tidy, they clearly took great pride in its upkeep.

Early in the evening, Fernando told me he would find me a casa particular, which is a private home that rents rooms to travelers, the Cuban version of a bed-and-breakfast. In the meantime, I helped hoist living room furniture up to the balcony from the street. New furniture— life is good, I thought. I came to find out the furniture was not actually new, but refurbished, and this was their first "new" furniture since the Revolution over forty years ago! I admired the resourcefulness of these proud people making do with the same furniture for forty years.

Fernando took me to a place outside of the city to a casa particular, which was the home of his girlfriend. Fernando was in his late thirties with a young son and an estranged wife. Although he was not living with his wife, the mother of his child, he made it clear to me that he didn't want his parents to know about his girlfriend.

We rode to the girlfriend's house in a light green Volkswagen Beetle that was accented with spots of rust. Getting in and out of it was always a challenge. It seemed like there wasn't a single car in Cuba that had totally functional doors and windows. Fernando carried a wrench in the car to operate the broken mechanisms. His resourcefulness was necessitated by the shortage of goods brought on by the U.S. embargo. Car parts, furniture and even toilet seats were in short supply.

The girlfriend lived with her six-year-old daughter and her mother. The small, spare room was decorated with plastic flowers and religious paintings and statues. The TV was a large box with a small rounded screen unlike anything I had ever seen before. Upon closer inspection, I noticed the branding and dials were in Russian.

After the U.S. embargo began in the early '60s, the Soviet Union became Cuba's major trading partner. Many remnants of that period remain. I discovered that many people had Russian names. For a period of time, Russian was taught as the standard second language in schools. To this day, English skills remain in short supply. They do a terrible job of translating the tourist literature and menus into English. The Russian legacy is also evident in the cars on the road. Cuba is like an automotive melting pot with a mixture of pre-revolution American classics like Chevys and Buicks to Soviet-made cars like Ladas and Volgas. All were held together with the same out-of-necessity resourcefulness that made a set of furniture last forty years. Necessity is the mother of invention and she lives in Cuba.

Unfortunately, Fernando's girlfriend's house was on the outskirts of town, which turned out to be impractical because I had no transportation and there was nothing to do except go to the nearby beach. The first morning I was there, I went for a walk down to beach. I was walking along and I saw three girls sitting and sunning themselves. They smiled at me and waved. I smiled back and kept walking. On the way back they motioned for me to come and sit down (You do the math, the odds were in my favor). Twist my arm. Every one of them was there with an Italian boyfriend, they told me, but the guys were off down the beach. They wanted company. So I sat with them for awhile and we all flirted and laughed, me doing my best to communicate in Spanish.

To my surprise, it took a provocative turn right away. They started asking personal questions. While I was trying to figure out how to answer them, one of the girls asked me what I was made of. Before I could respond, she reached right into my pants and found out for herself! Right there on the beach. This was my first morning here. I thought, "Hmmm. Cuba might be fun."

Cubans, in general, aren't very shy, and lack many of the puritanical hang-ups we have in the U.S. They approach sex with the same openness and enthusiasm they give to music and dancing. It seemed to me that music, dancing and sex were some of the few things in their lives not under strict control. They were a means of self-expression the government couldn't regulate, and the Cubans thoroughly embraced them.

I only stayed at the beach house for a couple of days, but I was there for New Year's Eve. Since I had come to Cuba for some excitement on the millennium, I didn't really feel like staying home alone. I took a bus into the city to look for some fun. I found a place where they were having an outside party at a big hotel in the town square. It was all for tourists, and there were different groups being shuttled into the party. It was a hundred dollars to get in, and I didn't feel like spending that much to go into a party by myself.

I wandered around outside watching the festivities gear up when I saw somebody from California whom I had run into earlier in the day. He was with about nine or ten other people, and he said to me, "Come in, come with us!" So I just jumped into their group and went in without paying. It was a Cuban cabaret show for the benefit of the tourists, which wasn't the exotic or cultural experience I'd been hoping for.

Afterwards I went out on the streets. There was music and dancing everywhere. I joined a party spilling out onto the street at the waterfront. I started dancing with two young women. One of them took a liking to me and we started making out on the dance floor. I still wasn't used to the forwardness of the women, but I wasn't complaining.

It was after 3:00 a.m. and I had no idea how I was going to get home. Luckily, the two young women I was hanging out with were headed back to my neighborhood. We loaded into a large Buick Sedan from the '50s. There were at least eight of us in the back seat. We were like sardines but this was a pretty typical mode of Cuban transport. The only unusual thing was me, a gringo in the car. Cuban authorities frown on the locals fraternizing with tourists so I had to hunker down below the window whenever we passed the police. Because it was so late, the women said they would find a place for me to stay for the night. The next day, I walked along the beach to get back to my *casa particular*. I walked among the locals on the beach and past the segregated tourist sections. I wasn't quite a part of either group. I was an observer floating between both worlds, but not of them.

Later that day, I asked Fernando if he could find me another place closer to the city. He got me another *casa particular*, the home of a retired lawyer and his wife. It was much more in the center of things. I stayed there for a few days until I ran into Luis.

Luis was a bicycle taxi driver who I met on a cab ride. He was a delightful guy who wanted to know everything about me and wanted to be my personal taxi driver for the rest of my life. He was extremely outgoing, just one notch shy of being obnoxious. When he heard how much I was paying at my *casa particular*, he said I could stay at his home for free. So I went over to his flat, met the family, and moved in! I went from an upscale neighborhood to the other side of the tracks. The lawyer's family was very cordial, but I was definitely a client. At Luis' home I was a part of the party. In fact, I was the reason for the party.

Luis lived with his girlfriend, Elsa, and her four daughters. There was the youngest, Maria Elena, who was three, as well as a nine-year-old and two teenagers. The baby of the family took an immediate liking to me. She would cling to me as though I was her teddy bear. She was my personal alarm clock each morning. Long before it was light, she would creep into my room to greet me. I would wake up nose-to-nose with her bright shiny face— how could I say no? After about a week, seeing how close we had grown, they told me that she had not been baptized and asked me if I would be her godfather. It was an offer I could not refuse. I was very honored, and said yes. She was baptized on the same Sunday afternoon of her fourth birthday party.

MARK'S ADVENTURE ALERT

Location: Havana, Cuba

Subject: My Favorite Cuban Girlfriend

I became an official part of my adoptive Cuban family today. At least in the eyes of the Church. I am now a proud *Padrino*, the godfather of my friends' youngest daughter. It was her baptism and the celebration of her fourth birthday. A big day for such a little girl. "*Una candela*," her mother calls the bright-faced little bundle of energy.

There was an instant connection between us when we met and I was glad to oblige her parents' request to be a part of their lives and the ceremony. I explained that I didn't know when or if I'd be coming back and that was fine with them. I had lunch at their house and then we walked to the church for the ceremony. It was a group event with 15-20 others "starting their lives as Christians." The ceremony was a little drawn out for my taste, sort of how I remember the Catholic Church from my youth. But hey, I hung in there.

The real festivities began back at the house. Cake, balloons, streamers, and a piñata decorated the Old Havana apartment. Built in the '30s, the three-story building is actually about six stories tall because the ceiling on each level is about 18 feet tall. Tall enough that parts of the apartment had been crudely subdivided to create additional upstairs bedrooms on the same floor. Lots of energy went into cleaning and decorating, but the music made it really happen.

A borrowed Backstreet Boys tape blasting on a borrowed boom box in the courtyard of the modified two-bedroom apartment that housed nine people and three little pigs. Not from a fairy tale, three little pigs in a small cement pen outside the kitchen in the courtyard. Yes, it smelled like a farmyard, but nobody seemed to notice.

One of the benefits of becoming a godfather was getting to know the godmother. Ony, Elsa's cousin, had chocolate-brown skin and a very appealing curvy figure. Her shy smile exposed a small gap between her front teeth. I was introduced to her prior to the baptism. Luis and Elsa were fairly direct about fixing me up with her. It was as though they were saying, "Here is dinner and here is a girlfriend if you like her."

I was enjoying my time with my new family, but I wanted to visit places outside Havana. Luis wanted to be my guide on a tour around the country. This turned out to be more difficult than I had expected. To the Cubans, constant change is normal and accepted. When the Soviet Union collapsed, so did their support for Cuba. The Cuban economy and people had to adapt. For example, Castro announced that Cuba was going to go after tourist dollars, a compromise from the socialist ideal. The people just had to roll with it. The social and economic systems seemed to be held together by duct tape and dental floss, just like their cars.

However, it was not the economy that drew most of my attention. Traveling around Cuba with Luis, I witnessed the many ways the system discriminated against the locals. It's sad, but the Cubans are treated like second-class citizens compared to foreigners. There are tourist locations where the locals aren't allowed to go. Tourists and locals are not allowed to travel together. The locals are not even supposed to approach the tourists on the street. If the police believed a local was approaching a tourist for some sort of monetary gain, they would intervene. The government strives to keep the two cultures separated.

That was the real problem with Luis and I traveling together. We couldn't check into a *casa particular* together. We either had to go to separate hotels, find somebody who would bend the rules, or stay with a friend. We had to do things under the table, because people who ran the *casa particulars* had to fill out government registration forms. When they found that he was a local and I was a tourist they would say, "No, no. Sorry. Can't do that."

Often we couldn't get on the same bus at the same time. One night on the way back from a day trip, we had trouble getting back to Havana. Around midnight we finally found a bus. Probably because it was the middle of the night and we were in the middle of nowhere, the driver looked the other way. Whatever the reason, I was thankful. The bus was jam-packed. There were no seats available and we had to step over passengers and dogs sleeping on the floor. We let them all lie. Finding empty spots toward the back, we slept in the aisle the rest of the night.

Even walking down the street was a problem. If we saw police ahead, Luis would tell me to cross over to the other side of the street. At times it was irritating, but sometimes it was kind of exciting. I felt as though I were part of an underground subversive movement. It was a challenge. However, Luis was such a fun-loving, easy-going guy, we always managed to find someplace to stay and something to eat.

I experienced this again with Luis, Elsa and Ony. We went out of town for the weekend and had the same challenges. The first night we went out to the beach to search for places we could stay, but by 1:00 a.m. we still hadn't found anywhere. Although we ended up staying in a public pool house storage shed, at least we had poolside lounge chair cushions to sleep on.

The next night we finally found someone who had an apartment attached to their house and was willing to rent it to us under the table. I'll never forget the little feast we put together that night— part of a roasted chicken, stale, bland crackers and a can of something that resembled Vienna sausages. While many things were rationed and scarce, Cuban rum was cheap and plentiful. Families get an allotment of free food each month (one of the "benefits" of being in a socialist society), but it's hardly enough. A family may get two or three chickens a month. Not realizing this, I ate my chicken the way I usually do, leaving scraps of meat on the bone. It was very sobering to watch as they ate my scraps, leaving behind absolutely nothing but the bones, bare and shiny! I thought about all of the things I take for granted in the U.S. I realized that my notion of quality of life was so misguided. It wasn't about the crackers, these people were having fun. Once I got over myself, I did too!

My time on the island coincided with an international news event involving Cuba — the saga of Elian Gonzalez. Elian's mother, along with others, had tried to escape Cuba on a raft to get to Miami, Florida. His mother drowned. Little Elian made it to the shores of Miami into the waiting arms of relatives. However his father, still in Cuba, wanted him back. After lots of press coverage and political wrangling, Elian was returned. I wrote this story while he was still in Miami:

MARK'S ADVENTURE ALERT

Location: Havana, Cuba

Subject: Cuban Mother's March

There is something about Cuba that is very hard to describe or define. I keep thinking that soon it will all be clear and easy to write about. But it only gets more mysterious. Today I experienced the Cuban Mothers' March for young Elian. It was a phenomenal display of harmony and an event that ran like a Swiss watch.

Yesterday, if you had asked, my opinion would have been that Elian was not a big deal to most Cubans and that Cuban organizations were slow and anything but organized. Not today. The home where I am staying in Havana is about a block from the American government office, what would be called the Embassy if there were diplomatic relations between our countries.

It was the focal point of the March and the location of previous Elian demonstrations. It is also the location of several billboards demanding the return of Elian. I wandered freely around the area with my camera and even into a high-rise building for a better vantage point. People were friendly and gracious to me even knowing that I was from the place where Elian is being "held captive."

"Return our child! Return our child!" they chanted in Spanish. But it was not aggressive or violent. Somewhere between 80 and 150 thousand women and children marched along the Malecón, the street that curves along the Havana waterfront. It stretched for miles, literally further than the eye could see. It was an awesome spectacle with the surf crashing against the picturesque wall that separates Havana from the sea. Were they obligated to attend? Perhaps. Was the entire event choreographed for CNN? Certainly. But whether or not it could be perceived in a sound bite or understood by American culture, the heart of the Cuban community was there on display. The irony of the situation, on this island of inexplicable contrasts, is that that the Cuban Mothers' March was for a child who was with his mother when she died while trying to escape."

An event involving 100,000 people in any major city in the U.S. might cause a huge disruption in the day and could lead to arrests. Yet this event was organized and peaceful. After the march the whole crowd quietly dispersed. Forty-five minutes later everything was back to normal.

In Havana, I found people willing to talk to me about politics, many of whom anti-Castro. Many disgruntled Cubans would prefer either to live in the U.S. or to have things change in Cuba. When I got out into the countryside, I found that opinions changed greatly. Most people were pro-Castro and willingly part of the system.

Like other countries, big city and rural life are very different. In Cuba, the citizens do not have freedom of speech and all of the news comes from government newspaper and TV. However, in Havana, residents are inadvertently exposed to magazines, cable TV and other media via the tourist industry. They learn about the outside world that the government shelters them from. Cuba is a great place to visit, but I wouldn't want to live there as a citizen.

I was fascinated by Cuba on so many levels. Physically isolated as an island, it's also been culturally and politically isolated for over 40 years. Because of this isolation, Cuban society has evolved distinctly— just like the plants and animals of the Galapagos Islands that are found nowhere else in the world. Castro's influence has created a bastardized socialist society completely separated from common worldwide influences. The Cubans' irrepressible nature has evolved in spite of, or because of, the traumas they've faced. They have an amazing zest for life. For me, there continues to be a thrill and mystery in uncovering all these layers, finding new depths of understanding. What am I going to find next?

Cuba is a seductive place, and I would be drawn back to her many times, but for now it was time to get back to Baby Blue in El Salvador and finish my journey to the end of the world.

Back in El Salvador, I took Oscar up on an invitation to stay at his beach house. It was a world away from San Salvador urban life.

Location: El Pimental Beach, El Salvador

Subject: The Inner Adventure Begins — Part 1

I woke up this morning to the sound of the surf on the beach. Occasionally during the night a particularly large wave would crash against the beach so as to startle me just a bit. I'm at a rustic beach cabin at the end of nowhere. A forty-minute dirt road followed by a fifteen minute sand road along the beach.

On one side of me is the ocean, just out my bedroom window. On the other side, about fifty yards away, is an estuary where the fishermen from this small village catch shrimp.

I've been reading two books on my journey, both about journeys of their own. The first is a journal of an expedition into the Himalayas. An American biologist and his friend, the author, a student of Zen Buddhism. There is an inner quest happening for the author along with the search for certain wildlife. (*The Snow Leopard*, by Peter Matthiessen)

"Just as a white summer cloud, in harmony with heaven and earth freely floats in the blue sky from horizon to horizon following the breath of the atmosphere-in the same way the pilgrim abandons himself to the breath of the greater life that leads beyond the farthest horizons to an aim which is already present within him, though yet hidden from his sight."

The Way of the White Clouds
Lama Anagarika Govinda

The second book is about a journey that took the author from his medical practice into the realm of metaphysics. (*Joy's Way*, by W. Brugh Joy, M.D.) He returned from his expedition to become a teacher of spirituality and healing with body energies. In the book he describes exercises that he uses in his teachings, some of which piqued my interest. He explained an exercise that involves isolation and searching for an inanimate "teacher" in the desert. I was not consciously thinking about the exercise as I walked along an isolated stretch of beach. A large seashell appeared in the surf and "spoke" to me. As I reached to pick it up, I recalled the exercise and thought, "My Teacher!"

As I walked along I felt that I had found something special in addition to a pretty souvenir from this part of my trip. It had a feminine quality to it as if a representation of one of the many pretty women I've met on my trip, or in my life, for that matter. Very soon thereafter, I encountered yet another shell in the surf. The same size and shape, but very different in color, texture, composition and age. Rippling undulations partially filled with coral growth made it fascinating to study more closely. As I walked along with one in each hand, they spoke volumes to me. I plan to spend more time with my two new friends to see what else they have to say.

MARK'S
ADVENTURE ALERT

Location: El Pimental Beach, El Salvador

Subject: The Inner Adventure Begins — Part 2

I read more of *Joy's Way* this morning, finding out the actual impetus for his journey. Different than mine, but some parallels are there. Following an inner voice without knowing the exact destination... After reading for awhile, I had an urge to interact with my teachers and meditate. The teaching had to do with a similar dynamic that occurred recently in Cuba and again in San Salvador. In Havana, my friends introduced me to their cousin. 28 years old, very pretty, friendly and sexy! And it didn't take long for her to let me know that she was attracted to me! In spite of all this, there was a tiny little voice inside my head that said "No!" No to what, I'm not sure. No, she's not "The One?" No, don't get involved?? I got involved. There was chemistry between us but we did not get intimate. At least for the time being.

I left Havana to travel with my buddy. In a very small town, the home of my buddy's father, I met another sweetheart. A big voice inside my head said "Yes!" I was overwhelmingly attracted to this girl. We were in a disco with loud music but we managed to communicate a little. But mostly we danced. At the end of the night she was leaving with her friends and I asked for her phone number. She wrote down her address and asked her friend how to say and write "I Love You" in English. What she wrote wasn't even close, but I got the message!

The next day on my way out of town I saw her waiting for a bus. I was very excited to see her but the enthusiasm did not seem to be returned. We chatted for a moment, then as we parted, I said, "I have your number." She replied, "And I have yours." It left me with some hope. When I arrived back in Havana, I planned to call her and arrange another visit, but I realized there was no phone number on the card! Only an address and "I Love You!" Did she not have a phone or had she forgotten in her attempt at her message in English? It was a long way back without a call for confirmation. What to do? Meanwhile, I reconnected with the cousin in Havana and had a great time! But in the back of my mind, I wanted to find my way back to the other. Time and money were running out and I stayed with what was convenient. In San Salvador the same thing happened with a different cast of characters. I chose ease and convenience over what I really wanted. And I used other people's feelings as an excuse not to follow my instinct and go after what I wanted. That certainly was a lot of words to describe a rather instantaneous experience. But hold on, there's more to come in a different area of my life...

MARK'S ADVENTURE ALERT

Location: El Pimental Beach, El Salvador

Subject: The Inner Adventure Begins — Part 3

I'm spending more quality time with my "teachers," enjoying some interesting and enlightening exchanges. I imagine I've lost some of my audience for lack of photos. And now I'm talking to seashells! There goes the rest of the crowd. Ha! So be it!

I want to expand on the insight I discussed recently and how it spilled over from my social life to photography and the creative impulse. Honoring that voice that says, "Whoa! That would be a cool shot!" It could be spontaneous or carefully planned. It doesn't matter. Following that impulse and making it happen is the crux of the artistic process for me.

However, more times than not, I'll find an excuse or reason not to go for the shot. My most common excuse is, "He/She won't want to have his/her picture taken." I'm projecting my feelings onto other people. Now I realize that I can go after what I want and still have respect for other peoples' wishes and feelings. I like that. And interacting with my subjects seems more effortless now!

A fascinating byproduct of this little internal episode is that I have felt more joy in my physical surroundings when I'm not taking pictures due to the disappearance of the thought, "I should be taking a picture of this..." That thought comes from a different place than the creative impulse. Yeah! Follow the inspiration and lose the nagging! I can live with that!!

MARK'S
ADVENTURE ALERT

Location: El Pimental Beach, El Salvador

Subject: The Inner Adventure Begins — Part 4

I received a specific request for reports on food. A review of the haute cuisine of El Pimental Beach. Move over Julia Child and Tom Veneklasen. Natural foods are the standard fare here, though not for reasons of health but availability. Food just doesn't get any fresher than what I've been enjoying here. Coconuts right off the tree. Fish direct from the sea. I was taking pictures of kids catching crabs in the estuary and they asked me if I wanted some for lunch. Half an hour later I was having crabs and coconut milk.

A regional favorite, and one of mine as well, is the coffee-flavored ice cream. OKAY, it's not Ben & Jerry's, in fact, it's just flavored frozen milk. But it did come direct from the cow earlier in the day. And mighty tasty, I must say!

Our featured item today is the Duck Soup Pimental! While enjoying *café con leché* for breakfast this morning I noticed a live duck lassoed by his leg to the open-air kitchen table. I returned from a short cruise in the estuary to find that the duck was being plucked!

An hour or two later I was having lunch. The delicately seasoned broth came with several manly sized chunks of unidentified vegetables and one large portion of our formerly feathered friend. A hearty corn tortilla and coconut milk served au naturel rounded out the meal. Simply delightful. Oddly enough, here in the country that produces the most coffee per square foot, I've been served a lot of instant coffee. But then, coffee doesn't grow at the beach.

After my stay at the beach cabin I headed back to Oscar's house in San Salvador. I had developed quite the extensive social network in the short time I had spent in the city. Oscar introduced me to his friends and they in turn introduced me to their friends. I enjoyed my status as the "interesting foreigner." There was something paradoxical about being around so many great people in the context and framework of this violent and depressing culture.

I spent a lot of my time with Oscar's friend Linda. We attended a few cocktail and dinner parties and soon I had more offers for social events than there were nights in the week. On one occasion, Linda gave me an interesting perspective on the violent nature of her country. Driving around in her car, I'd noticed a shiny silver revolver that had slid out from beneath her seat. I swallowed my initial shock and brought it to her attention. "Oh, yes, that. Isn't it cute?" she said, as if it were an accessory to match her earrings, her little bling bling, bang bang!

Her father had taught her how to use it and other guns. It led into a lengthy conversation about the war and violence that had torn her country and society apart. Linda had some very personal stories about family members and associates who had been abducted and later dumped on the street dead, with no fingernails left and other more grisly evidence of an unimaginable way to die. "But things are okay now," she reassured me. But the cute little revolver remained.

Another friend I made turned out to be both helpful and fascinating.

MARK'S ADVENTURE ALERT

Location: San Salvador, El Salvador
Subject: Salvadoran Cyber-Chick

In my quest to solve some computer difficulties and to archive my digital photos, I was introduced to Karla. I had been told that she was a crazy girl who spent her days at work on a computer and her nights at home online. A GeekChick. A Techie! But she certainly didn't look the part! In person she was very attractive and vivacious and talked a mile a minute. An unbelievably fast, nonstop cadence to her speech. "Stop and take a deep breath!" I would tell her so that I could understand more than one out of every seventeen words. It was no use though, she'd be back up to full speed within 15 seconds.

I told her about the programmers and tech people I knew at home and that they stayed up all night surviving on coffee, Pepsi, and pizza. She nodded quickly with her eyes wide open to acknowledge that I was describing her lifestyle exactly.

I think that computers have an effect on the human nervous system. No matter what my posture is I get a sharp pain between my shoulder blades after a certain amount of time online. I think the nervous system gets amped on some level by the electronic interaction, hence the "wired" lifestyle of the technical types.

Back to Krazy-Karla. At a coffee shop (wouldn't ya know?) she described her numerous online liaisons and a program called "ICQ" (Get it? "I seek you"-I didn't!). It's a sophisticated chat program that is very popular in El Salvador. Forgive me if this is old hat and I'm just a little behind the curve, but I was amazed at the functionality of the program and by the fact that the company says it has received requests for, and downloaded the program, 80 million times! Obviously a little more widespread than just El Salvador.

Again, back to KK and her international online lovers… Matus was the codename of her Honduran friend she knew only through her computer screen. They spent months getting to know each other online. Hours together every evening, then eventually at work, ICQ allowed them to be in touch ALL DAY LONG with an omnipresent little dialogue box in the corner of her screen, regardless of what she was doing or working on! A fairly intense relationship, electronic or not. After months of this, Matus finally decides that he must meet her in person and tells her he is coming to San Salvador for that purpose. She panics! She tells him that her real name is Ricky and that she's actually a guy!! No response for two minutes. Finally back across the screen comes, "I LOVE YOU!" This real life story continues, but gets too complicated and convoluted for me to begin to describe. The happy ending (or beginning?) is that they actually did meet and they have been seeing each other regularly ever since. In person! And yes, my computer is up and running, and my photos are nicely stored on CD!

In addition to Oscar's social network I made some friends on my own. Although Oscar's house in the city was in an upscale neighborhood, his street ran parallel to a main drag lined with businesses. Just behind his house was a casino, and down the block was another nocturnal establishment called *Lips*. Curiosity got the best of me and I decided to explore both places.

The casino did not hold my attention for long. It had none of the energy of Las Vegas— just one smoky room with blackjack tables and slot machines. The lighting was dull, the mood oppressive. I like to take my chances at blackjack from time to time, but this place certainly did not inspire me.

The *Lips* sign, with its large lipstick-smudge logo, made no attempt to hide the nature of its business. A broad-chested doorman in a pressed white shirt and black tie asked if I had any *armas*, firearms! I said no and passed through a doorframe-type metal detector. My pocket-sized digital camera made it buzz and blink. Uh-oh! As I removed the camera from my pocket the doorman motioned toward a desk and said that I would have to check it before I entered.

My eyes popped open as I watched other customers sliding their revolvers across the countertop. Guns were appearing from boots, under belts and out of coat pockets. Maybe this wasn't such a great idea after all. I hesitated, saying I didn't want to check my camera and that I would come back another time. Sensing the loss of some gringo cash, the white-shirted doorman interceded at the desk. He told me I could keep my camera with me but using it in the club was not allowed. I agreed and paid my cover charge, which included my first two drinks.

The place was lively and boisterous. It couldn't have been a bigger contrast to the casino next door. There were three main rooms, two of them with stages. The room connecting the two showrooms had four pool tables and TV's hanging from the ceiling in the corners. Damn! I couldn't believe all of the nearly naked babes in the place! Dancers everywhere and waitresses scurrying about serving food and drinks. I wandered between the rooms checking out not only the dancers onstage but also those scattered throughout the club. Clusters of four and five of them stood at the different bars, checking me out more intensely than I did them. They looked at me like I was lunch and they had missed breakfast! The attention was overwhelming, I didn't know quite how to handle it. I tried to smile and return their attention with eye contact but I was terribly out-numbered.

I found a table in the main showroom and ordered my first beer. A few tables away another gringo was surrounded by a small crew of dancers. He waved to me as I looked in his direction. He gestured for me to join him at his table saying, "We gotta stick together around here." Ted had a huge plate with a half-eaten burger, salad and fries in front of him. His small entourage of dancers smiled at me as they continued to munch on the fries from his plate. He introduced himself and the four girls at the table, making a valiant attempt to remember and pronounce all of their names correctly. He explained the social and economic workings of the club, an overview of how I fit in and what to expect.

At Lips the girls made their money by doing lap dances. Three songs for what was about ten dollars. Prostitution was expressly prohibited, as noted in various places in the club. The closest thing to an exception was what I'd call the self-serve booth. You'd pay a fee and enter one side. There was a girl on the other side separated by a pane of glass. The customer was on his own to, ahem, service himself. No thanks, not appealing to me.

Ted was struggling with the language as he spoke with the dancer to his right who seemed to have territorial rights over the others at the table. She was asking for help with some paperwork. He asked me to help translate and to be the bearer of bad news. It seems that unknowingly, he had agreed to help her get the necessary papers to get a visa to the States.

I did my best to explain that there was a misunderstanding and that he was not able to help with the papers. Caught in the crossfire! She was not happy with the news I tried to deliver so tenderly. She stormed away from the table in a huff. Ted was visibly relieved. Two other women closed in, happy to have the main competition eliminated.

As the only gringos in the place, we got lots of attention from the ladies. Most seemed to be in their early twenties. Most were single moms with several kids at home. For them this was very much a matter of survival. That didn't stop them from having fun, as well as making me feel welcome.

Dina was a friend of one of Ted's friends. She was not the most beautiful nor most vivacious woman in the place. In fact, sadness seemed to ooze out of her soulful brown eyes. Like big pools of shiny darkness, it was her eyes that drew me in. It was a very emotional connection from the beginning. What was it that connected us? Out of all of the girls in the club, all of the sexy smiles, why her? It was her eyes. I wanted to dive right into them. Something about the sultry sadness attracted me. Was it sadness in me that resonated with hers? Was it something in me that wanted to comfort and soothe her sadness? Whatever it was, it was strong and unspoken.

I visited Dina at the club three or four times before we got together after hours. Ted was in San Salvaldor on an extended consulting contract with a manufacturing firm. He was staying in a large suite in an American chain hotel. On two occasions, a small group of us piled into one taxicab and accompanied Ted back to his hotel room.

Ted had been involved with one particular dancer but had broken it off with her recently. In the process of dating one of them he had become friends with two others. Like an older brother, he was very protective of them. He empathized with them, caring about their hopes and dreams that often extended far beyond their current reality of surviving and feeding their kids. But their reality was just that, their kids and the struggle to survive. I was surprised and even impressed by his friendly affection for them without being sexually involved. There was certainly flirting and attraction but he had established an unusual level of trust and rapport with them.

With Dina and me, it was a different story. The sexual nature of the club certainly set the tone of our relationship from the start. Outside of the club, within the limited privacy of Ted's hotel room, our connection progressed. Our only real privacy was under the covers of our double bed or in the shower. It was a little awkward but exciting at the same time.

There was no language barrier between us as we whispered under the covers. That is, with the exception of one episode in the shower. We were enjoying ourselves when unbeknownst to me, something happened that made her think she was not pleasing me. It triggered an emotional meltdown in her with cascading feelings of self-doubt and despair. She cried and cried and cried. It was hard for me to understand what was going on. All I could do was hold her while asking what was wrong and telling her everything was okay. My kisses and caresses seemed to have no effect. When the tidal wave of emotion finally began to subside, she started to open back up to me. Between sobs, she explained that she didn't think she was doing it right. She thought she didn't know how to have sex! I comforted her and told her she was doing just fine!

I was shocked given her sexy confident persona inside the club. To my amazement, I found out that she had never received positive feedback from any of her previous lovers. How sad! I did my best to make up for the deficit.

I was making plans to leave El Salvador and I wanted to invite Dina to join me for a short trip to a mountain lake. I hesitated because I knew I would be leaving soon. I was telling Oscar about a conversation I had with Dina in which I told her I was leaving town. Oscar interrupted me mid-sentence and completed the sentence for me. "…and she started crying." he said. "Of course she did," he continued and shook his head in another "Markie, Markie, Markie…" moment. "Take her to the lake. Have some fun. Why do you have to think so much?"

Were the tears real? Was she working me? Perhaps both. Oscar did help to simplify things. Dina agreed to the weekend expedition. We went to the lake, about two hours out of the city. Her young son Alfonso joined us for the trip. He was a happy 18-month old with an easy smile and a head full of dark curls.

Being that it was the off-season there was plenty of peace and quiet. We visited a couple of mountain villages and got to see a softer side of El Salvador. I got to know Dina as a mom, exposing another dimension of her character. The weekend was completely comfortable, effortless and fun. Perhaps because of Alfonso, it wasn't torrid and passionate. However, it was very natural and real.

Unfortunately the weekend had to end and I continued with my preparations to head to Honduras. Dina wanted to go with me to the border and then take a bus back. We rode together for a couple of hours toward Honduras. It was the last chance we'd have to spend time together. I knew there would be tears at the border, but we would still have fun along the way.

We got to the border and had a little over an hour to wait for Dina's bus back to San Salvador. In the meantime, she helped me get started on the border crossing bureaucracy. One friendly bureaucrat was checking Dina out with a slightly lascivious eye. He looked at me with one raised eyebrow, a silent gesture that said, "You're one lucky guy!" I nodded in acknowledgement and gratitude, wondering to myself what I was doing leaving her behind.

I knew I could never live in San Salvador. Dina and little Alfonso on the road with Mark was not gonna happen either. I was clear that I was leaving but I was still torn. We got her ticket and waited together next to the bus as the engine rumbled and some of the final passengers boarded. She made a valiant effort to restrain her tears as her lower lip quivered very slightly. But it was no use. The ticket taker waved impatiently at us signaling that it was time to go.

It was the last thing I wanted to do but I almost had to pry her arms from around me or the bus would have left without her. She finally scampered up the steps into the bus. When she reached her seat she pressed her palm to the window as she looked out at me through teary eyes. I waved as the bus pulled away while she continued to press one hand against the window as if trying to reach through to me.

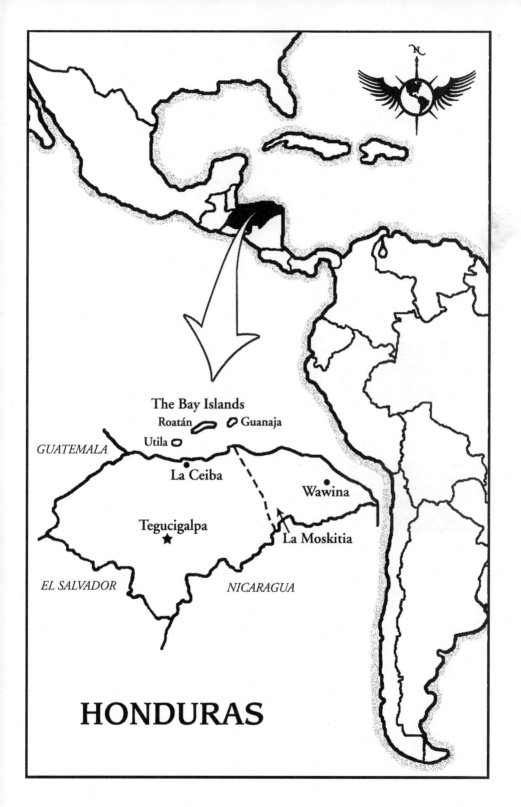

The Bay Islands
Roatán Guanaja
Utila

GUATEMALA

La Ceiba

Wawina

Tegucigalpa

La Moskitia

EL SALVADOR NICARAGUA

HONDURAS

The look on Dina's face as she left had an impact on me for which I was not prepared. Watching the bus trail off into the dust I couldn't figure out what I was feeling, but I didn't like it. The pain and anguish on her face? My own feelings of loss? Feeling guilty for causing her pain? My emotions were jumbled up and I didn't want any of them.

I just wanted to get across the border and drive. I didn't want to stand around and face what I was feeling, but I would have to. Continuing with my paper chase, I soon found out that I was short about thirty dollars for the fee for my car permit. There I was at the border between El Salvador and Honduras, late in the day and without enough money for a permit to get across. The only option was to drive back to a nearby town to get the cash. But that would get me back to the border after closing, leaving me in El Salvador for another night. I did not want to do that! I became possessed. I could not face the prospect of hanging out in this town in my current frame of mind.

I had to find a way. I started selling stuff out of my truck to raise the cash. I had a spare Walkman and a cooler I had never used and a bunch of other odds and ends. I just went out on the streets and started grabbing people as they walked by, asking them if they wanted to buy anything. I raised the $30 dollars and got my paperwork done before the border closed. I was still possessed, but now with fewer possessions.

I got in Baby Blue and headed into the rolling hills of the Honduras countryside. I tried to drive away from my feelings, almost cursing under my breath as I gripped the steering wheel. It was late in the afternoon. I passed a very small town with a hotel, but I didn't feel like stopping or talking to anyone face-to-face. I kept driving straight through that town, even though it was starting to get dark. I was actually breaking one of my traveling commandments: Thou shalt not drive at night in Latin America. This is because of problems with *banditos*, lack of proper signage and road markings, pedestrians, animals and more. But that night I wanted to take the risk, to push it, to get away from feeling lousy. Like maybe if I drove fast enough, and put enough distance between her and me, I could outrun the feeling that was tearing me up inside.

Darkness fell and the rolling hills had turned into mountains. Then I started to realize that my feelings were getting the best of me. I thought, "What the fuck am I doing?" I had no idea where I was going or where the next town was. It was totally dark. Lost in Honduras. Sad and alone. The road climbed further into the mountains. I was driving on a winding road, in the pitch-black of night, with a mountain on my left and a drop-off to my right. "This is stupid," I thought. "If I fall off this cliff they won't be able to look for my mangled remains until daybreak."

I came around a blind corner with a severe drop off only to see two sets of headlights barreling downhill straight for me! One truck was passing another, taking up both lanes! I had only three feet of dirt shoulder to my right before the road dropped into the darkness. For a fraction of a second I thought I was a goner. I swerved, straddling the dirt shoulder and the bumpy edge of the pavement. The two trucks, still in parallel tracks, managed to swerve enough to pass me safely. I was left there, stopped halfway on the shoulder, marveling that I was still alive— too stunned to even move. I had a broken heart and nearly a heart attack. Not the best introduction to a new country. There in the dark, on the edge of a cliff, I was physically and emotionally drained. I decided at that point that I was going to lower my personal speed limit by ten miles an hour. And in the future, remember my traveling commandment: do not drive at night.

It was another forty-five minutes before I came to a place to stay. I was thankful to be alive but still totally drained, devoid of emotion. I felt like a zombie checking into the hotel. My legs were stiff and I could barely speak.

I have other bad memories of Honduran highways. Once, while driving (during the day this time), I came to a small town shortly after there had been an accident. A big one, involving three cars and a bus. The bus was banged up a little bit and two of the cars were really crunched.

The bus and one of the cars were blocking the highway. The car was a small sedan, and the driver's side was completely crumpled. The driver was obviously in bad shape. The car door was punched in so he was not going to be getting out any time soon. There were no jaws of life, 911 or emergency road service in this little town, which is true of most little towns in Central America.

People came from a nearby mechanic's shop with hand tools to try to pry the door open and get the guy out, but it was not looking good. I was shocked by what happened next. There were two people lying on the ground next to the bus in obvious agony. Another bus came up to the scene and was trying to get through. The bus driver actually got out and dragged the two injured people to the side of the road, got back in the bus, and drove on through. I found it ironic that in the land of mañana, the driver had a schedule to keep.

There were throngs of people working on the situation, and I knew I couldn't be any help. It made me feel a little sick, but there wasn't much I could do but move on and get out of the way. I was again inspired to lower my personal speed limit another ten miles an hour. If I continued at this rate, before long I would be driving backwards.

The remnants of Hurricane Mitch were still very evident. Hitting the coast of Honduras in October, 1998, it left over a million people homeless, over 6,000 dead, and destroyed about 70% of the crops. The poor country was devastated, and though the U.S. helped out with immediate needs, there was still a great deal of damage to repair. Here I was, two years later, and the roads were still being worked on. Detours and temporary one-lane bridges delayed and frustrated me. Though decimated, the country seemed to be bouncing back nicely. I found it interesting that a lot of the businesses were re-named with titles such as "Mitch's Store" after the hurricane. It seemed like they were embracing the experience rather than pretending it never happened. I would be surprised to see a restaurant called "Katrina's Kitchen" in New Orleans.

Eventually, I made my way to the port town of La Cieba. La Cieba is the name for a tree native to the area. It's a large, distinctive shade tree with a round pattern of branches and leaves. The town is a thoroughfare that hosts travelers from throughout the country. It was a little bit rough around the edges. It had a certain gritty charm to it, but more grit than charm. Being a port town, La Cieba had a transient population and the sleazy feel of a border town. A guy like me could have been just the ticket out for the locals. I realized after awhile that starting up a conversation was easy, but it was a lot harder to get them to leave me alone.

My hotel was not far from an open-air market. I toured the area in the morning and found a café for the locals and shopkeepers. I sat down and made some friends. I was chatting with three or four people, all of them vying for my attention while I was trying to order food. They were explaining to me what was on the menu and I was introduced to the local custom of *Salva Vida* for breakfast. *Salva Vida* means lifesaver and is the national brew, taken along with a thick, loosely rolled Honduran cigar. The two of them will kick start just about anybody's day! Nicotine and alcohol, the breakfast of champions. I learned about the layout of the town and the lifestyle there, but I couldn't quite relax because I always felt like a target. It seemed that everyone wanted something from me.

There was a nightclub district near the water that was not too far from my hotel. The neighborhood was sketchy at best but I decided to venture out anyway.

The first club I went to was bizarre. It was a large dance hall and people were doing a strange local folk dance to really awful music. It was a weird, ungainly, unattractive thrashing. No rhythm, no beat, just a sort of slow-motion epileptic seizure. Okay, perhaps I'm being a tad judgmental. I latched onto some locals who became my guides and guardians for the next few days as I prepared for my trip to the Bay Islands.

La Cieba is the main gateway to the Bay Islands. There are three main islands, Roatan, Utila and Guanaja. Roatan is the biggest and most popular of the island chain. I tried hard to find a ferry that would take Baby Blue to one of the islands, but the cost was prohibitive. I decided to park Baby Blue and take a flight to Roatan. The process of finding a secure garage made me aware of what an important part of my life Baby Blue had become. After El Salvador, I didn't want anybody's hands in her glove box but mine.

The islands are distinct from the Honduran mainland. The people, the lifestyle, and the language are all different, almost like another country. They have a laid-back Caribbean style and you hear lots of reggae music. There is a thriving tourist industry that is completely non-existent on the mainland. The locals are multilingual — Spanish, English and even a French dialect.

MARK'S ADVENTURE ALERT

Location: Roatan, Honduras

Subject: ...here on Gilligan's Isle

It's very easy to remain shipwrecked on this little island named Roatan, in fact many gringos end up spending much, much longer than they planned. Unless you're a scuba diver there isn't that much to do. Perhaps doing nothing is the main attraction.

They say the attitude of the locals has more of an impact on the tourists than vice-versa. The gringos and the islanders seem to blend very nicely, unlike many other tourist destinations where the local culture is destroyed or remains distinct. The culture is multi-lingual with Spanish and English taught in most schools. This helps when it comes to being so gringo-friendly.

MARK'S
ADVENTURE ALERT

Location: Roatan, Honduras

Subject: Island Nightlife

I stayed in the town of West End, you guessed it, on the west end of the island. This is the area where most of the scuba diving happens. The town is basically one street along the water, lined with a number of dive shops, restaurants, and various lodging establishments. I did my obligatory dive, but I actually prefer the freedom and solitude of snorkeling by myself.

West End nightlife is loosely organized into three segments; the watch-the-sunset shift (I saw the green flash!), the mid-evening shift, and the wee-hour shift. Insert dinner before or after any segment you like... This schedule is supplemented by the Friday Night Blow-out at Fosters attended by locals from all over the island. The sunset shift is at one of several docks or establishments actually built on the water. The sunsets are worth watching for sure, even for someone coming from Arizona. A very enjoyable communal activity for West Enders. And as I said before, I saw the green flash! I had heard and read about it before but wasn't sure if it was a myth or some function of staring at the sun too long. But no, just after the sun went below the horizon, it was like a little puff of green smoke. Then the crowd clapped as if to salute the little green genie.

The Twisted Toucan has a lock on the mid-evening shift. It has a small thatched roof that covers a four-sided bar that only seats about 14 people being polite. That doesn't stop the dozens of others from crowding around and spilling into the street and the courtyard.

Salva Vida is the universal favorite, with many locals opting for rum and coke, while some tourists are compelled to overdo the more tropical concoctions. At around 11:30 p.m. the Toucan shuts down in favor of Loafers, the late-nite joint, built on a second level, overlooking a volleyball court on the beach. It's just out of town and away from the lodging to allow for all-night reveling for those not intent on diving in the morning or otherwise gainfully employed.

I ventured out of West End one evening with two local young ladies eager to show me their Island. I had a rental car so I was their friend! I had flirted with Nicki and she offered to be my tour guide. Cynthia came along as her bodyguard. They spoke an English dialect that was fun to listen to but often hard to understand. When they really didn't want me to understand, they spoke "Patou," a native tongue. They switched languages faster than I could change TV stations. They were both very reserved but managed to have a good time, especially when they learned how to use my digital camera. Then Nicki wanted to learn how to drive. I let her take the wheel and steer and she eventually ran the Suzuki Samurai into a ditch. No harm done, but Cynthia was not happy about the situation. She got over it.

MARK'S ADVENTURE ALERT

Location: Roatan, Honduras

Subject: Lobster for Lunch

One of the highlights of my stay on Roatan was a day cruise on a small sailboat. Captain Alex was a rasta-reggae-dancing-happy-as-you-can-be kinda guy with a black German Shepard as first mate. The main mast was handmade from a tree on the Island. It was anything but high-tech, but perfect for the occasion. We snorkeled at various locations around the Island while Alex looked for lunch. By mid-afternoon he had collected enough seafood for our feast. Shortly thereafter Alex emerged form the tiny cabin of the boat with plates of lobster, conch, and potatoes. Add lime, hot sauce, Salva Vida, and some reggae music and you've got your own tropical paradise!!

MARK'S ADVENTURE ALERT

Location: Roatan, Honduras

Subject: La Tienda Jose Maria

The next day, the dynamic duo took me to some tiny little towns around the Island including Flowers Bay, where Nicki seemed to be related to every other person there. It was Sunday morning and lot of people were strolling to or from church in their Sunday best. We visited lots of her relatives and I heard lots of stories about life and living in this tiny village.

The next little town along the water was Gravel Bay. Not a very romantic name, then again not a very romantic place. Rustic, perhaps. I came back by myself, late in the day to take pictures. I stopped to take a picture of a girl on a bike. She was at the window of a broken down wooden house that was the neighborhood store. By the time I got it together she was gone. But Alberto, the 83-year-old proprietor, was there to pose for me and introduce me to the neighborhood as they stopped by one-by-one. Alberto has been living in the same place on the waterfront since 1917!! His aunt willed him the place and he named the store after her, though you wouldn't know it because there is no sign, just a small window with a counter underneath. I asked for a soda and handed him a 100 lempira note (about $7). He didn't have change but said "Don't worry about it 'til next time." Faith in humanity after all those years! I visited with Ricardo, his young grandson, and then Ises, his studious granddaughter. An assorted cast of characters came, chatted, and departed, as they finished their shopping. It was a fascinating slice of life for me to enjoy.

I met someone on Roatan who would become a big part of the next segment of my adventure. The person was Laura; the adventure was a mysterious place called La Mosquitia. I was thrilled with the prospect of exploring the remote jungle region on the southern coast of Honduras that extends into Nicaragua. The maze of rivers through the wilderness area prevents the construction of roads. The inaccessible area's mystique was captured in Paul Theroux's novel, The Mosquito Coast, which was later turned into a film starring Harrison Ford. To Laura it was her family home, the place where she grew up. I would soon discover her love/hate relationship with the place. She was torn between two worlds, her current home in the big city of La Cieba, and her roots deep in La Mosquitia.

Like me, she was a visitor on Roatan. We had even more in common as single travelers, something of a rarity on the island. With only a small group of folks, the nightlife in the West End was still vibrant. It was only a matter of time before our paths crossed.

She was far from being a classic beauty given her slightly crossed eyes and her missing two front teeth! Though I never asked, it was my professional impression that she had lost them in an accident because the rest of her teeth seemed to all be present and in fine shape. Even with these, shall we say, esthetic handicaps, she possessed a wacky and engaging charm. All of the elements of her personality and person added up to an attractive package. She was quirky, she was fun, and best of all she had taken a definite liking to me. We got to know each other over the course of a few days. One particular evening, after a couple of drinks, we ended up in bed in my hotel room. Things progressed as you might expect between two people attracted to each other. Until, at the height of the physical and emotional charge between us, something happened that changed the direction of our relationship. Engaged in protected sex like a good boy should, she suddenly grasped at me and removed the protection, demanding that I continue without it. It was disconcerting to put it mildly. Her actions were not motivated by wanting more physical sensitivity, but by the desire to conceive a child! In that moment, I was not remotely interested in becoming a father. Being highly aroused and slightly tipsy was not conducive to a conversation about planned parenthood. The mood came to a crashing halt.

A cultural abyss had appeared between us like a bottomless crevasse. She felt hurt and rejected. I felt bewildered. My casual approach to this intimate situation had blown up in my face. Casual sex rarely is. Aren't I old enough to know this by now? Individual psychic energies are opened up and swirled together like unconscious ingredients in an improvised recipe for an unpredictable soup.

The intensity was too much for me. I felt isolated and unable to communicate. "Friendship," I thought, "Why don't we keep it right there." I did not want to create another goodbye-at-the-border scenario. Still in bed together, we each withdrew to our respective emotional safety zones and drifted off to sleep.

The next morning, we had somehow swept the awkward encounter under the rug and our friendship and plans to visit La Mosquitia remained intact. Later that day, we caught a flight from Roatan back to La Cieba to prepare for our excursion. From La Cieba we would require a plane and two boat rides to get the village of Wawina, deep in La Mosquitia. After making arrangements for the flight, we shopped for groceries to bring to her family. We bought a bucketful of meat. Literally. We filled a large green plastic bucket with fresh meat from the butcher, various cuts, bones and all! What about ice? A cover for the bucket? Laura was not concerned about those details. No one batted an eye about a bucket of meat as carry-on luggage.

Author's note: That's carry-on not carrion!
Editors note: Actually, it would be both.

We boarded the 15-seat twin-prop plane and I noticed the signage below the windows and on the seatbacks was in Russian. The interior was not in great shape. I wondered about the engine. The crew? Replacement parts? "Just a short flight," I rationalized irrationally.

The plane sputtered over a wonderland of green undulating terrain. Snakes of water divided chunks of land. Was it sections of land carved up by rivers or one massive waterway dotted with islands? In many places it was a toss-up. From a distance, the random lumps blended into an intricately woven tapestry.

We approached a runway that looked as though giant hair clippers had shorn the jungle's unruly locks. We coasted to a stop in front of a small weather-beaten wooden building with a boarded-up service window and a small antenna. The massive airport complex was not open for business. The only functional aspect was a bench against one side with four people calmly waiting for our flight. Next to them were a couple of rickety wooden carts to assist with the transport of luggage down a short path to the river and the small dock that served as an aquatic bus stop.

We joined a dozen or so other passengers and their baggage in a dug-out canoe with two inches of water in the rounded hull. There were no seats, but rather small, moveable split logs for keeping butts and bags above the migrating puddle. I shifted from one awkward position to the next, but my attention was riveted on the passing junglescape, in which land was not visible through the dense vegetation on either side. As the small outboard motor coughed and smoked, Laura and our fellow passengers looked thoroughly bored as if settled in for a dreary daily commute.

I however, was on the edge of my log, delighting in every flickering branch and peering intently at exotic birds and giant green iguanas. The prehistoric-looking lizards, larger and longer than baseball bats, angled their craggy faces majestically toward the sun. As we approached, some seemed content to watch us pass below like a parade, while others felt the need to leap from great heights into the brush or splash into the river. We would encounter more of them under different circumstances at our first stop.

When we reached a small outpost, the depot for the network of canoes and other small boats, three iguana hunters in a dugout canoe pulled in with a bounty of twenty or thirty iguanas. The ten-year-old lizard hunter inside me was jumping up and down. My reptile fascination went way back. As a youngster, exploring the desert near my home in Arizona, I had spent many hours stalking them. My pals and I caught and kept them in a makeshift terrarium that consisted of a large glass jar with nail holes in the lid. The biggest lizard we ever came across was a fraction of the size of these monsters.

These hunters had motives different than mine — putting food on the table. When Laura asked if I had ever eaten iguana, I had to admit, I was a virgin. I had never seen it in a supermarket or ordered iguana, fries and a coke! She offered to prepare one for me if I wanted. I plunked down 35 *lempira* (about $2.50) for a four-footer of my choosing. We'll call him Lenny the Lizard. I felt a twinge of guilt, as though I were sentencing him to death. I rationalized that Lenny's fate was already sealed at that point. I would come to find out that the death sentence was not the worst of it. The process of getting them to the table was cruel and unusual. To immobilize them, a claw from each leg is pulled out with the tendon still attached to the iguana, dangling like string with the claw on the end. Tendons from each side are tied together behind their backs like handy little handcuffs. Gruesome little handcuffs. This effectively restrains most of them, but a few of the feistier ones still thrash around and bite. These unlucky troublemakers have their heads stomped until they calm down. In transit, they are flung around by their tails like a piece of luggage.

In the U.S. we love our hamburgers and steak but we rarely get to know the cow or witness its final moments. We have refrigeration that allows some distance in that relationship. That luxury does not exist in Laura's little village. Groceries (in this case, Lenny) are kept alive and breathing as a method of maintaining freshness until the desired dinnertime.

I will finish Lenny's tale now, before we actually get to the village. When we reached Laura's house, Lenny was slid under a bed and forgotten about for a few days until the time came for iguana gumbo. I helped in the preparation of the dinner, wishing I could have taken back my decision to sample iguana. When I was served my bowlful, I had all the enthusiasm of a kid eating spinach. I had managed one bite then quickly passed my bowl to someone else. After all that, I had absolutely no appetite for Lenny or any other lizard.

Back at the depot, after we had bought Lenny, we boarded a smaller dugout canoe with a more powerful motor. Go figure! The canoes were made from local trees and came in sizes seating anywhere from two to twenty passengers. After 45 minutes, we stopped in a small cove with a well-worn path up the bank. Several people were bathing and doing laundry while youngsters frolicked and swung from trees. One of the youngsters greeted Laura enthusiastically. Soon, a small gang of kids was helping us carry our luggage the half-mile walk to the village. The jungle had been cleared for miles in every direction resulting in a hot and dusty barren wasteland. I couldn't tell if the dried-up little shrubs were weeds or an attempt at cultivation. We saw three young girls hacking away on a plot of land with machetes nearly as tall as they were. They looked about ten years old, and were working very hard in the sun. I paused to marvel at the young workers and asked Laura about taking their picture. "Sure, why not?" she said as she waved for the trio to come over to the path. With her reassurance, they approached cautiously while I got out my camera. They were big-eyed and curious, but painfully shy. Laura coaxed a few smiles out of them as they leaned against their monstrous machetes.

We continued on the path, passing a few houses as we approached the village. We reached Laura's family home on the outskirts. Constructed ten feet above ground, the family compound consisted of two buildings; one for cooking and dining, the other, sleeping quarters. The entire group slept in one big room divided into two sections by a curtain. Underneath the buildings were additional living spaces with hammocks strung across poles that supported the raised structures. Fifty yards away was another elevated wooden structure, an outhouse (bombs away!) shared with two other families. About twice as far in another direction was a communal well and laundry facilities. Perhaps "facilities" is not the best choice of words to describe a cement slab. Clothes were washed by hand in a bucket, and then pounded on the cement. I was sure our green meat bucket would end up there soon.

Laura took me on a tour that included several social visits to friends and family. The village did not have a general store and their one doctor was a resident on loan from Cuba doing his international externship. In the center of town was an evangelical Christian church with a shiny scuba tank that served as the church bell. Aside from the bottom being cut off, the tank was in better shape than the last one I had used.

Laura had 12 brothers and sisters ranging from toddlers to adults with youngsters of their own. Some of them had homes close by, including her grandparents who lived in a small, secluded house. Her grandma was losing her eyesight and her grandpa was completely blind. Laura's younger sister lived with them to provide assistance and companionship. I wondered if this was a cultural tradition for elder care. I had more questions that did not get answered back at the main family home. Her mother did all of the cooking, with five or six toddlers and infants constantly underfoot. I was shocked to see Mom set a bowl of food on the floor and watch the youngsters fend for themselves like farm animals. Some of the older ones cared for the younger children but, from my cultural perspective, they were not getting the kind of attention they deserved. Then I found out that one of the youngsters was Laura's! Her desire to have another child by me seemed all the more sad and irrational. Culture shock. It was hard to comprehend, much less pose a question or open a discussion.

Laura's father worked on someone else's farm many miles away and returned home to his family only a couple of days each month. I wondered how they could have had so many kids with the limited time and privacy available. I was apprehensive about meeting her Dad and unsure if our paths would even cross. It didn't seem to be a concern for Laura. He did show up and was extremely cordial and friendly to me. Both parents were hardworking and sincere.

The village was not at all what I had expected. I thought I would find a group living in harmony with nature in the jungle rather than people struggling to survive in a barren sun-baked clearing that was once a forest. Life was difficult and apparently without much joy. Maybe I just caught them on a bad week.

When Laura and I returned to La Cieba, we exchanged mailing addresses and promised to write. However, I got the sense that her city address was not a stable one. I felt sad and awkward about the promise, believing that this would be our last contact. There had been something between us, just not enough to get past the culture and geography.

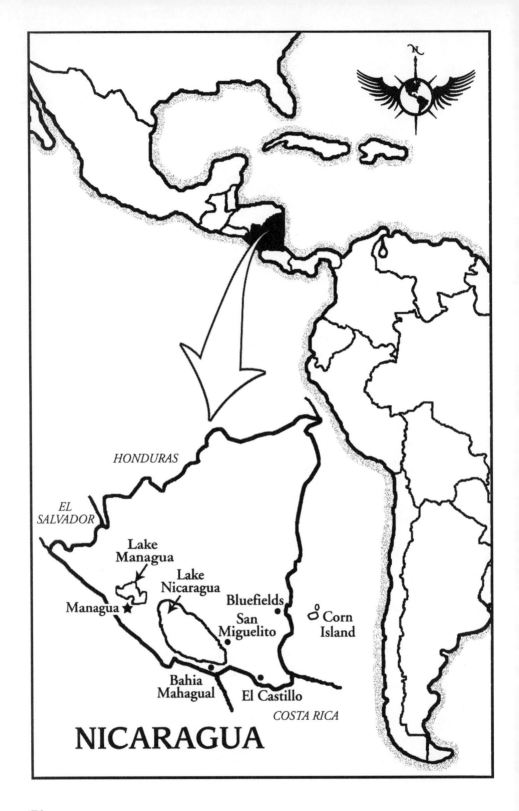

EL
SALVADOR

HONDURAS

Lake
Managua

Lake
Nicaragua

Managua ★

Bluefields

San
Miguelito

Corn
Island

Bahia
Mahagual

El Castillo

COSTA RICA

NICARAGUA

I crossed the border in one hour flat, destroying my previous personal best time by hours, thanks to the help of an eleven-year-old *tramitadore*. The aptly named Darwin helped my border crossing process evolve. Holding my place in line before the border even opened was as significant as the development of the opposable thumb. It inspired the creation of a new traveling commandment: Thou shalt arrive at borders early in the day.

I began my trip to Managua where I would be picking up my pal Scott who would be accompanying me on the road for a few weeks. The four-hour trip seemed a lot shorter and was certainly livelier in the company of two young ladies who I had picked up hitchhiking just across the border (those opposable thumbs do come in handy). They were hitching in one direction, but when they saw me coming down the road they crossed the street. They didn't seem to care where they were going— I would do my best to get them there!

Lorena was cute, lively and very flirtatious. She was wearing a short skirt, a tiny top, and a choker necklace. She was a little firecracker and knew it. She teased me about how I was going to be her new husband. I was flattered and played along. She was so vivacious, it was infectious. Christina was older with two kids at home. She was much quieter and definitely the more serious of the pair. They were willing to ride all the way to Managua with me if I promised to buy them a bus ticket home. I was happy to have someone to talk to, and they were ecstatic when I bought them lunch and sodas.

We arrived in Managua and went directly to the airport to pick up my good friend Scott. He is an adventurous world traveler from the San Francisco Bay Area, and since his business was seasonal he was able to join me for this part of the trip. I kept a lookout for Scott, who resembles a young Sting, but more rugged and less pretentious. I enlisted Lorena and Christina to be Scott's surprise welcoming committee. They hid on either side of the exit doorway. When he walked through the door, they jumped out and yelled, "Hola Señor Eh Scott," each kissing him on the cheek simultaneously. (In Spanish, every "sc" sound is preceded by a vowel, usually an "e." They had difficulty saying "Scott" so, for the rest of the trip, my amused and confused friend became "Eh Scott." Now let's eh-skip back to the story.)

On the plane, Scott had befriended Dennis, a former Peace Corps volunteer in Nicaragua. We invited him to join our party, which he did. We found a hotel and said our goodbyes to Lorena and Christina. I gave them money for their bus tickets home and thanked them for keeping me company. Scott, Dennis and I decided to check out the Managua nightlife.

We found a place close by that was a restaurant and bar with a live seven-piece band. It was loud and boisterous with lots of drinking and dancing. We met three local ladies who agreed to join us after hours. We walked a couple of blocks down the street only to find Lorena and Christina waiting for us in front of the hotel. (We did the math, fairly quickly. Six is company but eight's a crowd.) We three guys looked at each wondering, "What do we do now?" I felt kind of responsible for Lorena and Christina. After a short conversation, we decided to get them separate accommodations for the night and continue our party with the nightclub ladies in our rooms.

The woman whom Dennis had paired off with was ready for action and they took off. The two who remained with Scott and me were less committal. As soon as room arrangements were made for Lorena and Christina, the other two said they were leaving. "What? Wait! Everything is cool now! You gotta stay awhile!" They ended up staying for another beer or two but ultimately left Scott and me sleeping alone. Oh well. It had been an exciting first night for Scott regardless of the eventual outcome. The next morning we took Lorena and Christina sightseeing before taking them to the bus station. This time we made sure they got on the bus.

Scott, Dennis and I checked into a hostel that had an active international backpacker scene. We spent the next few days hanging out and exploring Managua with a variety of characters including Monica, a German lady that Scott had connected with. She had been on the road for over a year. Her sun-bleached hair and tanned face reflected the travels and adventures she had experienced.

Managua is not a resort town by any means. Earthquakes, war and the resulting poverty have ravaged the city; parts of it are still a wasteland. One evening, as we were eating at a sidewalk café, a group of kids came up to beg for money. They were very young, seven to ten years old, and looked extremely unhealthy. The proprietor had to come out and forcefully shoo the kids away. We found out that the kids were homeless and that many were addicted to sniffing glue. The owner explained the dire social dilemma.

They sniff the glue to get relief from the cold and loneliness. The glue wreaks havoc with their young lives making them incorrigible, like feral animals. Once they've had a certain amount of exposure to the glue it is extremely difficult to rehabilitate them. The unofficial solution in Managua (and in Honduras where this is also a problem) was to take them out in the desert and shoot them like wild dogs. It is an awful situation. Managua is not the cheeriest place in the world. We were ready to move on.

The following day we planned to head south out of Managua to the city of Massaya where they have markets for handicrafts. I had gotten up early and headed down to the banks of the lake to take some pictures in the early morning light. I saw an old church that was reflecting the light beautifully. I had parked in a no-parking zone, only planning on being there a moment. While I was taking the picture, a policeman showed up on foot. He asked to see my driver's license and wanted me to come downtown to pay a fine. I refused. I finally ended up giving him ten dollars. "Bitten" again! It would not be my last encounter with the Nicaraguan police that day.

After I got back to the hotel, the Gringo Gang (Dennis, Scott, Monica and I) headed out in Baby Blue. There was construction and traffic was slow. I guess things are the same all over. There was a policeman directing traffic and he signaled me out of the flow and directed me to pull over, but I really didn't want to do that. I pretended not to see him and continued on through the intersection. I didn't think much of it until about ten minutes later, when I noticed the driver of the car next to me waving frantically and pointing to the car behind me. The pedestrian policeman had hitched a ride in a vehicle and had caught up with me! It was a scene right out of the Keystone Cops.

I pulled over. He jumped out of the commandeered car and demanded my driver's license. He was livid. I got out of the car and Monica stayed in the passenger seat. Dennis, fluent in Spanish, got out of the camper shell to intercede on my behalf. He pleaded, "With all respect Sir, what did we do wrong and how can we correct this problem?" The cop was having none of that. He wanted Monica to get out of the passenger seat so he could get in and we could drive to the police station. Monica flatly refused.

In the meantime, Dennis was still trying to smooth-talk him. Finally the policeman realized Monica wasn't going anywhere, and that he was outnumbered by us *gringos*. He angrily stuffed my license into his shirt, stomped down the highway, flagged down another vehicle, and went back in the direction from which he came.

The license he had taken was an international license I had gotten from the American Automobile Association. I wasn't too concerned about losing it because I had another one from Arizona. The next time I went back to the States I went to the D.M.V. to get a spare license. I even thought about going to the library and getting a couple of extra library cards. Spanish-speaking cops wouldn't know the difference and if they told me to come to the police station to retrieve it, I can say, "Okay, see you there!"

We got back in the car and headed down the highway chuckling and breathing a sigh of relief. However, down the road we came to a police checkpoint and were stricken with fear. We thought, "Oh my God, he radioed ahead! We're dead meat!" Luckily it was only a routine checkpoint and we continued without further incident.

The Gringo Gang had a great time visiting the active Massaya Volcano and staying in the town of Catarina. The tiny town overlooks the pristine Lake Apoyo and is as picturesque and friendly as you can imagine. Famous as Nicaragua's greenhouse, Catarina is a town full of nurseries— there were flowers everywhere, but hotels nowhere! We were referred to a family that had begun construction of some rooms for rent, but they had abandoned the project. We rented the half-finished, unfurnished rooms and made do for the night.

Most of the Gang moved on after this, but Scott and I remained. The following morning we did a day hike down to the chilly mountain lake we had viewed from afar. It was immaculate — said to be the only lake in the country not affected by pollution. Our destination was a vacation lodge on the lake, accessible only by boat or foot trail. While enjoying the serenity of the lake, we discussed our adventure agenda for the coming weeks. We agreed on the remote Corn Islands off of the Atlantic Coast. The inaccessibility was a big part of the attraction for both of us.

To get to the Corn Islands we had to traverse a large expanse of Nicaraguan countryside. Our initial destination was Rama, where the road ended and the waterways began. After a day and a half drive through the sparsely populated desert, we finally made it to Rama and the beginning of the Bluefields Region. The region was an extension of the Mosquito Coast with the same plethora of rivers that prevented the construction of roadways. Rama was a small town with a sleazy transient nature. I was not at all happy to leave Baby Blue there, but I had no choice. Early the next morning, Scott and I boarded a boat with a dozen other people and were told to cover our belongings with an onboard plastic tarp. Tarps were provided for passengers also. We would soon find out why! Once we were all aboard, the boat took off. Under the power of two large outboard engines we were flying across the water. We remained dry and comfortable until we reached intermittent patches of rough water. By the time we docked we were all soaked in spite of our tarps.

At this point we had reached the Atlantic coast and the town of Bluefields. It was obvious that we had entered a very different part of Nicaragua. Since nearly all of the area's trade and transportation comes from the Caribbean, the locals had a very different dialect and culture from the rest of the country. In fact, there is so little traffic between the two regions that they were almost two separate countries. I even learned that during the Contra War of the '80s, the east coast of Nicaragua had different motivations and took different sides than the rest of the country.

I received more on-the-street lessons on American intervention in Central America from Señor Eh Scott. He spent his college days in the radical environment of the University of California at Berkeley. In the '80s the campus was a hotbed of protests against American activities in Central America. Scott was very tuned in to what was happening back then, while I was oblivious. Here in Nicaragua, he was constantly asking locals their opinions about events of that period— questions about the Contras, the Sandinistas and Samoza. I was silently embarrassed that I didn't even know who was who, or what was what. I hid my ignorance by saying, "Give it a rest, Scott! That was a long time ago." I didn't want to know which side the CIA was backing and why.

We spent the night in Bluefields and the next morning we took a ferry to our final destination, the Corn Islands. Just like Roatan the islands seemed to have more in common with their Caribbean neighbors than their own country. The Spanish pirates and the slave trade influenced the culture and makeup of the islands. The locals spoke a "Ya Mon" dialect of English, which was part of the laid-back reggae flavor of the islands. One of their main industries was lobster. It was only a couple bucks for a plate of lobster— sometimes we had it twice a day! Throw in some Nicaraguan rum and "Ya mon, we be jammin!" Definitely the good life!

There are two Corn islands: Greater Corn and Lesser Corn. Greater Corn is made up of three or four little neighborhoods. There are about ten hotels scattered about the island. You could actually walk around the island in less than a day. The main drag started near the ferry terminal and extended along the water for a couple of blocks down to a white sandy beach. A couple of restaurants, a bar, and a park were scattered among the tourist shops. There was also a small airstrip a few blocks away that doubled as a soccer field. A plane landing on the playing field seemed like a reasonable exception to the "no time out" rule in soccer.

The Corn Island version of a billboard was hand-painted on plywood. There were only two subjects covered, both addressing social responsibility. One told lobster fisherman not to fish during the off-season in order to let the population regenerate. The other was for AIDS education, encouraging people to use condoms to protect themselves.

Scott was very keen to do some scuba diving. Much to our surprise, there were no dive shops or rentals. We knew that the lobster fisherman used scuba tanks. We found someone who was willing to rent us the tanks, but I was a little bit hesitant. They didn't have any ancillary equipment. No weight belts, depth gauges, buoyancy compensation vests, or pressure gauges. Nothing! Just a tank, a hose, a regulator and someone's old leather belt to strap the tank around your waist! Scott was itching to do the adventure while I would have been content to just drink rum and snorkel off the beach. However, one of the fishermen agreed to take us on a tour of the Lesser Corn Island and to a couple of dive spots. We decided go for it.

We jumped in the fisherman's tiny wooden motorboat and headed out in the direction of Lesser Corn. Halfway there we strapped on the tanks with our makeshift equipment and jumped in. Diving with the lack of a proper harness was more awkward than I could have imagined. We had to swim down to the bottom against the buoyancy. I have no idea how those lobster divers did anything with the makeshift gear.

Forty feet under, we had to grab onto a rock to keep from bobbing back up like corks. There I was, hanging onto a rock by a couple of fingertips and wrestling with my tank that wanted to escape upward from its flimsy belt. Then I noticed I was struggling to breathe. I was having difficulty drawing air in from the tank. I thought the air line might be clogged. Then, the scuba diver's nightmare— no more air! Shit! I was forty feet down!

Now, I'm not an idiot, though it may seem so at this point. I never would have agreed to do a dive like this if it hadn't been for Scott. Borrowing rusted tanks from some unknown fisherman was all his idea. I looked over to Scott who was close at hand as a good diving buddy should be. With one hand on a rock and the other clutching the defunct tank, somehow I managed to get his attention with my convulsions. Turning purple may have helped as well. He realized what was happening and from behind his mask he seemed to be smirking at me while I squirmed for air. He handed over his mouthpiece to let me breathe. We floated back to the surface together sharing the one good tank. No big deal for him, but I was a little freaked. As we broke the surface, Scott looked over at me with a mischievous grin and said, "We cheated death once again!"

A little history on Scott will explain his comment and my confidence (however unfounded) that led me to the bottom of the ocean. You see, Scott had spent his childhood summers on Grand Cayman where his father struggled to run a small resort. Scott was scuba diving at six and teaching it to the resort guests at twelve (that's years of age, not o'clock). Scott's father was a flamboyant character living large in south Florida and the Caribbean. He was involved in the early days of water skiing and scuba diving on a grand scale. He set world records as a water skier and was involved with the production of two TV series: Sea Hunt with Lloyd Bridges and Flipper.

Scott regaled me with stories of his youth and adventures with his father, both above and below the water. His father would always rebound from some near deadly mishap with the catch phrase, "We cheated death once again!" As Scott and I bobbed there in the open water, he appropriately appropriated his father's expression.

From there we made our way to Lesser Corn, and like two Robinson Crusoes we explored the tiny, nearly uninhabited island. Our guide pointed out a small eco-lodge up on a hill but we never actually saw any humans. We ate our packed lunch on the beach before heading out to another underwater location.

Scott finished his tank while I snorkeled safely and contentedly nearby. In fact, I had a memorable encounter with a pair of beautiful underwater creatures. Eagle rays! They were about four feet across and spotted like leopards. In about thirty feet of water, I dove down toward them with a disposable waterproof camera in hand. The disclaimer on the camera said that it would only operate down to twelve feet. I figured out why. The pressure on the case made the film advance mechanism inoperable. You could take one shot before having to ascend to advance the film. I repeated the up-and-down process a number of times without scaring them away and did manage to get one great shot.

They are arguably the most graceful and elegant of all underwater creatures. I was awed to be in their presence. They glide through the water like a giant bird with a long pencil-thin tail trailing behind. The pair allowed me to come fairly close to them for quite some time. I finally got too close for their comfort and they decided to leave me in the dust (so to speak). But they left something behind; a remora, a small fish that accompanies sharks and rays.

Remoras attach themselves lightly to their companion, eat parasites, and scoop up any food their big buddy might miss. This one was five inches long, greenish-brown with a triangular head. The stranded little guy (actually I prefer to think of it as a girl!) was obviously distraught all by herself. Apparently I was the next best thing to an eagle ray. She stuck with me for about 15 minutes. I felt like the ever-so-proud papa as she followed me, staying very close to my stomach and chest. Eventually she swam off in search of a new companion. Apparently I was not able to fulfill her needs. I was heartbroken, but I know there are other fish in the sea.

We completed our seafaring adventure and it was time to get back on the road. As I've said before, "The road less traveled is often that way for a reason." We decided to go down the center of Nicaragua to cross into Costa Rica rather than go down the main corridor on the Pacific coast. Once we got back from the Corn Islands we headed south past the two large lakes, Lake Managua and Lake Nicaragua.

In that region, the border between Nicaragua and Costa Rica is the San Juan River. In my guidebooks, I had found information about crossing the river and the border. I assumed there would be a bridge or ferry for Baby Blue— but no! That would be too easy and convenient. There was only a ferry for people. We had driven twelve hours and reached a dead end.

We decided to make the most of our predicament by taking a side trip. We caught a boat down the river between the two countries to the little town of El Castillo (The Castle). It is an interesting part of the world because of its history and geography.

It was the main tourist stop along the river. It was originally a Spanish fort overlooking the river and was used to ward off pirate attacks. This region was part of the "Gold Route" and was very important to the Spaniards. It was the easiest place to cross the continent (since there was no Panama Canal yet). Ships could go from the Atlantic, up the river into Lake Nicaragua, and dock at the far side of the lake. Then they would offload their cargo onto horseback (since there were no automobiles yet either) for a short trip to the Pacific.

With the river on one side and the jungle on the other, there were no roads to the town of El Castillo. It was car free and carefree; just bicycles and little paved paths all around the village. The fort is now a sleepy but picturesque museum. The people in town were delightfully friendly, and the climate seemed perfect to me. Not an easy place to get to, but an easy place to get used to. We found a hybrid hotel high above the river. Designed into the hill, there were balconies overlooking the water like a luxury resort. However, there were communal showers and three bunk beds in each room, just like summer camp.

One day, in the late afternoon, I went out wandering by myself to take some pictures. I saw a cemetery at the top of the hill right next to the town dump. I started climbing the little path up. I had passed a few homes when I saw a little boy running around with a palm frond between his legs, pretending it was a horse. He was about five years old wearing one blue rubber boot. He was as curious about me as I was about his missing boot.

He started following me. He was a confident little guy and he tried to engage me in his game. I played along. We passed by his house, and sitting outside were members of his family. They saw the kid wandering up the path with me, but just nodded and waved. I marveled at the situation. I was a perfect stranger hanging out with their very young son. I thought about the contrast of this situation to that of other kids in Central America or even the United States. Having just come from the glue-sniffing street kids in Managua I was struck by what a wonderful childhood this kid had in comparison. The sense of family and community that these people enjoyed was beyond the imagination.

He followed me all the way up to the cemetery. The setting sun cast long shadows over the crucifixes and gravestones. Smoke from burning trash filtered through the cemetery creating a ghostly mood. The little boy put his chin on a cross and gazed off into the distance like he was a million miles away. I captured the moment in one of my most memorable photos.

The next day, Scott was up to his old tricks. Always looking for excitement, he suggested that we run the rapids that curved around the fort. We checked around for rafts or inner tubes to no avail. Undeterred, Señor Eh Scott decided to give it a go with just flippers. He picked a route that looked safe and dove into the water. Once he got into the rapids, he disappeared. "Oh my God! Where did he go!?"

I only saw him briefly as he bobbed amidst the twisting rapids. At the end he jumped out and waved up at me. He rejoined me at the top of the rapids. There was an unspoken challenge, so of course I got into the water. You might have thought I would have learned my lesson from the rusty scuba tanks, but nooooo! I tried to position myself as Scott did to avoid smashing into any big rocks. Nonetheless, the speed of the current threw me down the river, uncontrollably and dangerously out of position. Sucked into the rapids, I tried desperately to avoid obstacles. Holy shit! I was out of breath, off-kilter and beginning to think that this was really stupid. The prospect of splitting my skull and ending up at the bottom of the river seemed altogether too real. Okay, so maybe I am an idiot.

The rapids eventually spit me out into the calmer section of the river. I managed to haul myself to the shore and collapse on the bank thinking, "Yes, I am an idiot." But a proud idiot. Scott greeted me with a high five and the catch phrase that was becoming our own: "We cheated death once again!"

Our stunt caught the attention of two *Nicas* (Nicaraguan women) who were staying at our hotel. That evening, the security guard let us hang out in the lobby area after hours. Irma and Elisa shared a bottle of rum with Scott and me. We took pictures with my digital camera, playfully daring each other and capturing the provocative antics. Then we went back to our separate rooms.

Irma and Elisa had to return to their hometown of San Miguelito. There was going to be a festival there and they invited Scott and me to join them. Being that our social calendar was not entirely booked up, we agreed! The four of us took the boat back to Baby Blue and headed north to their hometown.

San Miguelito was a very small community, but every year they hold a huge festival called *Festival del los Patronales* (Festival of the Founding Fathers). When we got to the festival we caught sight of incredibly beautiful horses. They had ornately decorated saddles and the vaqueros (cowboys) had matching outfits. The horses did a special step that made them appear quite regal. It looked as if they were dancing.

Another interesting part of the festival was a combination rodeo and bullfight. Every afternoon of the four-day festival, people would pile into the grandstands. The bleachers, about thirty benches high, went all the way around a corral. There was a live band at one end, and live bulls at the other.

A rider would mount the bull and they would open the chute, just like a rodeo, and he would ride it for as long as he could. That's where the similarity to a rodeo ended and the bullfight began. After the bull bucked the rider off, the people from the stands would jump in and start taunting the bull with shirts or anything else they could find. Drunks risking life and limb in the name of fun. Some were getting gored and tossed into the air! It was quite a spectacle and a very bizarre community tradition. I am certainly glad that Scott didn't do anything imprudent that I would, of course, have had to follow.

Each evening of the festival, the town was transformed into an outdoor casino and dance hall. There was live music, carnival games and lots of food and drink. It was a huge gathering for such a small town. It was small enough that everybody knew each other, and the two gringos stood out like a couple of sore thumbs. However, that was a good thing— we were treated like VIPs. This corner of the country didn't see many tourists, so everybody wanted to know our story, how we ended up there, and what we thought of their little town. We were very impressed by their friendliness and told them so. As the night progressed, people got more and more drunk (at least the ones who hadn't been gored). We danced with Irma and

Elisa late into the evening. We split off as couples and went to their respective houses for the night.

The next morning we all met for breakfast before Scott and I headed out of town. Scott and Elisa were obviously smitten. Scott had more adventures on our agenda so we needed to head out that day. We exchanged e-mail addresses with the ladies and headed back north. We keep in touch with them to this day.

We backtracked to the Pan-American Highway. After a long day's drive, we ended up at a little resort outside of San Juan del Sur. The resort is on the Pacific, just north of the Costa Rican border. The majestic coastline has a number of outstanding surfing spots that Scott wanted to visit.

One afternoon, I was returning from a surfing session when I spotted something in the sand. It was a sea snake that had been thrown up onto the rocks. He was a strikingly beautiful navy blue and bright yellow. His tail, instead of coming to a point, widened out into a fin. I picked him up with a stick and examined him, as any young boy would do. Then I put it back in the ocean. Weakly, he started to swim away, but a little later I saw him back on the shore. He didn't make it (cue funeral dirge). When I got back to the hotel and described him, I found out it was a Pelagic Sea Snake! Rare and deadly poisonous! Unknowingly, I cheated death once again!

MARK'S ADVENTURE ALERT

Location: Bahia Majagual, Nicaragua

Subject: Eskimo Hospitality

An Australian guy named Paul runs the resort we're staying at. He was a metallurgical engineer who quit his job and sold everything he had so he could run this resort on the beach. Calling it a "resort" is being really kind; it was about 5 ½ stars short of a 5-star rating. It was more like glorified camping. When Paul sold all he had to follow his dream it apparently wasn't enough to capitalize his venture. Nevertheless, he was happy— he was living in paradise.

He had hired a lot of local Nicas (including his live-in girlfriend Danni) who had absolutely no experience in customer service. They didn't even know what service was. It made his life challenging trying to train them. They didn't even know the difference between a refrigerator and a freezer. And they had no idea how to take an order. The concept of waiting on somebody was totally foreign to them. They seemed to put in about two hours worth of effort into each shift, unless of course, flirting was part of their job description.

Paul's employees were mostly young women who seem to come and go quickly. They are friendly and flirtatious, including and especially, Danni. Paul shocked me when he asked if I wanted to take Danni with me to Costa Rica. How extraordinarily cordial of my host, I thought, to offer to share his woman with me! But no. It seems that Paul and Danni have grown weary of each other and Danni's mother won't take her back into the house so she (and he) are kinda stuck. Nonetheless, I still appreciated the gesture, even though I would become the one with the obligation. Paul is in a bit of hurry to find a home for her because he is already in the process of replacing her with a younger, prettier version. And things could be getting a little tense under the peaceful veranda on the beach. Things are never simple, even in paradise.

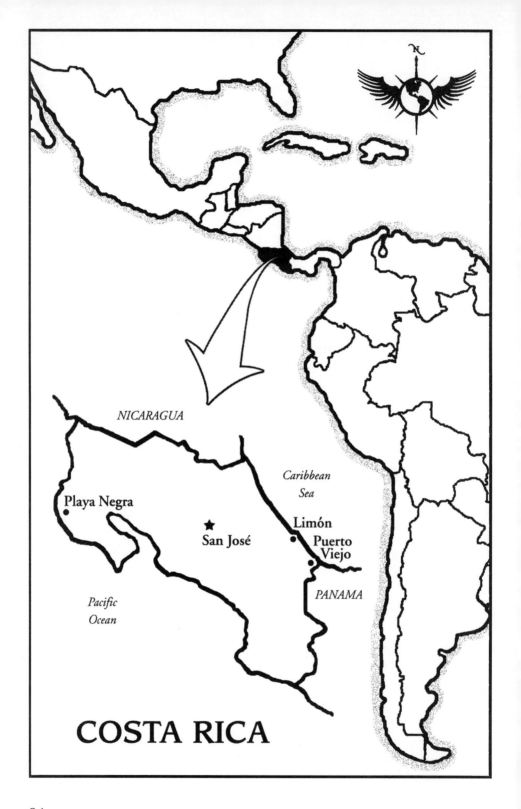

NICARAGUA

Caribbean
Sea

Playa Negra

★
San José

Limón

Puerto
Viejo

Pacific
Ocean

PANAMA

COSTA RICA

Scott and I crossed the border from Nicaragua into Costa Rica. There was a sharp contrast between Costa Rica and other Central American countries. The previous countries had an underdeveloped tourist infrastructure. Therefore, it was unusual to see a foreigner. On the other hand, Costa Rica has a highly developed tourist culture.

As soon as you cross the border into Costa Rica, you become "just another tourist" and are treated as such. They're used to you and are not overly friendly. One of my first experiences in Costa Rica was in a bar surrounded by a bunch of European and American tourists drinking Coronas. I thought, "OKAY. Next country please." Costa Rica has gone out of its way to develop international tourism for good reason. They are blessed with many natural wonders— volcanoes, waterfalls, beaches, jungles and exotic wildlife. But their roads suck! With their emphasis on tourism, you'd think they would spend a little more money on roads.

Scott and I spent a couple of weeks exploring the beaches along the Pacific coast. We spent some of our time snorkeling and scuba diving. We got connected to the traveling surfer community and were directed to some legendary surf spots including Ollie's Point (named after Oliver North of Iran-Contra fame). Our favorite spot was Playa Negra. We stayed at the resort that overlooks the world-famous surf spot featured in surfing movies and magazines. It has a very clean right-handed reef break which delivers a consistent and "gnarly" wave.

The resort was exquisitely designed into the landscape. It consisted of seven cabanas scattered around a dining pavilion and swimming pool. There were iguanas everywhere. Of course the main attraction was the beach and beyond.

Pedro, a retired Swiss investment banker, founded the upscale resort. Years earlier he had wisely purchased a big chunk of land adjoining the beach. Pedro was in his late sixties with short, silver hair. Without his even saying a word, I could tell he was an accomplished individual. He had an aura of strength balanced by a humble nature.

Scott and I enjoyed lengthy conversations with Pedro. Topics ranged from philosophy to business. He still had close ties to the San Francisco Bay Area from his investment banking days. He spoke seven languages and seemed to be starved for intellectual interaction. Our discussions often took place during meals, which were prepared by a European chef, imported to set the resort apart from other Costa Rican resorts. The incredible cuisine in the open-air, natural setting was hard to beat. It was a cross between camping and a five-star resort, the best of both worlds.

We pried ourselves away from Playa Negra and headed inland to Monteverde where we did a canopy tour. Basically it's a cross between eco-tourism and a carnival, the worst of both worlds. As a carnival ride, it was not the ultimate thrill. As for the jungle-eco aspect, any exotic fauna were not going to stick around with the intrusion of cables and throngs of tourists. Still, the throngs were eating it up. It was plenty exotic for them.

The countdown to Scott's flight home was ticking, so we headed back to San Jose, the nation's capital city. I dropped Scott off, bidding him a fond farewell. I had mixed emotions. We had been together nearly 24/7 for weeks. It had been a blast, but I was ready to get back to my solitary mode of travel. With Scott on board I got much less writing done, but more than doubled up on death-cheating adventures.

Scott and I had explored the Pacific coast and the central part of the country, which left me the Atlantic side to explore on my own. I was looking forward to the rustic and remote character of the east coast. On my way down from the mountainous region of San Jose, I stopped at a bus depot restaurant.

From my seat at the open-air restaurant I could see passengers waiting, and the comings and goings of buses. I spotted a particular young woman who was wearing tight blue jeans and a little red top. She was having an animated conversation with her friends. I found it hard to take my eyes off of her. As I ate my *pinto gallo* (black beans and rice) I wondered if I could muster the courage to introduce myself. How could I steal her attention from her friends? I told myself that I would do it as soon as I finished eating. But, I waited too long. A bus pulled up and all four girls climbed aboard and were gone. Why had I hesitated?

Something about her animated personality and cute figure captivated me. I couldn't get her out of my head. As I continued my drive eastward, I had a powerful flight of imagination that entailed jumping on that bus with her. In my mind, we would meet and talk. She would crave adventure, desperate to leave her controlling and abusive home life. I would rescue her from the horrors at home and take her on an exciting adventure while being chased by her domineering, land baron, drug-lord father. Later that night, the vividness of the fantasy compelled me to record it in my journal as the beginning of a novel. Over a period of weeks, I continued writing in the evenings and finished four or five chapters. Then I just stalled. Looking back on it now, the rest of the plot wasn't there yet.

This wasn't the only time I'd been struck by a similar fantasy. Many years ago, I was traveling down a highway in Arizona when I stopped at a Dairy Queen in a podunk town. Working behind the counter was a beautiful girl. I remember thinking that I wanted to sweep her off her feet and take her away, rescuing her from the dreary roadside town. The fantasy was strong but a long way from reality. I paid for my chocolate shake and left having hardly exchanged a word with her. But I remember the powerful fantasy to this day.

I continued my journey toward the Atlantic coast. I made my way through Limón, a large poverty-stricken port city. The drive south from Limón to Puerto Viejo scooted right along the coast. I weaved through palm trees with the beach on one side and the jungle on the other. There were wild banana trees growing in the jungle— a different variety than you would see in the supermarkets of the U.S. These bananas were smaller with a spicy cinnamon taste. The solitary drive along the water was a pleasant change from the non-stop action of previous weeks.

Puerto Viejo is the biggest tourist attraction on the Atlantic side of Costa Rica though it is relatively minor compared to the west coast. There were a number of great restaurants in one neighborhood and then a row of open-air bars along the beach. The laid-back Rasta-reggae influence from the Caribbean clearly distinguished the atmosphere from the rest of the country.

The bars on the beach showed American movies during the dinner hour. It seemed like <u>The Matrix</u> was playing everywhere I went. I couldn't help but feel as though I had taken the blue pill (or was it the red?) and left the matrix behind — my American culture and homeland. Travel is an effective method of stepping out of and recognizing one's cultural hypnosis.

I continued south to the smaller community of Cahuita where I would soon find myself deep in the jungle, guided by a crackhead. I had befriended some locals hanging out in the town square, or more accurately, they befriended me. There was not much tourist infrastructure so I relied on my new friends as guides. They seemed to be ever-present; "Can I help you with this?" "Can I help you with that?" I'd give them a few bucks for their services.

I made plans with Peter, one of my crackhead friends, to guide me on a rigorous hike to a nearby ridge. Long sleeves and pants protected us from the insects and thorns, but smothered us in the heat and humidity. We would search for the elusive two-toed-sloth. Thus began Mark and Peter's Excellent Adventure. I know I am mixing my Keanu movie metaphors but gimme a break, this is my first book!
Editor's note: It's actually not a metaphor, it's a reference.
Author's note: I said gimme a break! I like the two "m"s. I'm trying to be illiterate.
Editor's note: It's alliter... ah forget it.

Peter knew where some sloths "hung" out and we spotted one in very short order. It was about 30 feet up in a tree. In order to get a good picture, I needed to get closer. Peter gave me a boost and I pulled myself up to the first set of branches. Once I was in the tree, Peter used a long stick to pass my camera up to me. As luck (or lack of preparation) would have it, I only had a couple of shots left on the roll. Peter searched my bag and tossed another roll up to me. With trepidation, I climbed toward the sloth. Peter called up to me, telling me not to worry.

I had disturbed the sloth from a deep slumber. I wasn't sure how he would react to my presence in the tree. He didn't seem too concerned about me. In fact, within a few moments, his eyes drifted shut. He was sound asleep again. I was in close range for a great shot but there was no eye contact.

Each time I shook the branch to wake him up, he would glare at me as if to say, "Hey dude! Can't you see I'm snoozin' here?" Then he would quickly fall back to sleep. There I was, 30 feet up, hanging onto the tree with one hand and my camera with the other. I didn't know much about sloth behavior (that is, aside from my own personal tendencies). Would a grumpy sloth bite? Although he looked as cuddly as a koala bear, he had three-inch claws that I didn't want dragged across my face. Every time he opened his eyes I got a couple more shots. Finally, I decided not to disturb the little guy anymore and slid down the tree feeling victorious.

Looking back on it, I should have guessed sooner that Peter and his friends were crackheads. Every time I would give them a couple of bucks they'd disappear. One evening I was drinking rum and Coke at a local bar. The next thing I remember was waking up in my bed with a hangover from hell. It seemed much worse than just a hangover— I was dazed and confused. Had I been drugged? Really tough to say since I couldn't recall how much I drank. I reached down to scratch my butt only to find a pot seed stuck to my left cheek! "How did that get here? For that matter, how did I get here?" I had no recollection of the latter part of the evening.

I looked down to find that my camera bag was still next to my bed. I was relieved to see everything was there. I checked my wallet. It was empty! I didn't have much money, maybe forty dollars, but it was gone (Forty minus forty equals broke. I did the math, even with a headache).

Little by little, portions of the evening started to come back to me. I remembered being out on the street with my new friends and then in my hotel room with them and some strangers. I didn't know if I had spent the money on drinks or if they robbed me. If they did rob me, at least they had been kind enough not to take my camera equipment. The thought of what could have happened really shook me. Hence, a new traveling commandment: Thou shall not drink hard liquor with strangers (or alone for that matter).

My research told me that the Bri Bri Indians were some of the only indigenous people left in Costa Rica. They were located close by, in the southeast corner of the country. I wanted to continue my quest for more National Geographic moments. I was directed to the proprietor of a hotel who had contact with the Bri Bri. I got to the hotel only to find that she was out of town. I contacted her by e-mail and she said she might be able to arrange a visit for me. It would be an all-day hike to get to one of the villages. Then fate intervened. I got an e-mail from my buddy Joel in the U.S. that said he wanted to tour Costa Rica with me. I put the Bri Bri Indians on hold and headed back to San Jose to pick up Joel at the airport. Our first destination— the beach!

Joel is an interesting character. He is a Certified Public Accountant who still manages to spend almost half his time traveling the world. This particular trip, Joel brought a bunch of his files with him. In the mornings when I was working on my journal entries, there was Joel, preparing tax returns for the grandkids of an American business icon. He's able to do the tax returns on the beach! However, he knew when it was time to put down the calculator and pick up the Corona. It was a great work ethic for me to emulate. Actually, more of a play ethic.

Joel had also served as an international traveling mentor to me many years ago. We did a three-week whirlwind driving tour of Germany, the Czech Republic and Holland with his Swedish buddy, Patrick. As an accountant with a photographic memory for maps, Joel handled the finances and navigation effortlessly, taking a huge load off of my mind. The travel experience with Joel and Patrick was a blast. It certainly fanned the flames of my travel fever.

One of the most memorable parts of the European trip was visiting the famous Dachau concentration camp museum in the morning and then the Oktoberfest in Munich that night. We experienced one of the horrors of humanity, and then one of its most exalted celebrations in the very same day.

Joel's skill in navigating his way through a foreign culture came through again in Costa Rica. His ability to communicate in a language he doesn't speak is amazing. He knew very little Spanish and his pronunciation was absolutely abominable. I took four years in school, plus an immersion program, but he still seemed to communicate better than I did. With all of his traveling, he has gained knowledge of international issues including, but not limited to, sports. One time we jumped into a cab in San Jose and after the cursory grunts and nods we found out that the driver was from Nicaragua. Joel simply blurted, "Marvin Bernard!" (the name of a Nicaraguan baseball player who played for the San Francisco Giants). Instant rapport! Thumbs up, high fives and big smiles from then on. Language skills and communication are two different things. Also, the value of a friendship with a cabbie in a foreign city can't be overstated. It's like a concierge, bodyguard and drinking buddy rolled into one.

As Joel's communication style certainly proves, words are not necessarily the most important aspect of communication. Not being totally fluent in Spanish helped to refine my intuition. I needed to listen, watch and take in everything. Does this person want to help me? Does this person want to harm me or take advantage of me? I started using a gut feeling to read people beyond their words. If someone truly wants to help you, somehow the message will get across.

People would speak to me in very plain and simple Spanish, using words I knew, yet I would not understand them. The opposite experience also occurred. I would have a conversation with someone whose accent was so strong, or who spoke so fast, that I literally didn't understand a single word. Still, I knew exactly what they were trying to communicate. There was rapport and the message came across loud and clear. My intuition and language skills developed slowly but I got a jumpstart on real communication from Joel. For him, not knowing the language was just a minor detail.

Joel had been to San Jose before, and when it came to the nightlife he knew all of the clubs. We set up camp at a Holiday Inn. It was conveniently located and had a large pool that was perfect for late afternoon swims. The contrast in the preferred activities of Señor Joel and Señor Eh Scott were quite literally night and day. With Scott I would find myself almost drowning in some outdoor adventure. With Joel, it was a nocturnal adventure, chasing women and drowning in drink.

Over the next few days we spent our nights on the town and our days unconscious. We met women from many different countries. It was a bit of a Latin American melting pot. They would come to San Jose in search of a better life. The most interesting women were the Colombians. Of course they were beautiful, but that wasn't the most striking thing. They each had a warm and engaging presence that made me melt inside. These personality traits were so common amongst all the

Colombianas, that I reasoned it must be cultural. Hence, my plan to avoid Colombia was up for reconsideration.

Joel had booked his flight into San Jose, Costa Rica and out of Managua, Nicaragua, planning on touring one-way between the cities. His trip had been planned at the last minute so we didn't have a chance to match itineraries. Since my original six-month schedule had been obliterated, I was flexible and didn't mind backtracking. We crossed the border into Nicaragua, which seemed like an innocent thing to do, but there were some negative consequences.

I got Joel to the Managua airport with some side trips along the way. I headed back to the Costa Rican border where I discovered a little-known law that nobody had informed me of. Costa Rica only allows a tourist vehicle into the country once every twelve months. I tried to explain to the bureaucrat at the counter how I was the exception to the rule. He didn't care about my situation. I was in no-man's land again. Checked out of Nicaragua, but unable to get into Costa Rica. I couldn't drive Baby Blue back into Nicaragua without a couple of hours of paperwork. The best I could do was to park her under some bright lights near a government building. I had to take a half-hour cab ride to get to a hotel. It was an exasperating day. I splurged on a nice hotel with a hot shower and cable TV.

The next morning I was back in the fray, another descent into the bowels of border-crossing bureaucracy. The clerks were still saying, "No way, Jose!" No way for me to get to San Jose. The tramitadores said they could arrange a black market permit for $400. It seemed like I had no other options. But, finally, I got referred to an upper-level administrator who had a solution for me.

I got another transmigrante ("just passing through") permit like the one I had gotten in Mexico. This one had a 48-hour time limit attached to it. Plenty of time to get across to Panama, but not time for much else. So much for visiting the Bri Bri Indians. I was released from purgatory the next morning and headed to San Jose, the halfway point to Panama. I found my way back to our familiar Holiday Inn. My guide and good friend was gone, but I decided to venture out into the night on my own.

MARK'S
ADVENTURE ALERT

Location: San Jose, Costa Rica

Subject: The Lost Entry

I had passed the Parthenon Club a couple of times on my way to and from the hotel. An exact description of its nature was totally absent from the outside of the building, making it more than obvious that its purpose had nothing to do with family entertainment. It was, of course, an exotic dance club. Peering in the door from the street, one could tell that it was certainly not a dive, although it was not situated in the best of neighborhoods.

On this particular late afternoon I decided to poke my head in the door and find out what the scoop was on this place. A friendly young man pointed the way for me to go in and take a look. The layout was long and narrow with a small stage in the middle of one of the long walls. The bar was against the opposite wall at one end of the room, closest to the entrance. There were only two or three patrons and a barmaid, and no show going on nor any dancers to be seen. I glanced around and then took a seat in front of the barmaid who was dressed in a black skirt and white tuxedo shirt. She had enormous brown eyes and long brown curly hair. She was happy to tell me a little about the club. Shows started at about 7:30 and happy hour was until 10:00. Her invitation for me to stay and have a drink was gracious and sincere. I declined with a promise to return later in the evening. I had lots of packing and organizing to do, so this gave me some incentive to get something accomplished so I could return and have some fun!

And have some fun I did! As I walked back in the bar later, my first thought was to say hello to the friendly barmaid. As I walked toward the bar I surveyed the room quickly to find a moderate number of customers who were outnumbered by dancers sitting around chatting. One in particular had a great big smile for me. I smiled back and then looked away toward the barstool I was headed for. I sat down and glanced back at the smiling face. The smile was bigger than ever and soon she was blowing a kiss my way! I laughed and she motioned for me to join her on the couch with some other dancers. I paused for a moment but could not resist the pull of the eye contact from across the room. I headed over and kissed her on the cheek as if we had been friends forever.

Her name was Deborah and she was from the Dominican Republic. The contrast with her dark complexion made her teeth seem to glow in the dark. She had long bangs that covered her forehead and a head full of tiny braided extensions that fell all around her shoulders and down her back. Her face was narrow with high cheekbones and Asian looking eyes, dark with long lashes. Sitting down it was hard to judge her height and body type. It didn't matter because I was only looking straight into her eyes.

Sitting next to each other on the couch, both turned slightly to face one another, her arm was draped over mine as she gently stroked my wrist. We exchanged the usual pleasantries in Spanish but it was like extraneous static compared to the sexual current that was flowing between us. I was entranced.

I bought her a glass of champagne and we toasted. Soon we were holding each other's glasses. She was feeding me rum and coke and I was teasing her with her champagne. The DJ was playing mostly romantic ballads from the likes of Aerosmith and Bon Jovi. We were both swaying to the music when suddenly but smoothly she slid one of her legs across both of mine and she was sitting on my lap facing me. She was straddling me with her knees on the seat and we were nose to nose. The swaying continued except we were rocking against each other instead of side to side.

I was in another world! The room had faded away and I may as well have been in another galaxy. It felt like Heaven. She took a quick look around the room every once in awhile to check the location of her manager and the waiters. She was leaning over me, her head higher than mine, her long hair hanging down around me like a curtain for my privacy. She reached down between my legs and was pleased to feel that she was having the desired effect. She whined playfully because it was pointing straight down and out of her reach. I gladly cooperated in a joint effort to get it pointed in a northerly direction. Soon she was grinding against me and I was off to an even more distant galaxy!

After awhile she stopped to get me a sip of my drink. She had me pinned down pretty well but I was not complaining. She set the drink down and did a quick surveillance check. Then she reached down inside my pants and started stroking me. Again, it seemed as though we had been intimate friends forever. I couldn't believe the sensual pleasure I was experiencing with someone I had met less than an hour earlier. And it was in a semi-public place!

The intensity of the pleasure escalated over the next few songs until I was ready to explode. I tried to get her to slow down or stop but she wouldn't hear of it. "Don't worry, it's okay," she said in Spanish. She knew I was about to come and she wanted it to happen. I took her advice and just leaned back and relaxed. I stared up into her eyes and she gave me one of the most powerful orgasms of my life.

For the next few moments she just looked down at me and smiled. She was extremely proud and happy about her accomplishment. She told me later that what she had done was strictly prohibited by the management. And that's what turned her on so much, *"el peligro,"* the danger!

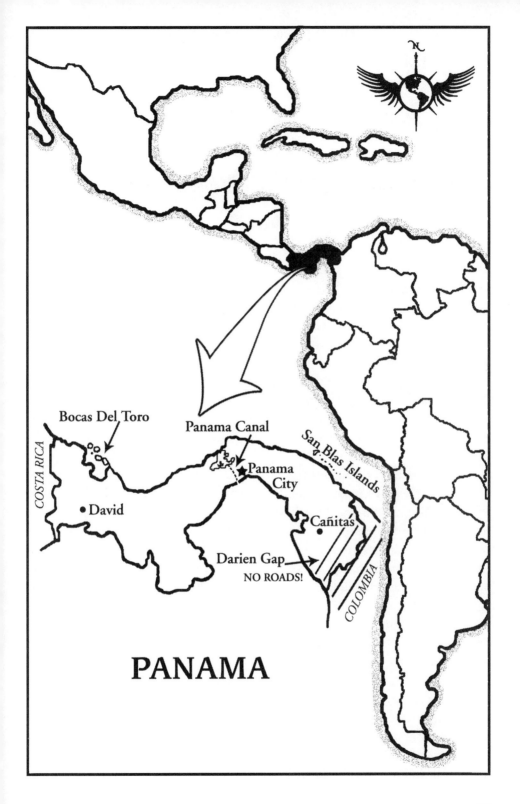

Bocas Del Toro

Panama Canal

San Blas Islands

COSTA RICA

David

Panama City

Cañitas

Darien Gap
NO ROADS!

COLOMBIA

PANAMA

95

The next day I took a leisurely drive toward the border in order to cross first thing the following morning (Thou shalt arrive at borders early in the day). My traveling commandment worked. I was in Panama by mid-morning! It was pleasant to cross over to Panama because of the American influence on the roads, such as lane markings and good pavement. What a contrast to Costa Rica! Another nice change in Panama was a return to dollars and gallons. No more liters or pesos or messy calculations (You know how I hate to do the math)!

There were a lot of other Americanisms I noticed right away. I went to a restaurant in the northern city of David (pronounced dah-veed). It was one of the fanciest in town, with white tablecloths, crystal glasses and sterling silverware. There was a little table set up in the foyer displaying their "gourmet" specialties— Sara Lee and Budweiser!

Panamanian geography was a challenge. Coming from a U.S. point of view, you think of driving through Panama as going from north to south. But in fact, the continent takes a little dogleg right (well, right on a map or left if you're on the road). If you're mixed up now, that's my point. When driving through Panama, you're actually driving from the west to the east. Whenever you're talking to the locals about north, south, east, or west, you always have to do these little translations in your head. The Atlantic Ocean is north and the Pacific is south (So where am I again?).

I asked around about indigenous groups, and found that the Guaymí (pronounced why-me) tribe was in that part of Panama. I endeavored to find a way to visit some of the indigenous folks in their native villages. In David, it was obvious that the plight of the Guaymí Indian was very similar to that of the American Indian. A distinct culture, they did not integrate well into the rest of Panamanian society. In the cities they lived on the social fringes and experienced a high level of poverty and alcoholism. I had taken some not-so-cheery pictures of the Guaymí Indians in town; mothers and babies panhandling. The bright vibrant colors of their dresses contrasted with their bleak situation.

I did my research to find out where their little town was and how to get there. I made my way into Hato Chami and asked if there were any guides to take me into the backcountry. It turned out there weren't. I saw a young kid asking for a handout in front of a small general market. I gave him some change and told him what I was up to. He introduced me to a cab driver who introduced me to someone who would take me where I wanted to go.

MARK'S ADVENTURE ALERT

Location: Northern Panama

Subject: Guaymí Indian Experience

I'm sunburned, exhausted, covered with bug bites, and have a mild case of the runs. But was it worth it? Heck Yeah! A two-day jaunt turned into a six-day adventure in the hills of Panama with the native Guaymí Indians.

I had arranged to have a guide take me into the Indian Reservation to meet and photograph the indigenous people living high in the mountains. As it turned out my guide was not a guide, but just a guy. A guy who lived in the area and has family in the hills. He is 34 years old and goes by Alfredo. We'll call him Al from here on out.

As it turns out, there are no guides or even maps to the myriad of small villages and foot trails scattered throughout this region of Panama set aside for the Guaymí people. And the Guaymí are not keen on outsiders, even Panamanians, visiting their land.

At one point it got a little tense, with one particular *Cacique* (Chief) checking me out before finally consenting to our passing through his territory.

The first day was an adventure in itself. Al and I headed into the mountains toward the village of Chami in Baby Blue, my trusted transport thus far on my trip. The four-wheel drive aspect of the little blue pick-up was essential for this rain-damaged mountain road. I am truly a novice at four-wheeling as recreation but I tasted the thrill of the avocation in a big way. It's sort of like a clunky form of skiing or snowboarding. You have to pick your line to avoid the biggest bumps, holes and other hazards. You must also control your speed. Too slow and you will lose momentum and stall or get stuck. Too fast and you could roll or bounce right out of the truck. And getting stuck is a very real possibility, one that we experienced.

During the current rainy season the road is not passable without four-wheel drive. Erosion and other vehicles had formed huge irregular ruts. Boulders and mud added another dimension of excitement. We were on a steep incline when I slid sideways and planted the back axle firmly onto bedrock. The wheels were spinning freely and so was my brain. Al and I got busy with the jack and lots of rocks. We raised the truck little by little as we crammed rocks under the tires. Eventually we were able to roll back out of the jam and continue on a slightly altered course.

Baby Blue became a taxi for several folks along the route, including Betice, a young woman in a beautiful black dress. The dress was typical of the Guaymí women. Guaymí men have no corresponding native attire; most wearing modern, though tattered clothes.

But back to Betice! She seemed to be enamored of my new pal Al. They seemed to hit it off well, although the cultural and language differences made it hard for me to tell what exactly was happening between them.

Many Guaymí speak two different dialects and some Spanish. Betice and Al were speaking a dialect and Betice wasn't speaking to me much at all. She was friendly to me but shy.

When we reached the end of the road for Baby Blue, Betice said she knew of an alternate route to our destination that could involve a night's stay with her family. It was getting late in the day and we had to plan for the probability of rain. Al and I agreed to go for it.

The trek to her small village was yet another challenge for the day. We walked for about four and a half hours and arrived at dusk. The hike was exhausting and exhilarating. Up and down lush green hills and in and out of an ever-so-rapidly changing cloudscape. Billowy balls and wispy wisps fingering between ridges in the distance became an enchanted wonderland as we entered them. The banks of cool moisture greeted our faces and left behind its light residue.

The next morning, sweet black coffee never tasted so good. I hadn't slept well on my bed of bamboo slats and was not even close to being rejuvenated from the previous day's toil. A bowl of rice and some kind of squash, and we were on our way.

We had to get an early start to make some progress before the rain that often comes at around 1:00 p.m. I was surprised when Betice joined us in our departure from the small group of huts. She did so in spite of the cries of her year-and-a-half old daughter. I asked her if she was sad to be leaving her daughter. She smiled and said no. I didn't understand but didn't ask any more questions.

A few hours later it became obvious that we were going to need shelter from the rain very soon. We inquired at the next hut we came to and we were directed to a larger dwelling not much further along the trail. We spent the rest of the day and the night there. I needed rest but did not feel totally welcome and couldn't really relax. A plywood plank on the dirt floor was my bed. We shared our food with them in exchange for their hospitality.

The next day we parted company with Betice and she headed back to her village alone. I was sorry to see her go. Each day she had reached into her little pack and donned a new colored dress. At the end of each day I was covered with mud and drenched in sweat, she looked like a picture from a page of Guaymí Vogue with a matching flower in her hair.

The next two nights were spent at a very friendly little village in an exquisitely beautiful spot. I felt very relaxed and welcome. Still no mattress and box springs but I was getting used to the bamboo.

We went for a day hike without our packs and I felt like a gazelle, well no, perhaps a buffalo with some really sore hindquarters. It was a beautiful day nonetheless.

This little village consisted of about eight huts on a grassy saddle between two hills. There were some more huts within a few minutes walking distance and a "grocery store" about ten minutes away.

We stopped at the store on the way home from our hike. I was dumbfounded at the price of a bottle of soda. Twenty-five cents! It wasn't exactly cold but I still would have paid five dollars!

On our second morning our plan was to head for Baby Blue. I was more than ready to head back. It had been an incredible cultural and wilderness experience. But I was dreaming of a cold beer, a hot shower and a mattress. No one else was involved in this fantasy, just me and my mattress! But it was not to be! A two-hour estimate turned into four hours and we still were not even close. I was not in any condition to continue in the heat of midday. But we were very close to our first night's stop, Betice's village! Coincidence? I think my guide/guy had designed the last part of our itinerary around seeing Betice again. He denied any such intentions. It didn't matter; I had to get over it. We were in for another night of bamboo!

I had some pork stew for dinner that night. The first animal protein of the trip! My bowl had a piece of pig hide with hair on it! Not quite ASDA approved quality. Must have slipped by the local inspector.

Speaking of animals, I asked Al if he could find someone from the village who would rent out a horse to help me back to

Baby Blue. Yes was the answer. I had to pay for the horse and
for the owner to come along to bring the horse back. I would
have gladly paid five times the price. I felt very guilty and
spoiled for the first mile or so. It was not a big horse and
he wasn't used to such a big rider as myself. I rationalized
that he did this every day and that if I had done the walking,
I would have been in much worse shape than he was going to be
at the end of the day. And the owner was very happy to get the
money. Okay, okay, so I wimped out. But I added horseback
riding to my adventure.

　　All in all, Al was a champ. We spent a tremendous number of
hours together. He gave me a window into a world I never could
have seen on my own. He may not have been a guide but he was
one heck of a good guy and he took care of me. My food,
shelter and safety were his main concerns. Interestingly we
never discussed money until the trip was over. In the
beginning, he picked out the groceries, I paid for them and we
took off. I was happy to make sure that he was more than happy
with his compensation.

After my Guaymí Indian adventure, I backtracked to David to recuperate and work on my journal entry about my expedition. I had absolutely no experience with Microsoft Word though my computer was equipped with it. "Cut and paste" for me was literally "tear and tape." It amazes me now that I had all this technology at my fingertips and yet I was using scissors and scotch tape. To organize my story I rearranged pages from my yellow pad on the floor of my hotel room. It was a tedious and solitary chore with which I struggled for several days.

Though it was a substantial city, David had no tourism to speak of and the nightlife was limited. I had made acquaintances around town in the process of my normal activities. Having been secluded in my room, I needed human contact. I found some at an Internet café a couple of doors down from my hotel.

She caught my eye through the storefront plate glass window— a momentary connection. The contact was fleeting, but in that fraction of an instant, very definite. She was inside the café at one of the computer stations. I entered, got my time slip, and looked for a station close to hers.

I sat down at my station and wondered how to start a conversation with her. I wrote down my e-mail and web site address and passed it to her. Before I knew it, she had visited my web site and sent me an e-mail! I replied, asking her if she wanted to join me for lunch. We kept e-mailing even though we were only a few feet apart. It was a strange and new dynamic for me. It eliminated that initial social awkwardness. A few minutes later we were walking out of the café, talking face-to-face. We made arrangements for lunch the next day. It was funny that as backwards as I was with word processing, throw in a pretty girl and suddenly I am a regular techno-geek.

It was in David that I began to recognize a definite pattern with the single women I was meeting.

MARK'S ADVENTURE ALERT

Location: David, Panama

Subject: "Are You Married?"

"Are you married? Do you have any kids? Do you like to dance?" is how the line of questioning usually begins. Eyes light up at the favorable responses. "Do you want a companion to travel with you? Can I go to Arizona with you? I want to have your green-eyed babies!", is the eventual progression.

One such encounter started during a needed haircut, led to a friendly manicure and pedicure, then continued with an invitation to cerveza and salsa! (Dancing, that is.) A female Nicaraguan friend now living in San Francisco warned me that the local Latinas would do anything to get their hooks into me and that I had better watch out!

Poor innocent me?? Oh no, far from it. Cross-Cultural-Flirting-R-Me! A sly, shy smile and just enough Spanish to be dangerous. I love the attention. And I've felt the hooks sinking in... and I liked it!

But wait! I'm on a mission! Tierra del Fuego or Bust! A postal or even an e-mail address will have to do for now... and perhaps if the hooks are in deep enough, I'll still feel them when I reach land's end.

MARK'S ADVENTURE ALERT

Location: Chiriqui, Panama

Subject: Nancito Petroglyphs

I was cruising the Pan-American Highway south of David, Panama and I noticed a small sign announcing a point of archaeological interest, the Nancito Petroglyphs. The sign was small and poorly placed, such that by the time I realized what it was I was already past the turnoff. I decided to turn around and check it out even though the sign gave me the impression it would be less than a major monument. My hunch was dead on.

Three kilometers into the hills I found the tiny town of Nancito. It took all of thirty seconds to tour the entire town twice. No petroglyphs. Upon inquiry I was directed to a local home. I was greeted by Abraham. A larger than life, delightfully animated character with a magnificent mustache. The mustache was salt-and-pepper blonde and was just as dramatic as his personality. I would soon find out all about his grandiose plans for his little town and the collection of boulders on its outskirts. He was the perfect pitchman for his pet petroglyph project.

There may be some significance to the curious carvings, but as yet, it seems serious scientific study has not occurred. The pre-Colombian carvings have a Keith Haring kind of flare, simple yet lively. They are scattered about on some Volkswagen-Beetle-sized boulders, in a saddle between two hills. The guide's presentation, with his exuberant enthusiasm, was an event in itself. His fanciful theories and explanations included people and religions from far and wide. Babylonians. Phoenicians. Hebrews. He called in connections to the Bible, astronomy and astrology! "After all," he exclaimed, "Panama is THE center of the World!" Come on, Abe, you're close to the equator, and a bridge between continents, but the center... Okay, who am I to judge? Aren't we all the center of our own universe? He invited me back to his home to regale me with more of his theories and plans. A national park, a visitor's center and hotel. He wants to write a book to put Nancito on the map. He asked if I would take the pictures and be the co-author. I counseled him to perhaps start with a brochure and a better road sign. He brought out a reference book and compared the Sphinx to one of the Nancito carvings, assuring me that the same people were responsible for both. I like to think I have an open mind and an active imagination, but Abe, babe, it's a stretch at best.

Back there between some of the boulders, I spied something that fueled my own personal theory to explain the glyphs. A small toadstool growing out of a deteriorating cowpie!! My experiences in the Yucatán Peninsula years ago taught me that it was no ordinary mushroom. The carvings just may be the work of some pre-Colombian ancestor of Keith Haring munching magic mushrooms and getting crazy with a chisel.

Bocas, Bocas, Bocas, I fell in love with Bocas. Bocas del Toro, "mouths of the bull," refers to three things: a Panamanian province, an archipelago, and the main town on one of the islands. On the coast, I packed Baby Blue onto a ferry for the two-hour ride to the town of Bocas. The archipelago consists of five main islands, most of which are covered with tropical jungle. The vegetation is dense, in most places extending all the way down to the water. In fact, the mangrove actually extends into the water, blurring the distinction between land and sea. Exquisite white sand beaches dot the archipelago, contrasting magnificently with the crystal turquoise water. There is good snorkeling and scuba diving in the region, plus surfing at certain times of the year.

The region is a safe haven for sailboats because of its location just south of the hurricane belt. Sailors and traveling backpackers account for a significant proportion of the population and add to the flavor of the Caribbean island.

The town has one main street and a central square where you can sit and count the number of cars going by on one hand (I counted six). There were a few taxis in town but most people walked or rode bicycles. Strolling the length of town took less than ten minutes. About eight blocks from the central square, reminiscent of the Corn Islands, a tiny airstrip doubled as the municipal soccer field. Rundown, tilting wooden buildings added to the rustic personality of the place. The main drag had a couple of good restaurants while other tourist establishments dotted the waterfront. With just enough homegrown infrastructure to handle the essential needs of travelers, corporate tourism had not arrived in Bocas. I loved the homey casual ambiance, but it seemed on the verge of being discovered and developed, hanging in a fragile balance. I'm afraid I might come back in ten years to StarBocas and McBocas (not to be confused with Boca Burgers, those would be okay).

The island mentality really appealed to me. Kids played in the parks and streets without adult supervision. Isolated by the water, it felt very safe and secure. Of all the places I'd visited and enjoyed this was the first time I'd felt, "I could live here!"

The focal point for many travelers and expatriates was the Wreck Deck, a bar officially named *El Barco Hundido* (the sunken boat). Located on the waterfront, the deck extended over the water so one can look down at the underwater wreckage. Lighting from the deck shined into the water so you could enjoy your libation while watching fish swimming through the colorful eco-system that permeated the wreck below.

The proprietor was a colorful character named Benson who was raised in Southern California. He had completed medical school in the U.S., but before doing his residency, he headed to Bocas for a year off, which promptly turned into three. I predict he's never going back.

At the Wreck Deck I connected with a loose-knit international gang of young travelers. Israeli, Egyptian, Swedish, Norwegian, and French Canadian delegates made up the United Nations band of bohemians. By virtue of being the owner of the only means of transport, I became the Secretary General, the designated driver, and overall leader of the gang. In the afternoons, we explored every accessible corner of the island in Baby Blue. Most people traveled by boat, hence the roads were not well developed. A close bond developed rapidly among the gang of backpackers. It made me wonder what all of the global conflicts were really about. Even with our different cultures and languages, we shared an undeniable human bond. There was an intense curiosity that connected everyone like unique points of a star. We were fascinated by each other and our explorations.

With the encouragement of Benson and the gang, I put together a digital slideshow from my travels. The gang assisted me by distributing flyers all over town. With some help, I connected my laptop to the TV screen at the bar. Thirty to forty curious travelers showed up for the casual event. Much to my amazement, the event proceeded without a hitch.

In Bocas, I hit my stride with my writing, photography and my on-the-road lifestyle. I was welcomed as a part of eclectic community. I felt at home and at the same time free! Wandering alone in the jungle with my camera, I stumbled into a rich emotional state. I reconnected to the feelings of 10-year-old little Markie, snorkeling in Mexico for hours on end. In Bocas, my camera was my excuse to get lost in another natural wonderland. Time ceased to exist in my own private world. My childhood-wonderland experience in the jungle unexpectedly intensified. Whenever I encountered a vibrantly colored frog, my inner child broke loose and took over my adult mind and body, like a werewolf during full moon.

Back in Costa Rica, I'd had my first electrifying experience with a fluorescent frog. Trekking down a jungle path, I spotted a tiny flash of red and blue in the crevice of a decaying log. When I realized that it was a frog, I flipped out. There was no rational explanation for how excited I got seeing this brilliant creature. As a youth, during the summer rainy season in Arizona, I had chased frogs, but they were dull, drab shades of green and brown. My childhood thrill of tadpole and frog hunting was amplified ten-fold by these supernatural colors. I became Markie the Frog Prince of Bocas.

The most famous beach in all of Bocas is called Red Frog Beach. A visit was at the top of my to-do list. Located on the backside of the nearby island of Bastimentos, it required a short trip across the water, followed by a 15-minute hike through the jungle. Red Frog Beach was a destination unto itself. For many people, the presence of the frogs was merely incidental to the gorgeous beach. But not for me! A few steps up from the beach and into the jungle, you could hardly help but step on a Strawberry Poison Dart Frog. Less than an inch long, they have deep shades of orange and red, with black polka dots optional. Strawberry Poison Dart Frogs forever....

The scientific name for the frogs is *Dendrobates pumilio*. I learned that from a grad student named Mark, studying the frogs under the auspices of the Smithsonian Institute. We were introduced by Dixon, the manager of the local Internet café. He had already nicknamed grad student Mark, "Jungle Boy." I became Jungle boy #2. We both spent inordinate amounts of time in the jungle chasing frogs, him with his tape recorder and me with my camera. He spent his mornings in the jungle recording the sounds of the little leapers croaking at each other. He recognized them by the subtle distinctions of their voices but needed a better way to identify large numbers of them for his study. Since a collar won't stay on their necks and their wrists are too small for a bracelet, frog scientists have another slightly grisly method of identifying them. They slice off a finger pad or two! With 18 pads to choose from (four on each front leg and five on each back), using just one snipped pad you could positively identify eighteen subjects. Using a combination of two snipped pads you could identify another....

Author's note: I need to hire a mathematician for this one.

Editor's note: No you can't, you're already over budget. It is 18 x 18 = 324.

I winced (as you may have) at the explanation. Mark (the first) rationalized that the frogs get along fine missing a finger pad or two. All in the name of science? I suppose I would survive without one of my pinkies, but I damn sure wouldn't give it up willingly.

He explained how the same species of frog could be found throughout the archipelago, but on each island, their colors have morphed independently. Colors and patterns vary from island to island. I made it my mission to find as many variations as I could.

I heard about an elusive blue specimen. Dixon directed me to one of his many cousins to help me locate one and photograph it. We mounted a canoe expedition up a river on another island in search of the mythical blue amphibian. We never located the legendary, perhaps imaginary, croaker (the Bocas Bigfoot! I realize that Bocas sounds a lot like bogus). Our expedition was not in vain; our efforts turned up a variety of other exotic wildlife including what the locals call a Jesus Christ lizard. When you see one of the lizards engaged in their astonishing trademark activity you are likely to exclaim their name. The activity I am referring to is walking on water. More accurately, running on water, on their hind legs, with their head and front legs upright and their tail dragging behind. Their high-speed disposition could not have been more contrary to another creature we encountered.

As we motored slowly around a bend in the narrow waterway, we came upon a three-toed sloth hanging very low in a tree, just feet away from our boat. He was freakishly slow, like a Disney animatronics animal at one-tenth speed. He turned to look at us with a confused look on his face as if to say, "Whoooooooaaaaa! Yooou'rre nooooot froooom arooound heeeeeerre," before inching his way up a tree. With a squarish head and long, lanky, humanoid arms ending in three claws, the creature seemed to be George Lucas' inspiration for the Star Wars character, Chewbacca. The two-toed variety I'd seen in Costa Rica was a round ball of fur compared to this gangly guy (Two toes versus three? Oh no! Could this be a part of some scientific ID system?).

MARK'S ADVENTURE ALERT

Location: Somewhere, Sometime in Panama

Subject: Aimlessness as a Virtue

Or maybe "Aimlessness and Inspiration" would be a more acceptable title. But since I'm not running for office, I'll keep the one I like. Aimlessness has a certain negative connotation, but for me the positive aspects outweigh them. Openness. Freedom. No particular place to be. Available for a spontaneous, fortuitous adventure. With a person, a butterfly or a wave in the ocean!

It is in this particular state of mind that I find myself blessed with the most creativity. Unfettered by the

```
distraction of desires and intentions my mind is open to
receiving the divine download, that flash of inspiration from
the heavenly hard drive!

    "A good traveler has no fixed plans and is not intent upon
arriving."

    I saw this quote many weeks ago and it has been my motto
and mantra ever since. Presumably from the Tao Te Ching by
ancient Chinese philosopher Lao Tzu, it has application in all
areas of life, not just traveling.

    Getting the mind to that state of aimlessness, into
uncharted territory, that's the trick. Sure, I have lots of
goals and intentions. But I am training myself not to cling to
them. To be open to the possibility of something even grander
than I had even imagined. Oops! That's yet another intention!
But no worries, there will always be more to let go of.…
```

In regards to my life, I had faith that I was headed in the right direction but was unclear exactly where I was going to end up. Which is intriguing, living life inside of your own mystery. I was preparing to leave Bocas feeling as though it had been a turning point, a defining destination for me but not fully understanding exactly why. A big part of me didn't want to leave, but still the impulse to move on won out. This time I was torn by the pull of the place, not one particular person. The island had been my mistress, tempting me to stay. Had there been a specific sweetheart as well, I may not have been able to resist.

On the ferry back to the mainland, I stared back toward Bocas as the wake dissipated to each side and the town got smaller and smaller. My visual connection to the place, the people and the good times, was fading into the horizon. It was the perfect metaphor, reflecting on the very recent past as I headed backwards into my future. Soon I would have to turn around and look forward, but for the moment I was content to dwell in the sweet sadness of the end of some good times— great times— in fact, the highlight of my trip to date.

Little did I know that the good times would begin again at my next stop. The rustic charm of Bocas would give way to the energy and excitement of Panama City.

Once on the mainland I made the long drive to Panama City. A friend from Tucson had given me the name of an acquaintance there. I called Jose, who told me to give him a call when I checked into my hotel. However, it was booked up. A Miss Universe-type pageant was being held there! What are the odds that I would have chosen a hotel that was hosting the most beautiful women in the world?! "All right, then," I told the clerk, "I'll be willing to share my bed with one of the contestants, or two if that helps." Oh well, I tried.

I called Jose who said, "Just come over to my place and we'll see what we can do." The 26-floor high-rise condominium was not far from the hotel. His two-story condo included the penthouse and the story below. The views were spectacular. A large deck wrapped all the way around the upper floor. He had huge couches outdoors — big white pillowy couches. It was like sitting in a white fluffy cloud, floating high above Panama City. From one side you could see the boats lining up to get into the Panama Canal. In the other direction you could see the lights of the city and all of the downtown bank towers.

He offered me a drink and we sat down and started talking. It turned out we had common interests in literature. We really hit it off, and he said, "Why don't you just stay here? My cousin lives on the top floor and he's out of town. So stay here as long as he's gone, don't worry about a hotel." Talk about the kindness of strangers. Wow!

Jose was an entrepreneur working on the launch of an Internet infrastructure project for businesses in Panama City. He was very busy "entrepreneuring" during the day. Still, he managed to be a great host and guide. I showed him my digital slideshow from Bocas del Toro and he was impressed. He said something like, "I'll have to get you to meet this guy 'cause he could do this for you, and another guy can do this, oh, I'll just have to invite all of my friends over for a party and you can meet them all at once." A few days later the party was a reality. I felt like I was the center of attention on the set of Lifestyles of the Rich and Famous! There were eight or ten guys, nearly all of them doing something on a grand scale. There were also an equal number of beautiful women, mostly from Colombia. Woohoo! I was beginning to think I would run the risk of kidnapping to visit a country full of women like these.

I met Roger, who ran a massive web site on expatriate living called escapeartist.com. Soon after, he began publishing my stories on the site. I met another gentleman who owned a vacation home near Bocas. It was like something out of Architectural Digest, completely isolated and built on the water in its own secluded cove. He was trying to sell it, and offered to let me stay there and hang out as long as I wanted in exchange for promo photos. Later, I would take him up on the offer.

I also met Edgar Noriega, the nephew of deposed dictator Manuel Noriega. We became good friends. Edgar was a great tour guide for the club scene. On several occasions, we partied into the wee hours of the morning. I was intensely curious about his life and his perspective on the U.S. invasion of Panama. I had seen a documentary entitled <u>The Panama Deception</u>. It presented the U.S. media's version, contrasted with what actually happened. There were stark differences. I wanted to compare Edgar's story with the two drastically different depictions. I assumed the events would have had a devastating effect on him and his family. Many years had passed since the invasion, but I sensed it was still a touchy subject. Out of respect, I couldn't just blurt out my most burning questions. Over time, we got to know each other and a dialogue opened up.

Again I was silently embarrassed, even after seeing the documentary, that I didn't know enough details to ask more intelligent questions. Edgar had been in school in the U.S. at the time of the invasion and had to change his name to avoid the press. He did not hold CNN in great esteem, to say the least. He talked about CNN running footage of his uncle's residence, rebroadcast over and over. "It was totally fabricated," he said. "Someone else's home entirely." CNN had focused on voodoo and drug paraphernalia to demonize his uncle. Edgar also spoke of CNN camera crews coaxing the locals to ignite piles of tires in the street so that the crew could get interesting footage. Of course, the General was no angel, having been on the payroll of the CIA for many years. If he had continued to act in the best interests of the U.S., there may have never been an invasion. The U.S. interests were certainly not the same as the interests of the Panamanian people. Contrary to the treaty signed by President Carter, the first Bush administration wanted control of the Panama Canal back from Panama. With each country I visited, my eyes opened a little wider.

My social network was still expanding and I was having a great time. Even so, it was time to leave the big city and the parties behind. From Panama City, I took a fascinating side trip by air to the southern Atlantic coast.

MARK'S ADVENTURE ALERT

Location: San Blas Islands, Panama

Subject: Kuna Indians

Fiercely independent fighters for their freedom, yet physically very small individuals. Most of them under five feet tall, they are proud of the four "revolutions" they have survived. They call attempts to subdue or otherwise destroy their nation, "revolutions." Other Indians, the Spanish, and the Panamanians have all made their unsuccessful attempts.

They exist almost as a separate nation from Panama, with their own ways and even their own laws. They welcome tourism but on their own terms. There are about 360 islands in the region with only forty inhabited. Most are very small with the highest altitude a few short feet above sea level!

The hotel I stayed at was on one such island. You could just about spit from one side to the other yet it was home to a village of over one hundred. A stay at the tiny Hotel San Blas included all meals and daily tours to other islands. I will describe a few of the many stops I made on my tours.

Pelican Island had thirty-seven palm trees, three huts, and is about twenty paces across and perhaps sixty long. A ring of white sand and patch of green grass shaded by the palm trees! Four permanent residents and four tourists for the day! Every romantic cliché about a tropical desert isle applies here. I was in awe for the first ten minutes after we were dropped off.

Isla Perro, or the "Dog Island" depending on your particular persuasion for language, was similar to Pelican with the added attraction of a sunken Colombian contraband boat just a few yards off shore.

The only residents were two friendly brothers, probably in their sixties, who collected a dollar from every visitor and told the forty-year-old story of the shipwreck. When I asked about the lack of women on the island, Ramon replied that they had every thing they needed on the island and that "women are just very expensive."

A one-hour boat ride and a two-hour hike got us to a small village back on the mainland and situated on a river. This village was not accustomed to visitors. The original intent of the outing was a search for frogs, but the isolated little village became the main event.

The villagers cultivated bananas and sugarcane. The raw material for their traditional makeup also grew in the area. Red for their cheeks like rouge and black lines on their noses that resembled tattoos.

A neighboring island with a much larger village was the home of the Kuna Museum and Aquarium. The aquarium was actually just a small pen built at the water's edge that held about seven sea turtles. Not quite up to the standards of the Monterrey Aquarium in California but they did allow close-up photography!

The museum was one room with many Kuna artifacts, posters and drawings. The guide spoke some English and Spanish and was very passionate about the history and rituals of his people. The guide was also the artist who created most of the exhibits.

The modest little museum experience communicated the independent spirit of the people. Their mythology is very connected to Mother Earth and her gifts. If you mess with the Kunas' relationship to her, you'd better watch out!

My last adventure before I headed out of Panama and into South America was a family affair.

MARK'S ADVENTURE ALERT

Location: Canitas, Panama

Subject: Love Panamanian Style

My cousin Molly was a Peace Corp volunteer stationed in a very small town in southeastern Panama. There she met and fell in love with a handsome young man named Victor. At the end of her stay they returned to the States together. They made plans to return to Panama to formalize and celebrate their relationship.

I was invited to the wedding but did not plan to attend, thinking at the time that my itinerary would put me somewhere in Brazil by now. Needless to say, I am long way from Brazil and I was happy extend my stay in Panama to attend the special event.

Molly is a saint in this tiny town. And as the cousin of a saint, I automatically had special status too. I was welcomed into the family and the community.

The ceremony took place in the Catholic Church and the reception was in the open-air town hall. It was a combination of customs from both cultures. Panamanians apparently do not spend six to twelve months planning a wedding. Most arrangements were made in the two days prior. Decisions about many details were made by the bride while her hair was being done!

Panamanians like their music loud and their beer cold! Atlas was the beverage of choice. The only choice! The visiting family was in charge of stocking the freezer! The local family lovingly prepared the food. Gallina de Patio, chicken from the backyard (Guess what? Tasted like chicken)! Ceviche, raw fished "cooked" by the acidity of limejuice! Perhaps not so artistically presented, but very tasty!!

I must admit my extreme disappointment about one Panamanian custom: you can't have your cake and eat it too! There was a large cake and a cutting ceremony but it is not served at the reception. Portions are delivered to the homes of the guests the following day. It was a pleasure and a privilege to be accepted and included in the culture and customs of Canitas. I was indeed touched by the open-hearted innocence of the townspeople! What a treat! Congratulations Molly and Victor!

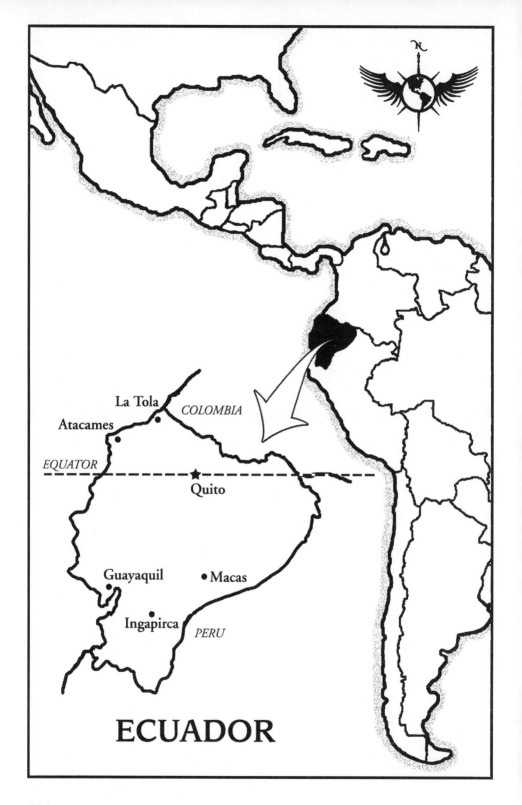

La Tola

COLOMBIA

Atacames

EQUATOR

★ Quito

Guayaquil

• Macas

Ingapirca

PERU

ECUADOR

Unbeknownst to many people, you cannot drive from Central America to South America in spite of the so-called Pan-American Highway. The highway stops at the Darien Gap. Heavy seasonal rains, as well as dense jungle and political considerations, have prevented the completion of this last segment of the highway. My solution? Baby Blue goes for a boat ride.

Shipping a vehicle added a new level of complexity to the border crossing bureaucracy. In addition to the mountains of paperwork, vehicle inspection, verification of ownership, fees to be paid and permits to be issued from two different countries, there is also the shipper. They have their own rules and regulations. There are companies whose sole function is to process the paperwork for their clients. Fortunately, I didn't need to hire a company because I had Edgar Noriega on my side.

Edgar worked for a shipping line that would transport Baby Blue. It was smooth sailing, at least as far as getting my truck onto the boat. However, getting Baby Blue off the boat and back into my possession was a completely different story. While she was tucked into her container, sailing through the Panama Canal and around the Pacific side of Colombia to Ecuador, I was on a plane. We were both bound for the same port city.

Guayaquil, a huge industrial city, is the center of commerce in Ecuador. I tried unsuccessfully to find a place to stay near the docks, but eventually had to settle for a hotel downtown. I got up bright and early the next day to retrieve my trusted friend. However, it would be quite some time before I took her back into my possession.

The paperwork that Edgar had so smoothly handled on the other side was nightmarish on this one. I didn't have anyone I could trust to help me. The dock was a rough-and-tumble area and the dockworkers weren't friendly. It was a long way from the dock to my hotel, necessitating many long cab rides to five or six different offices. The Ecuadorian officials were requesting documentation from the American Embassy.

Ironically, the American Embassy was the most difficult of all the agencies I had to deal with. I went there on a day the regular staff was on holiday. I tried to explain my situation to the gentleman on duty and he very bluntly said that they were not in the habit of handling that sort of paperwork and he simply couldn't help me. I tried to explain to him that this had to be a normal sort of thing because the agency that sent me did it rather matter-of-factly, as if they do it every day. He didn't want to hear any of it. He was being rather rude, telling me he couldn't help me and that I should leave. That really pissed me off. "Wait a minute," I said, "I'm an American citizen and this is the American Embassy, and you work for me!" That didn't sit very well with him. He threatened to call security. I left. Typical rude American!

Editor's note: You or him?

That meant another round back at the docks. I was mired in paperwork purgatory. I wasn't even free to sightsee. Not that there was much to see. Guayaquil had the depressing ambiance of a metropolitan capital and the transient feel of a border town. It was overgrown, overcrowded, hot and humid, with a layer of industrial grime. I worried that Baby Blue was never going to be released and she would just rust away right there on the dock.

I ended up going back to the Embassy on a regular business day and spoke to somebody who knew what I was talking about. It was so simple. The clerk said, "Oh you just need this form. Just go right over there and they'll take care of you." It still took another 48 hours to spring Baby Blue.

I was relieved and delighted to be out of Guayaquil. The lush landscape was more exotic than anything in Central America. Ecuador and South America seemed a little further away from home in more ways than one. It's difficult, even now, to put it into words. Everything from the vegetation to the roads seemed different. The houses were made of native materials and built on poles up off the ground about a story high. Every once in awhile I'd see a house completely painted yellow, or even turned into a political billboard.

I turned into one of the houses and said hello to the people sitting out front. They were delighted to have a visitor and I was amazed by the plethora of bizarre fruit trees. There were five or six kids between the ages of five and sixteen. Once they saw I was interested in the different fruits they started running in every direction to pick fruit for me. I was blown away by their enthusiasm, not to mention the wide variety of unusual produce.

One of the samples they gave me was cacao, the source of chocolate. I had seen cacao seeds drying on the hot pavement on the side of the road. Farmers spread the seeds out in a section about three-feet wide and thirty-feet long, right there on the shoulder of the highway with all the diesel fumes. My new friends explained the process from the tree to the pavement and finally the sale to Nestlés.

Later on my drive, I came across a fruit stand that had seven different species of banana. They ranged from red, to green, to brown, and from two inches to 14 inches long. I was fascinated to see so many varieties of bananas hanging all in one spot. Diversity! The word that best describes the geography, climate and culture of Ecuador. There are more than twenty distinct indigenous groups in Ecuador. Imagine the diversity of these groups that live from the beach, to the jungle, to the Andes. The diversity of the exotic fruit was just a taste of what I would experience in all of the different realms of Ecuador.

I spent several days meandering up the Pacific coast. The roads were not well marked so I never quite knew if I was headed in the right direction. I wasn't overly concerned; I was enjoying the ride. I was in my "aimless" mode, exploring new towns. As I got closer to the capital city of Quito, the nature of the drive shifted dramatically. I was at the foothills of the Andes. All of the roads from the lowlands funneled into one main highway up the mountain into Quito. Suddenly, I was moving at a snail's pace among trucks and buses up a narrow winding mountain road. It was midday, but it would be long after dark before I would reach my destination.

High in the Andes, Quito is nestled between peaks in a 22-mile valley referred to as the "Avenue of the Volcanoes." There is both a modern area and an historic section within the city. The "old town" is designated as a World Heritage Site for its Old-World history and architecture. Quito is just miles away from the Equator. One might think that it would be hot year-round; but, in fact, it is generally quite cool due to the altitude. I visited *la mitad del mundo*, the middle of the world, and got a picture of myself straddling the equator with a foot in each hemisphere. I was at the middle of the world, on my way to the end. These thoughts were swirling in my brain, clockwise in one hemisphere, counterclockwise in the other.

I found a hotel in *Gringolandia* (Gringo-land-ia). This neighborhood is the center of tourism, a hub for the comings and goings of the entire country. The main artery, Avenida Amazonas, runs through the eight-block district that is home to more than sixty travel agencies booking tours to the Galapagos Islands and jungle destinations. Across Amazonas from my hotel hung a two-story, bright yellow, vertical banner with the bold inscription, "Eco-tourism." Curious, I wandered over.

The walls up the creaky stairway were plastered with photos and glowing reports from the company's expeditions. The walls of the second story reception area had more of the same. Within a few minutes, Maximilliano Moreno, the founder of Ecotrackers, was explaining the details of the locations and the philosophy of the organization. His enthusiasm was contagious. Over the next few months I would become great pals with this wonderfully wild-eyed crazy guy who I called Mad Max.

The agency specialized in what was referred to as "community eco-tourism"— a mini-Peace-Corps-type placement agency, with programs in numerous indigenous villages all over the country. The idea behind Ecotrackers is to create sustainable tourism that will keep the jungles AND the cultures intact. Hence the term, "community eco-tourism." By finding a way for the indigenous villages to get income without selling out, without selling T-shirts and without selling precious trees from the rainforest, Ecotrackers addresses a major issue throughout Ecuador and other parts of Latin America.

The agency places volunteers in indigenous villages where they stay with the locals for a small fee that covers room and board. Volunteers teach English, make trails to special sites, help put up buildings, and do other projects. Most people go for several weeks. You can choose where you want to go and how long you want to stay. Max had many locations around Ecuador where he had gone and preached his mission. Little by little, he was convincing the locals that they could sustain the forest, their lifestyle and culture, and make some money in the process. Max was struggling against a lot of forces. He had to go into villages and enroll them. Then, he had to do the same to the volunteers to get them involved. He had his work cut out for him.

Ecotrackers offers Spanish lessons for their volunteers to ready them for their assignments. It also had affordable housing a few blocks away from the office where volunteers could stay. It was a four-bedroom apartment with a couple of bathrooms, certainly more upscale than a lot of hostels, but below the level of a nice hotel. There was a communal kitchen and room for about eight volunteers. Max and his family lived upstairs in another unit. I decided to give it a try.

The apartment buzzed with the excitement of adventures to come and adventures completed. It was a lively place, like a college dorm but with a little more privacy. The living room had a TV and a VCR. Max and his family often came down in the evenings to watch TV with the volunteers. Max had a wife and three daughters. Dominica was about five years old. His other two teenage daughters, Antonella and Veronica, were actively involved in the organization and worked in the office. They swore they learned their English by listening to the Backstreet Boys. It's not Shakespeare, but better than Snoop Dogg, Fo' Shizzle!

The Ecotrackers' apartment was my base camp over a period of months. I got to know Max and his family quite well. A visionary, Max imagines the world as a better place. He's also a missionary, a salesman, and a very curious scientist absolutely in love with life.

One afternoon we visited the local university during what could be described as a combination labor strike, protest and annual convention of an association of indigenous groups from all over Ecuador. Max was beside himself with enthusiasm for the photo opportunities I would find. In addition to the photo ops, I got my first whiff of tear gas, a remnant from a confrontation earlier in the day.

In Ecuador you'll find huge regional differences because of the variations in geography, weather and cultures. It is a mosaic of peoples. Groups living in the mountains in Otavalo have very little in common with the Shuar living in the rain forest of the Amazon basin. Unfortunately, these differences mean that many indigenous groups are not well represented in the national government. Diverse and distant from each other, they often speak in different tongues. However, they manage to come together to throw a strike. And for one reason or another they're always on strike!

They get their way because of their effective demonstrations. They can immobilize the country by burning tires on the highways, which in turn, shuts down traffic. It's curious how they wield their power, and how well it works for them. They don't get their voice heard unless they do something drastic.

Hundreds of folks, mostly in their native regional garb, were camped in the main square of the university. The media was there along with the military. Max was in fine form, networking to add more locations to his Ecotrackers' network. He spoke to people from numerous groups about their plights and what they hoped to accomplish at the meeting. Genuinely interested and concerned, he shared his knowledge of their history and customs with me between each encounter. I was astounded by the depth of his knowledge. He knew the details of one tribe's struggles against international oil companies and another group's struggles with drug addiction. He pointed out curious distinctions in their clothing that I would not have otherwise understood.

As we walked off of the campus the police were stopping a small pick-up truck carrying food and supplies to feed the masses of humanity camping on the grounds. Max interceded on behalf of the nuns driving the truck, asking the officials to let them through, but they refused. There were plenty of sympathizers around. Max began to organize volunteers to carry the bags in on foot. The police told him he could not do that either. "These people are hungry," Max persisted in a polite and diplomatic manner. Perhaps just to get rid of Max, they finally consented and waved the truck through. Compassion in action. I was proud of my new pal.

On another occasion, I came home at 12:30 AM to find Max and two volunteers in the living room. "Let's go take pictures of the church," Max blurted,

"The lights are beautiful at night. It's just a few minutes away!" So began our two-hour trek through the streets of Quito. Max, his three daughters, the two volunteers and I took off on a tour that included colonial architecture, a cool little café and a 566-step staircase down to the church.

I came home even later on another night and was enlisted in yet another adventure. The office manager, Dave, a long-term volunteer from England, was departing in the wee hours of the morning for his homeland. Max and some other volunteers figured, "Why go to bed?" A lengthy cross-cultural exchange continued over wine, rum and Coke until we woke Dave up for his ride to the airport.

The lively goodbye at the airport was followed by a sunrise hike through Quito's equivalent of New York City's Central Park. Max insisted that we remove our shoes as we walked and he talked. He had a highly developed interest in medicinal plants. Walking along, he'd grab a plant or flower, grind it between his finger and thumb, and hold it under our noses to demonstrate its aromatic quality. We spent a couple of hours, barefoot and drunk, traipsing through the park as the sun came up. I went back to the apartment to crash. To my amazement, Max went directly to the office for the day.

Max is a rare individual who is just crazy enough to believe that his work with indigenous people and the environment can actually make a difference. The world could use a few more people like Mad Max.

"Never doubt that a small group of thoughtful, committed individuals can change the world. Indeed, it is the only thing that ever has."

Margaret Mead

Author's note: The next five chapters are a story within a story, entitled, My Ayahuasca Diary.

The seed was planted by a headhunter with a blowgun, decked out in full war paint. I was at the South American Explorer's Club in downtown Quito. Every Wednesday evening the club had a meeting featuring a different speaker with a topic of interest to members and guests. I had the privilege of being the speaker the previous week, presenting a digital slideshow of my journey up to that point.

But this week I was part of the audience, listening to Rodrigo, a Shuar Indian, a descendant of those who fought fiercely against the Spaniards. Though he dressed the part, Rodrigo was anything but ferocious. His nomadic tribe was never conquered, perhaps in part because of the fear inspired by their reputation as headhunters. It was their practice to behead their enemies, sew all the orifices closed, shrink their head, and keep it as a trophy. The theory behind the practice was to catch the spirit of the enemy to prevent it from doing any further harm.

Rodrigo was at the club to attract tourism to his remote village of Macuma, located in the Amazon basin in southeastern Ecuador. It was a tough sell because of the remote location of the village— a ten-hour dirt-road drive from Quito, followed by a seven-hour trek through the jungle. An adventure just getting there, coupled with an indigenous cultural exchange? It was hard to get much further away from the beaten path. Sign me up!

As the evening progressed, Rodrigo talked about the shamanic culture and their ceremonies with the native plant Ayahuasca. Rodrigo was a village elder but not a shaman. He spoke about the medicinal and spiritual uses of the Ayahuasca ceremony. I was fascinated as he explained how visiting participants often had visions of the local snakes and panthers and received spiritual guidance from them. That would certainly add another dimension to my adventure.

The Ayahuasca ceremony piqued my interest, but I was still leery about participating and diving that far into their native practice. I would already be in relatively uncharted territory, geographically speaking; psychologically speaking, I might feel the need to remain on solid ground.

The next day I discussed my trip with my pal Mad Max. By then, I had visited a couple of off-the-beaten-path destinations under the auspices of Ecotrackers. Over a bowl of *sancocho* (a pork-based stew), and a plate of *habas* (native beans), Max shared many details about the Shuar Culture. "They live in a world of magic," he explained in Spanish.

The conversation drifted in the direction of the Ayahuasca ceremony and my possible participation. Max was an excellent resource on the subject because of his background. As I have mentioned, Max was immersed in eco-tourism, but he was also trained as a medical doctor and had a strong interest in the area of medicinal plants. In fact, he is an expert in the subject, having taught it at the Central University in Quito.

Max had never tried Ayahuasca himself and was actually neutral on whether or not I should do it. Nonetheless, he spoke of some of his other Ecotrackers clients who had participated in the ceremonies. Some had only been looking for an exotic way to party while others had a more personal or spiritual agenda. He spoke in particular about one individual who came back with a lightning bolt kind of clarity about his life and his relationship. Max wasn't selling anything but I was sold. I decided then and there that I would do it.

I had done some research and read accounts of Ayahuasca's use in various Amazon cultures. The name Ayahuasca is translated as the "vine of the soul" or sometimes the "vine of death!" The first translation made sense and even had some appeal. But the "vine of the death?" Yikes! In my research I found no accounts of any deaths from Ayahuasca, but the translation was still somewhat disconcerting.

I came across a book in the library at the South American Explorer's Club entitled, The World is as You Dream It, by American John Perkins, who led trips into Shuar country for Ayahuasca ceremonies. It gave me a nudge in the direction of participating. Little did I know at the time that the author led a bizarre double life and wrote another book called, Confessions of an Economic Hitman. Much, much later I would read that book, meet the author, and get another significant nudge in a different area of my life.

"Until one is committed, there is hesitancy, the chance to draw back..."

W. H. Murray

I was committed (or perhaps I needed to be). Though I never signed on any dotted line, I had made a promise to myself. However, it was not a total blind commitment. That would have been unwise in this circumstance. I needed to have a sense of safety and security. I needed to leave myself an out if something did not feel right.

I thought about three possible optimistic outcomes for my Ayahuasca experience:

1) That I would have an ecstatic experience with startling revelations about my life, love and passions.

2) That I would go through with the experience and realize that my own spiritual practice creates more clarity for me. I'd get confirmation that I am already on the right path.

3) That I would choose not to follow through for any number of reasons: lack of rapport with the shaman, not feeling safe in the environment, or even some irrational fear. In this case, my intention and activities leading up to that point would give me all the clarity I was looking for.

4) My head would blow up.

Any of the first three would be well and good, but what about the darker possibilities? Some kind of toxic reaction. A psychotic one. My head blows up. I would be a long, long way from professional help. Beneath my enthusiasm and excitement was the knowledge of the risks and a definite undercurrent of FEAR.

When you register for personal growth seminars, they tell you that the seminar begins the moment you register (commit yourself) regardless of the actual start date. This rang very true for me in this instance. Immediately my life took on a higher level of intensity. I dove more deeply into my daily practice of journaling and meditation.

Looking back over my life, I see a pattern. I do something every couple of years to clear away the psychological cobwebs and start fresh, some new adventure in awareness or consciousness. In my journaling I reviewed the personal growth techniques and spiritual practices I've been involved with since my high school days/daze. I began with smoking pot and dabbling with psychedelics in high school. Leaving the drugs behind, I learned Transcendental Meditation the summer before my senior year, which I practiced daily for twelve years. Later, I got into hypnosis, yoga and breathwork. Living in the San Francisco area in the '80s, there was always something new to try, such as sexuality and intimacy seminars or exploring consciousness with another.

The Ayahuasca adventure definitely fit the pattern. I had done a lot of things in the name of self-discovery, more and more finding myself on a spiritual path. The reader might be asking, not to mention the writer, are drugs a part of a spiritual path? That is a question I was asking myself. Was this really some pious pursuit or was I, like those others Max had mentioned, just in it to party? Would that be such a bad thing? A part of me said yes. The truth is that there was a little of that. One could certainly find safer and easier ways to party. But for whatever reason, the desire was there.

The set and setting— that is, the mindset and the environment in which the experience happens— have much to do with a psychedelic experience. The writings of Aldous Huxley and Ram Dass about the relationship of psychedelics to mystical states had piqued my curiosity. As a youth, I never had a great experience. I did get a sense of the possibility of a good experience, perhaps more from what I had read of other people's descriptions. My experiences were tainted by the paranoia that comes with doing something forbidden and the need to pretend nothing was happening. If you couple that with an underdeveloped self-esteem, and the personal uncertainties that come with being a teenager, you can imagine that my experiences were not the greatest.

The idea of a similar exploration as an adult held some appeal for me. Having a guide, with expertise in shepherding others through the experience for a positive outcome, added even more appeal. Instead of going off on a fearful teenage paranoid tangent, the guide would help to make the journey a joyful and ecstatic one.

I sought input from someone I trusted at home— my brother-in-law Kevin. When I told him about it, he was very excited for me. "You'll never be the same," he said. That scared me a little bit. He said I would be more in touch with my own reality. But what if I was out of touch with everyone else's? He counseled me, "Don't let the shaman take over authorship of your experience."

"Huh?" I replied.

He phrased it another way, "Keep in mind that you are the one creating your experience." He told me that it would change my perspective, and give me a glimpse of a world that is there, but our conscious mind blocks us from seeing.

"If the doors of perception were cleansed, every thing would appear to man as it is, infinite."

William Blake

****

In order to get to Rodrigo's village of Macuma I first had to reach the city of Macas. I wasn't looking forward to a ten-hour drive on a dirt road. I discovered another option that was more appealing, a 35-minute flight! I would need to pack carefully for the seven-hour hike that followed. I would be in backpack mode without a serious backpack. I only had a small pack for my photo gear and a duffle bag with a shoulder strap for everything else. The relative luxuries of Baby Blue would remain in Quito.

"It doesn't get interesting until something goes wrong"
Unknown

Our guide is a no-show.

My plane arrived early in the day. I was joined in Macas by a Dutch couple, Marcela and Miguel, who had taken the bus. Both in their mid-twenties, they spoke English fairly well and were working on Spanish as their third or fourth language. They were on a six-week holiday through South America.

We were supposed to meet Rodrigo at 5:00 p.m. to catch a bus to the trailhead to Macuma, where we would stay the night and hit the trail first thing in the morning. Well, at least that was the plan. However, at 6:00 p.m. we were anxiously looking around town and making phone calls trying to locate Rodrigo. He was an elusive character, though not intentionally, there was just no way to reach him at his village other than going there.

Eco-trackers had a contact in Macas other than Rodrigo, a family that acted as a host to volunteers on their way to various Ecotrackers destinations in that part of the country. The Flores family was on the phone with Max in Quito trying to come up with an alternative plan for our slightly stranded threesome. Not to worry though, the Flores family had hosted many Ecotrackers volunteers on their way to other locations. They would help to activate plan "B". Whatever that was.

The Flores family ran a small pharmacy that had been designated as our meeting place. I needed some mosquito netting and hoped to find a pair of lightweight, long pants. So I went off on my own to shop and explore the town.

Macas is the largest city in eastern Ecuador, though it is really just a big town. The main downtown market area was limited to three streets that ran parallel to each other. Though Macas is remote, the construction materials and techniques were sophisticated and it had a modern feel to it. With its tiny airport and more substantial bus depot, Macas is a hub for the remote villages of the region. Many of the bus stops leading from Macas were simply trail heads that lead to villages.

I got my shopping done and went back to the pharmacy. Manuel Flores had contacted another Ecotrackers location and made arrangements for us to take a bus to the village of Pablo Sexto first thing in the morning. It would not be the distinct indigenous village we had planned on, but rather a comparatively modern agricultural village.

Oh well. It was a disappointment for sure, but it was also a relief from the undercurrent of fear that had gripped me since I had committed myself to the Ayahuasca adventure. But I hadn't heard any fat lady sing. There was still a possibility that we could do the trip after our visit to Pablo Sexto.

We spent the night in the Flores' home, getting to know the two young Flores boys and their parents. Both of the boys were very serious chess players, with trophies as tall as they were. Their very sweet and warm parents worked hard to maintain their pharmacy and provide for their family.

They genuinely seemed to enjoy their involvement with Ecotrackers. I was inspired by their commitment to their community and to their environment. They grasped the need for environmental conservation in this out-of-the-way corner of Ecuador. It gave me further hope that the Earth just may have a chance.

Surprisingly, I was alive and wide-awake at 5:00 a.m. The boys had each vacated their bedrooms for the visiting travelers, and were sleeping in the living room. I began to meditate in the privacy of my temporary room. But the privacy only went as far as the top of the walls. The walls didn't reach the ceiling. The construction of their home was such that none of the internal walls reached the roof. The top of the U-shaped roof was at least six feet higher than the walls. Gradually, as I meditated, the entire home came to life as a lively radio station was inadvertently broadcast throughout the dwelling.

While it was still dark Mr. Flores drove us to the local bus station to get us on the first bus to Pablo Sexto. He was willing to drive us all the way to our destination and actually wanted to visit some friends there, but for some reason there was no gas available in Macas, he dropped us off for the two-hour bus ride.

The dirt road ran almost completely uphill and was close to being washed out in several locations by recent seasonal rains. Pablo Sexto was frequently cut off from all means of transport for weeks at a time during the rainy season. Though we had climbed up considerably from Macas, we were still in dense forest vegetation.

We arrived in Pablo Sexto mid-morning. It was home to only about 500 people, so it was not difficult to locate the home of our contact. We settled into our respective quarters, two different families that lived a few doors away. The homes were either constructed from the local timber or of the newer version, cement with thin corrugated metal roofing. When it rained, you knew it.

Behind my house was the family *cuy* pen. Guinea pigs. When I was a child my family raised guinea pigs as pets. Here, they raised them as a supplement to their diet. They were a delicacy of sorts. They often had cuy for dinner on special occasions. Wouldn't you know, visiting Ecotrackers volunteers qualified as a special occasion. Tasted like chicken.

We got a tour of the town and school, and set up a meeting to discuss our volunteer activities. The school had a huge agricultural vocational training component to it, complete with their own farm that raised livestock (cuy included!) and crops. Animal husbandry and farming technology were very practical skills for life in the village.

We spent a full day touring three neighboring villages. They were smaller, much more primitive and only accessible by foot. The first village was the smallest, consisting of about eight rough-hewn wooden shelters in a large clearing in the woods. The residents were delighted to have visitors in spite of our language barrier. Four of them actually joined us in a circle as we rested from the forty-minute hike.

Rudolfo, our guide from Pablo Sexto, was translating the conversation from their native tongue to Spanish. "Would you like some refreshments?"

"Sure, thank you. That would be great."

Well, it sounded great at first, until Rudolfo explained what it was we were passing around. It was *chicha*, a fermented beverage made from corn. Well, okay, so far so good. Then came the explanation of the fermentation process — mastication. That's a 25¢ word for chewing. Yes, the women of the village chew the corn to release the juice and start the fermentation process. Stomping grapes seemed positively civilized compared to pre-chewed corn hooch! In the interest of being polite, I think we all faked a couple big gulps while we kept our lips tightly sealed against the large gourd that was being passed around.

The second village we encountered was significantly larger. We arrived in time to disrupt what appeared to be the school lunch break. Rudulfo was a friend of the teacher and introduced us. He was dressed in gym shorts and a tattered soccer jersey. He explained the challenges of being the only teacher in the school. He had thirty children under his care, all at completely different educational levels. Generally, they did not have access to pencils or paper — challenges indeed. The children gathered around curiously, but mostly kept a safe distance. A few of the bolder ones posed for photos.

As we headed towards the next village, the sun had risen almost directly overhead. Though the morning had been brisk, the heat was now bringing out exotic insects in full force. I trained my macro lens on multi-colored grasshoppers and spiders. With their intense red and yellow markings they seemed like animated bits of jewelry.

Arriving at the final village was like walking into a ghost town. It was on the bank of a small stream. The only sound we heard was the gentle rushing of the water. The town was entirely deserted with the exception of an elderly man in poor health and two young boys who were caring for him. The remainder of the villagers, we came to find out, were tending crops in the nearby hills. We chatted with the boys at some length and shared some of our snacks with them.

We had reached the last village of our tour, but we were still several miles from our home base of Pablo Sexto. Our guide promised another stop that we would enjoy, keeping us motivated and moving forward. We came upon a stream flanked by large boulders, deep enough for a cool dip. A perfect spot to bask in the sun and enjoy the snacks we had packed for a picnic.

The weather had been ideal for us that day. The immersion into nature and our interactions with the villagers had totally distracted me from my preoccupation with the ups and downs of my potential Ayahuasca experience.

At the swimming hole, I stripped down to my shorts and waded in up to my thighs. The water was very cool, a few degrees shy of cold. As I relaxed into the experience of the water streaming around my thighs, my legs disappeared and became part of the river. For several glorious moments my body melted into the environment. There was no separation between me and the river, or the rocks I was standing on, or the boulders and trees that surrounded me. The mystical and wondrous experience seemed so very natural. It was as if I had accessed a state of pure experience— stumbling into non-judgmental paradise.

My companions were certainly enjoying the moment, basking on the large rocks and dipping their feet into the cool water. We shared the treats of our communal picnic and the intensity of my experience began to fade. I was left with a warm glow and a big smile.

We made it back to Pablo Sexto and the next day we launched into our Ecotrackers volunteer activities. At previous Ecotrackers locations I had taught English. I met the stringent job requirements: the ability to count to ten and say "good morning".

At Pablo Sexto, discussions with schoolteachers and administrators pushed me down a different path. They saw my computer and camera equipment and asked if I would give a lecture on computers. Who, me? A computer expert? Less than two years before I could barely turn one off and on. But I indulged their request. I gave a primer on the Internet and digital photography to four different classes. About forty kids attended each class, which was basically every student from the entire village.

The Internet had not yet reached Pablo Sexto but it was probably not far away.

The village had but two phone lines. Most homes in the village had TV's and some had video games. The school had two computers for administrative purposes, but the personnel lacked the training to utilize them properly. If anyone knew about lacking computer training it was me. I was an expert in being untrained.

My digital photography demonstration was very well received. I took several photos of each class. In one class there was a cute couple sitting in the front row. They were, no doubt, the village equivalent of the homecoming king and queen, both attractive and looking so happy together. I connected the camera and explained to the class that the first photo I would show would be the two lovebirds in the front row. Instead, I brought up a photo of two colorful frogs sitting together. The kids nearly fell out of their chairs laughing.

I felt like I was very successful explaining the concept of the Internet to the older students. With the help of a diagram on the blackboard I explained how, "your computer is connected to the phone, the phone is connected to a big computer, connected to other big computers, connected to people all over the world!" I fielded questions that told me that they were engaged. I was amazed to watch the light bulbs go on in their little heads.

During one lecture I had an epiphany. Another mystical experience. For a moment I felt as though I was in the perfect place doing the perfect thing. It was like a feeling of déjà vu that went on for several minutes instead of a fleeting moment. It was as if I had established some sort of divine connection that was electrifying me and illuminating a new path. Inspiring the young villagers was a powerful experience. It seemed like a significant piece in the puzzle of my life, but I still couldn't see the whole thing.

The temporary distraction from my Ayahuasca adventure ended on the bus ride back to Macas. I was reading, At Play in the Field of the Lords by Peter Matthiessen. My uncle had recommended the book, knowing I was headed for South America. I checked out a copy from the library at the South American Explorer's Club. The novel is about a conflict between missionaries and indigenous people in South America. I was startled to come to a passage involving Ayahuasca.

It described the nightmarish experience of the central character. A large dose of Ayahuasca was the catalyst for a decisive action that changes the course of his life. Under the influence, he steals a plane and flies away into uncharted jungle wilderness with the knowledge that there would be no fuel for the return flight. Wow! How real was this disturbing depiction? Had the author had a personal experience? My mind raced, fueled by the undercurrent of fear that had been suddenly reactivated. Suddenly my roller coaster was back on track and picking up speed.

Our plans to visit Macuma had been rearranged. Preparations had been made for us to depart for the jungle early the next morning. Another night in the Flores' household in Macas was all that separated us from our adventure.

The next day we were at the bus station for an early morning departure. Instead of Rodrigo, we were greeted by his 19-year-old son Mauricio. He arrived at the bus station only moments after we did. We were certainly not hard for him locate, standing out from the crowd like three tall white lampposts.

Mauricio had the same soft-spoken manner of his father. He was short, with a sharply chiseled nose and a long ponytail. His youthful enthusiasm, tempered with shyness, replaced the wise but humble self-confidence of his father.

I shared a seat with him on what was the proverbial Latin American chicken bus. Our luggage was stowed behind the driver next to two crates full of young chirping chickens. Machetes and the occasional rifle were brought on board without drawing the least bit of attention from anyone other than the three wide-eyed gringos. We weren't in Kansas anymore and this wasn't a Greyhound.

Mauricio was fluent in Spanish. In his village of Macuma many of the young people were bilingual, speaking both Spanish and their native tongue. After the cursory exchange about my life and the weather in Arizona (yes, but it's a dry heat), I dove into an inquiry about life in the jungle village. It did not take long for me to steer the conversation to the subject of shamanism and Ayahuasca. He asked me if I was interested in doing it. I said I was thinking about it. My young guide smiled a knowing and mischievous smile.

The bus meandered through the jungle, making numerous stops along the way. I felt like I was in a theater, watching a movie of the locals' lives like a spectator— removed but fascinated. People gathered and socialized at the stops before making their way to their respective villages. Ours was the final stop— the end of the road— a river, thirty to forty yards across, both cold and very swift.

To reach the trailhead we needed to get to the other side. Okay, no problem, where is the bridge? No bridge! A rusted cable was suspended 40 feet above the river. Hanging from the cable by two large rollers was an iron cart with a decayed wooden floor. Crossing the swift river in the rickety cart seemed to represent the point of no return. "Remain seated at all times. Beware of holes in the floor. Keep your hands away from the rollers. Your ride has begun."

The crossing required some energy because the landing on the other side was at a slightly higher elevation. Besides our gang, there were five locals headed on the same trail. After helping us cross over, the five others disappeared into the wilderness ahead of us, carrying boxes and bags, with only one pair of shoes among them.

We arranged our packs and prepared for our trek. I slung the single strap of my duffle bag over my shoulder. Marcela and Miguel had proper backpacks and were better prepared than I in this regard. I was uncomfortable, but my years of backpacking with my Dad had kept me in good shape. Marcela and Miguel, however, were not used to the rigors of backpacking.

Mauricio told us that most visitors take six to seven hours to complete the trip. The pace of my two companions with their packs turned out to be painfully slow for me. I used it to my advantage to take photos along the way. Again, colorful insects captured my attention at nearly every turn. I lagged behind for a few moments interacting with a suitable subject. I usually would catch up with the gang shortly thereafter. If they could travel so slowly, I could surely stop for 1/500th of a second here and there. However, I got waylaid when I came across one particularly brilliant beetle in a cluster of exotic flowers. It was photo opportunity I did not want to leave behind.

Mauricio backtracked to see if I was okay. I told him I would be a few more minutes. I knew I was being selfish but I felt justified because I had to accommodate to the extremely slow pace of my fellow travelers. I felt they could cut me some slack and allow me to indulge in a photo opportunity that I might never have again. Marcela didn't see it that way. She was quite irritated that I was holding them up. This would come back to haunt me later in the day— much, much later in the day.

Several groups of locals had blown by us like we were standing still. A few stopped to chat with Mauricio. We encountered long stretches of foot-deep mud. Crude but useful paths of logs were fashioned across these stretches. Measuring three logs across, they stretched for hundreds of yards. Attention to foot placement was essential so we moved slowly. Still, it was far easier than extracting your foot from thick mud every step.

Late in the afternoon it became obvious that we were behind schedule. Miguel and Marcela were getting tired. Marcela was avoiding eye contact with me. In her mind, the three or four times I had kept them waiting as I snapped away with my camera was the only reason we were behind schedule. We were now nine hours into a trip that should have taken seven. Mauricio, in his own passive way, was trying to speed up the pace.

There I was, with two tourists from Holland and a local guide, trekking through a dense and intense rainforest. After nine hours on the trail, our packs weighed heavily on our shoulders. Sunlight was fading quickly and we were still miles from our destination. Our guide looked scared. That's never a good sign. The sounds from the surrounding vegetation began changing as the various creatures of the night awoke. As darkness slowly took over I began to feel as if the jungle was closing in on us, trapping us. My mind raced, "What the hell am I doing? I could die out here! Ooh look at that bug (click)!"

In the jungle, in the mud, and in the dark it was creepy and unnerving. I'm sure Marcela took some comfort in blaming me. Had I known it was to come to this I would have passed on the photo opportunities. I wondered who would take care of my pet pig if I never made it out of the jungle alive. Would I ever see Baby Blue again? (Oops! Sorry Mom, I'd miss you too!)

Finally, we saw some relief ahead on the trail. There was an intermittent glow of a flashlight in the distance. Eventually we could see a horse and rider coming our way. Mauricio's younger brother and his young friend had come from the village looking for us. They greeted us, and thankfully, loaded our packs on the horse and left a flashlight behind. Then they headed back to the village with a full load.

It was a relief to have our load lightened but the mud and the darkness was not a good combination. As the light diminished, the sounds from the forest increased. The symphony of birds, frogs and insects enveloped us along with the night.

With one flashlight between us, we teetered on the logs, stepping blindly and hoping not to fall in the mud. We all eventually fell in, and extracting ourselves was not enjoyable. Though Mauricio was managing to maintain his composure, the three of us were very much on edge.

Finally, after more than an hour of tedious progress we came to a clearing, and Mauricio pointed out a glimmer of lights in the distance. The village. Closer yet were some smaller flickering lights. The lights were rapidly moving towards us as we approached them. What a relief. It was Rodrigo and several villagers coming to greet us and guide us in.

Rodrigo was pleased and also very relieved to see us. His presence was more than comforting. We still had not arrived, but finally reconnecting with Rodrigo felt like an accomplishment. We continued on solid ground that turned out to be a rudimentary airstrip for the village. An airstrip?! I had not been aware that an airplane was an option. Would have been nice to know.

One of the boys with the group walking ahead raised his voice to call attention to an anaconda crossing the trail. It was certainly less than man-eating size, but exciting nonetheless. The boy grabbed the snake so we could get a closer look and some photos. I was glad we didn't meet it in the forest, alone in the dark!

We were exhausted and it was late in the evening, so a tour of the village would have to wait until morning. At a large outdoor table we were treated to crackers and soda. For them a bottle of soda was something for special occasions, as if it was a bottle of fine champagne reserved for esteemed guests. The soda was standard lemon-lime but the sentiment was genuine and appreciated.

Soon we were shown to large huts with bamboo slat beds built out from the walls. There was some flex in the bamboo but not much. It didn't matter at that point, I could have slept on a rock.

I awoke the next morning feeling mildly refreshed and excited about the new day. The fears of the night before had given way to the familiar fears of Ayahuasca. The day began with a baptism ceremony. Our own! With great seriousness and reverence, Rodrigo explained many of the customs of his tribe regarding red face paint and body adornments of feathers and beads made of various seeds. My baptismal Shuar name was "Wajaral," relating to strength and wisdom. Sure beats "Dark Cloud!!

In spite of the somber manner of his explanation, I couldn't help but feel the tourist show aspect of the ceremony. The cynical salesman in me questioned Rodrigo's motives, but his sincerity was unmistakable. I would learn over the next few days how the tourist trade fit into the overall scheme of development he foresaw for the village.

He was wise on many levels and understood the potential impact of different directions of progress for the village. He believed that the construction of a highway to the village would destroy the culture of the tribe very quickly, plus have a terrible effect on the surrounding environment. His vision, similar to that of Ecotrackers, was that eco-tourism could bring economic development to the village without a significant impact on their culture while preserving the environment that sustained their connected style of life.

The village was close to a small river. The second item on our agenda was a tour by canoe. We were not just passengers, but also expected to provide rowing power to get upstream. That wasn't in the brochure! We reached an island of sand and rocks where we took a welcomed break. Rodrigo continued to share details of his tribal culture and its relation to the environment. He pointed out birds and the locations where armadillo and tapir could be found. We were even given nets to catch small fish for a future meal.

We were advised that we would be meeting the shaman at lunch and told that if we wanted to partake in the Ayahuasca ceremony we could do it that evening. Whoa! I thought I would have a day or two to settle in. Oh well, here we go. My Ayahuasca roller coaster was approaching the last big incline.

Back at the village we prepared to hike along the river to a beach where we would have a picnic. Rodrigo's extended family and friends would be joining us, including the shaman. I was introduced to him in Rodrigo's family hut. He spoke absolutely no Spanish. I felt no connection whatsoever when we met, not the slightest hint of rapport. That's cool, I told myself. It's a cultural thing, we will certainly warm up to each other.

The hike to the beach was a short one. We carried pots and pans, produce and a live chicken! The picnic itself was not very comfortable for me. I was being eaten alive by sand flies. I could not even see them, but they were having no trouble finding me. Whose picnic was this anyway?!

The food was served in courses, but I was not relaxed enough to enjoy the cooked bananas and yucca. I kept looking at the shaman, who looked ridiculous to me in a big furry hat that was totally out of place in the warm sun. He played a flute with no pleasing tones or any sense of melody. He just struck me as goofy and a bit thick. I was having second thoughts about trusting my mind to this fellow.

Later in the afternoon there was yet another local expedition, this time to a sacred waterfall. About fifteen of us crossed two rivers to get to the special spot. The second river was over waist high, and chest high for some of the group. We crossed together as a chain, linked firmly wrist-to-wrist. Crossing alone would not have been easy.

My cynical mind wondered if the waterfall ceremony would be another tourist show (been there, done that, got the wet T-shirt). To my delight we were included in the ceremony, but not the focus of it. It appeared to be the real deal.

The shaman brought a gourd containing a liquid derived from a locally grown herb similar to tobacco. A semi-circle was formed around the waterfall; we were standing knee deep in the pool below the 30-foot cliff. The shaman chanted incantations, which we repeated. The shaman then poured the potion into the cupped palms of the participants. They held it for a few moments then ingested it through the nose and the mouth, slurping and snorting it all at the same time. I did my best to do it like they did. It had a medicinal taste but was not unpleasant. Individuals took turns walking into the waterfall as the group focused their attention on that person.

Not everyone entered the waterfall but the three of us gringos took the opportunity to participate. The cool water crashed down firmly on my head and shoulders, an exciting little rush, but it wasn't enough to knock me over. The waterfall ceremony was enjoyable on a variety of levels. Getting there, crossing the rivers in a group effort, the natural beauty of the waterfall, and the intimacy of their sacred ceremony. It was hard to tell if the potion had a mood-altering effect because of all of the positive circumstances. The overall effect was joyful. I felt very alive and privileged to be there.

On the way back to the village I started to reconsider my opinion of the shaman. Perhaps I had judged him harshly based on my first impression. The Ayahuasca ceremony was feeling like a better idea, my confidence was back up again. I was ready for the evening.

False alarm! The rug was pulled from beneath me again. The evening's Ayahuasca ceremony was not to be. This time it was in the form of an emergency patient that the shaman had to attend to. Definitely a good reason to delay! The patient would take Ayahuasca as part of her treatment, and there was not enough remaining for our use. The roller coaster dipped down again.

We were allowed to watch the shaman's session with his patient. She showed up in modern dress and sat in a chair across from the shaman the entire time. There was dialogue throughout the two hours, in between chanting and prayers. Halfway through the session, the shaman brought out a wine bottle and a cup-sized gourd used as a glass for the Ayahuasca. It was more than obvious that the taste did not appeal to the patient. She needed lots of encouragement to finish drinking the dose he had poured.

As a spectator not understanding the language, it brought up more questions than answers. Yet another delay, seemingly a last-minute stay of execution. Execution? Vine of death? Underneath the confidence remained my fear. Still, the delay would provide an opportunity to become more involved in the process. The Ayahuasca vine had to be gathered to make another batch of the elixir.

The next day, I found myself wandering in the forest with a hatchet gathering branches. The leaves of the plant were not used, but rather the branches. We gathered roughly a bushel basket full of branches and proceeded to chop them into sections. Each section had to be smashed with a hammer to crack open and expose the inside. The pulverized branches were placed in a large cauldron of water set to boil over an open flame. It looked like the quintessential witch's brew. There I was, the sorcerer's apprentice, in the smoky cave (okay it was a hut) churning the bubbling potion with a giant stick (might just need a little more eye of newt).

I tended the pot throughout the day with Mauricio, adding water as the level dropped. At midday the leaves of another plant were poked into the thickening liquid between the branches. The leaves were necessary to activate the chemical compounds from the vine. When you think about the thousands of different plants in the Amazon Basin, it boggles the mind that someone, generations prior, managed to combine these two for the resultant effect.

Toward the end of the day, after removing the branches, the contents of the cauldron had been reduced to a runny, greenish-brown sludge. The shaman poured it into two different empty wine bottles. I felt a sense of satisfaction and completion. Part of the stage was set for the evening.

But there was another bump in my roller coaster ride that afternoon. A plane had touched down on the village runway. This plane came to the village every two weeks or so. It was several days ahead of schedule. The three of us had hoped to catch a ride on the plane back to Macas, avoiding the long trek back to the bus. But not today! At least not me. Not when I was so very close to my date with Ayahuasca.

We had been traveling as a group but we were not obligated to stay together. Marcela really wanted to take the plane back to Macas. I was lobbying with Miguel for them to stay for the ceremony. However, if the plane left without us, our return trip would be very much in question. There was another plane that showed up only sporadically and sometimes had limited space. Even if it was available, the fare was much higher.

The flight was tempting, but I had decided I would stay even if it meant hiking out. Miguel agreed. Marcela was furious. She had little interest in the Ayahuasca ceremony and had not planned to participate. She was a nurse, and certainly had justified reasons to decline, but Miguel was caught up in my enthusiasm. Once again, I was impeding her progress. It wasn't my intention to ruin her day, but for me the ceremony had become the major focus of this trip. I told her I was sorry but that it was very important to me.

It was getting late in the day and this would be my last chance for meditation and journaling before the adventure. My meditation was clear and calm. In my journal I asked myself the same, "Why am I doing this? What do I want from this?" questions. At that point, I was tapped out for answers. "You are ready," I wrote, "You'll get what you get." "Relax. Let go." I was ready even with the tiny butterflies fluttering in my gut.

When I emerged from beneath my mosquito net, everyone was busy preparing for the evening. The middle of the hut had been cleared. Mauricio was there and the shaman in his furry hat seemed to be in an extra-jovial mood.

They were setting the stage, literally, for a traditional dance production. Eight young women donned costumes of matching blue dresses with elaborate fringes and beads. The show began with the youngest dancers showing off their awkward, shy steps. The music intensified and the more experienced dancers joined in.

The production included mostly female dancers, with three young males in full painted regalia joining in selectively. Throughout the rest of the performance the men contributed with musical talents — four distinct percussion instruments plus the shaman on his ever-ready flute. More than once I could have sworn he played a few notes from Jethro Tull. Thick as a Brick seemed to fit.

At the end of the performance everyone was on their feet participating in a dance step, stomping twice on one foot, then the other, then stepping over a symbolic log placed in the middle of the floor.

The show ended and the energy settled as most of the people went their own way for the evening. Remaining in the room were Rodrigo, the shaman, Marcela, Miguel, myself, Mauricio and one other villager. There would be four of us taking the Ayahuasca — Miguel, Mauricio, the villager and myself.

I was pleased that Mauricio would be joining us. I had gotten to know him well and developed an appreciation for his gentle and sincere personality. I had developed a strong rapport with him, something that still had not happened with the shaman.

The shaman brought out the recycled green wine bottle and motioned for us to gather around a small table. He passed the bottle around ceremonially. When I took it in my hands I could feel the excitement well up in me. Yes, I was afraid, but much more so, I was excited. Excited about the experience I was about to have, and moreover, excited that I had made it all this way. I had stood up to my fears and trepidations and moved ahead. I was proud.

The same small gourd cup was used to dispense a dose to each individual. The taste was worse than I had imagined, like forcing down rancid mud. I was told that almost everyone vomits as a part of the process. I shuddered and choked it down. No turning back now. The ceremony had begun.

I was eagerly anticipating the festivities when the shaman gathered his things and made for the door. "Huh?! What?!" I thought, "What's the deal?" He wasn't supposed to be leaving! I intercepted him at the door, with what had to be a very confused look on my face. I wanted to say, "Hey, you're not leaving, are you?" but I knew he wouldn't understand a word of my English or my Spanish. I think he understood my sentiment and he motioned towards Rodrigo and Mauricio as if to say "Sorry Bud, I gotta go. But don't worry, they'll take care of you." (Perhaps he had to exorcise a demon in the next village, or maybe he just had a date).

Another rug jerked out from under me. An assumption. The shaman would not be guiding us through the experience. Just a strong preconceived notion I had. I had to deal with this new situation as it was. Soon Mauricio was gone as well.

Rodrigo would be my caretaker. There would be no further ceremony per se. We were each left to our own experience. Rodrigo counseled me on what to expect, including the vomiting part. He said he would be close by if I needed him. It was comforting to know he was there.

I sat by the fire with Miguel and waited for something to happen. The conversation progressed something like this: "Do you feel anything?"

"I think I feel something. Do you feel something?"

Thirty minutes or so passed and we heard someone outside heaving. Perhaps Mauricio. Whoever it was, I didn't like the sound of it, or the thought of going through it myself. I told myself I would be the exception to the vomiting part of the process. Soon it was Miguel's turn to take a trip outside. This was turning into the lamest frat party ever!

Marcela came out from under their mosquito net to comfort him outside. Miguel came back in looking a little woozy. By then I was feeling the effects, but still hoping I wouldn't need to vomit. Just then the feeling intensified and suddenly my body felt out of control. It was scary and not at all pleasant. I finally realized it was happening to me, I had to barf. I got outside and my body took over from there.

Phew, what a relief. The out-of-control feeling was gone and I was left with an expansive feeling of being in my body and at the same time floating around and above it. Miguel had retired with Marcela under their mosquito net. I sat down by the fire to marvel at the beauty of the flickering flames. The warmth of the coals penetrated my body supernaturally. I felt as if I was glowing back in communication with the coals.

I fumbled through my things to find my pen and notebook. I wanted to capture the experience on paper. Would my writing be intelligible by the light of day? We would just have to wait and see. It seemed clear as I wrote. But soon it became heavy, laborious. Enough writing, I just wanted to feel. I stayed by the fire a little longer before finding my way to my bunk, in my own kingdom under my mosquito net.

I was in my own little cocoon, but I was connected to the stars. I had an extreme sense of well-being. Perfection. Words pale and just don't do the job. As trite as it sounds, I felt at one with the universe. At the same time, I could feel every inch of my body like never before. I could feel my entire vertebral column flex from top to bottom as I inhaled and exhaled. With my eyes closed I could see colors and shapes taking form and coming towards me. I saw faces and other objects emerge momentarily in bright colors, not photo-realistic or dreamlike, but a colored light show that disappeared when I opened my eyes.

I felt supremely comfortable in my body, even on the rigid bamboo slats. From time to time, I would shift from my back to my side feeling equally at home. I wrapped my arms around myself and put one hand on the side of my face. I caressed myself as if I was in the arms of a lover.

I was very content to lay awake in my bunk most of the night, enjoying the expansive feeling of oneness. I don't recall getting tired but eventually I drifted off to sleep. When I woke up late the next morning, I took a moment to check in with myself. There was no hung-over feeling, in fact, it was quite the opposite. I did not feel like I was still under the influence but I felt rested and very, very peaceful. The tranquility was quite amazing.

I was greeted with big smiles from Rodrigo and the family. I found my way to the spring bath and leisurely started my day. I was curious to read my notes from the night before. My handwriting varied from crystal clear to barely legible. Nothing earth-shattering. The content was simple and basic and the tone was very positive. Clarity, self-esteem and optimism about life. "I like my life! I'm a pretty happy lucky guy! Life is good just the way it is! I seem to be composing pretty good sentences! It will be fun to read this tomorrow." A little sappy, but sincere.

When I returned to the hut there was a group of five kids playing by the front door. I sat down and sank into their little world. I was startled by a profound connection with them. I was interacting with five small beings rather than playing with kids. It was at once both eerie and uplifting. It was almost as if they knew what I had been through the night before, and now I was a member of their club. Were they different than the day before? No, but I was. Connecting with the stars had reconnected me to myself.

My Ayahuasca Diary Epilogue

Was I glad I did it? Most definitely. Would I want to do it again? Probably not. The growth I experienced leading up to the actual ingestion of the Ayahuasca was as powerful as the event itself. In contrast, Miguel's Ayahuasca experience began that afternoon and consisted of throwing up, falling asleep and waking up groggy. My set and setting had been entirely different. Making the commitment ten days prior in the café with Max initiated a process. That process provided the lessons. I filled 70 pages in my journal with my observations and insights. I experienced a heightened sense of clarity and focus. I became the river. I had an epiphany in front of the classroom. I confronted my fears. And finally, I completed my quest in the jungle. What a powerful drama I had created for myself.

Back in Quito, I received an assignment to boldly go where no tourist had gone before! Not Spock and Captain Kirk in the Starship Enterprise, but Mark and Tim in Baby Blue. We were going to be eco-tour pioneers. Max entrusted us to make contact with a new village and establish another location for Ecotrackers. Usually he visited a location before sending volunteers, but this time we were blazing the trail — being guinea pigs instead of eating them. My eco-partner Tim was a twenty-something Canadian who had been caught in Max's web of enthusiasm during a two-month adventure through South America. A thoughtful and friendly guy, Tim was thrilled to be a part of our mission. With minimal instructions, we were sent off to the Rio Cayapas and the village of San Jose.

From Quito we drove down out of the mountains to the coastal town of Esmereldas. After Esmereldas, the paved highway ended and we continued on a rocky dirt road north along the Pacific Coast toward the Cayapas River. The town of Borbon, nestled at the mouth of the river, was a hub for the transport of cargo, human and otherwise. Like a Wild-West frontier settlement, Borbon felt like it was on the outskirts of civilization, about to leave it all together.

Max had instructed us to contact a woman in Borbon named Zelda. She was supposed to give us specific directions to San Jose. Zelda was nowhere to be found. With Borbon's decrepit phone system, we were not able to reach Max.

We checked into a hotel and continued to look for Zelda. We were nearly at the point of giving up when she arrived back in town. Zelda was in her 60's and was involved in social work in Borbon. She was happy to facilitate our efforts and the expansion of Ecotrackers. She gave us instructions to get up the Rio Cayapas to San Jose. Zelda had a contact in San Jose who she felt would be open to Ecotrackers and helpful to us. Even with the connection, in sales terms we were pretty much making a cold call.

The next morning Tim and I got in an oversized motorized canoe and took the eight-hour trip up the river to San Jose. With four seats across, the boat was like an aquatic minivan, stopping at villages along the way where people waited along the shore for a ride upriver. At one stop, we were amazed to witness three men wrestling a full-size cow. They tied its legs against its body and proceeded to stuff the struggling animal into a canoe that was barely big enough for two Boy Scouts. Although he didn't look sick, he certainly was a "mad cow!" We crossed our fingers for the safety of the captive cow on his journey upstream.

The rustic and primitive village of San Jose overlooks the river from high on a bluff. A crude stairway, fashioned out of cement, led from the water up to the village. There were no vehicles in town, save a couple of rusty bicycles. Being situated on the river in a jungle, the town had a plentiful supply of wood, which they used for all of their buildings.

Our contact in San Jose was easy to find even though she had no idea we were coming. She was a prominent member of the 200-person village and she quickly arranged for us to give a presentation in their "town hall." She also arranged a place to stay — the top story of a local home with vacant rooms where guests were housed. Our rooms had beds with mattresses, enclosed with sheets of mosquito netting to keep the giant insects away. We made arrangements to join a local family for meals.

That evening, Tim and I got up in front of a group of 20 diverse residents, including two nuns from Italy, to give our Ecotrackers presentation in Spanish. I was more fluent than Tim and better versed in the basics of community eco-tourism, so I was elected to do most of the talking. A part of me felt like the rain forest version of Tony Robbins, the other part felt like some kind of imposter. How did I end up here? I'm a dentist! I'm not a missionary! My head was spinning. The villagers looked up at me with great expectations. I was just learning the concepts, would I be able to get them across in Spanish? The audience held a range of attitudes from cynical to hopeful and excited. After we spoke and fielded questions, a dozen locals enrolled in a week of English classes. The lessons are used to help small communities interact with future visitors.

So there we were, Tim and I, eco-tour pioneers having a blast. We were teaching English classes in the morning and exploring the region with the men of the village in the afternoon. We bushwhacked through the jungle to a secluded waterfall and swimming hole and made trips to mountaintops with magnificent panoramic views. We attempted to communicate the value of their natural resources to our guides. The potential for eco-tourism was ongoing, but once the forest was gone, it was gone.

The village does have some contact with the rest of Ecuador. Though it is a long trip, treks to Esmeraldas were not uncommon. Many young people left for the big city, only to find that living in the heart of nature offered a better quality of life. Just like kids from Small Town, USA, quite a few would find their way back.

San Jose had a primitive electrical grid, powered by a small gasoline generator. When they had fuel, they turned on the generator for a couple of hours in the early evenings. I had my laptop and camera and was desperate to charge up their batteries. I offered to pay for the fuel and give a digital slideshow if they turned on the generator

That evening I hosted an informal show with pictures of villagers and the surrounding area. By then, we had been accepted by the community and dozens of people attended. Their curiosity and restrained enthusiasm about the foreign technology was evident. Their comfort level grew and soon, every time a picture of somebody would come on the screen they would howl and laugh, "Ah! There's Fred, there's Fred!" (Okay, there was nobody named Fred, but you get the picture).

Overall, San Jose was a rich cultural experience and I felt as though we had done something worthwhile. Would Ecotrackers gain a foothold here? What would the impact be in twenty years? Had our presence made a difference? I hope so.

I was still not finished with Mad Max and Ecotrackers. I saw the need for a better way to communicate the Ecotrackers experience to potential volunteers. The photos and written trip reports on the walls were good, but video footage would have had so much more impact. In fact, I had a brand-new, mini digital video camera with me, which was a parting gift from a business associate who had helped make my departure possible (Thanks again, Fred!). I had been so involved with my still photography that I hadn't even taken it out of the box. It was time. I took on the responsibility of creating a promotional video as my volunteer project. Max was all for it.

I asked Juan Carlos, who was part of the staff in Quito, to come with me. Twenty-two years old, energetic and outgoing, he was from the coastal town of Atacames, and had come to Quito to work for Ecotrackers. He was keen on improving his English and himself. We cooked up a plan to tour the country filming Ecotrackers locations along the way. He would be my co-pilot and cameraman. I was the on-camera host, producer, and director of what eventually became a 20-minute piece.

Juan Carlos (who I will call J.C. from here out) jumped at the opportunity even thought it was without pay. I covered his expenses over and above the generosity of the Ecotrackers hosts. As in other countries, I'd found that the locals had very limited travel experience, even inside their own country. J.C. knew Quito, and his hometown on the coast, but the rest of his country was unexplored territory to him. We chose seven Ecotrackers locations in a large loop around the country. Max spent many hours briefing me on the specifics of each location.

J.C. mastered the basics of the video camera quickly and became quite proficient at zooming and panning as per my requests. I could never have gotten the same candid shots on my own. I would go in with my fairly large 35mm camera around my neck, while Juan carried the little video camera in the palm of his hand. People would look at me and run. "Run from the tall gringo with the big camera!" However, J.C. and the tiny camera blended right into the human landscape with no one batting an eye, as if he were invisible.

Our grand adventure was under way. First stop, Ingapirca! It took us about a day and a half to get this agricultural area high in the mountains. I don't know how anything could grow in such cold weather— we froze our *cajones* off.

Editor's note: I'll spare you the translation.
Author's note: I won't. It means, "balls!"

Our hosts, Jose and Asura, put us up in a room with chilly concrete floors and walls, and no heating. We slept under our blankets, inside our sleeping bags, with our clothes on. Every morning we had to crawl out of our sleeping bags and scurry across the yard to the unheated concrete bathroom. Bordering on cruel and unusual, this was everyday life for them.

Jose and Asura spoke of the peculiarities and customs of the region. Similar to Guatemalan villages with their different bright fabrics, the indigenous groups in Ecuador can be recognized by their peculiar hats, specific to each region and group. In this particular area, the locals wore white, rounded, felt hats with two little furry white balls hanging down from either the front or the back depending on their marital status.
Editor's note: Are they cajones?

Choclo, a staple in their diet, is like corn with oversized kernels and a dense, meaty texture. As in Pablo Sexto, another staple in their diet is cuy. You would see the rodents skewered and roasting over a fire at the roadside stands. What seemed like a dead rat on a stick to me was their equivalent of a Big Mac.

I found the infrastructure of the village a little odd. In the middle of a row of modest homes, a "mansion" would appear out of nowhere. Most of the homes were one or two stories made of mud, in an adobe-type construction. Others were made of concrete like the one owned by our host. The "mansions" looked like Main Street, USA. This was the result of a phenomenon called *hermanos lejanos*, meaning, "brothers from afar." A member of a family would go to the U.S. to work and send money home. Compared to the small scale of the local economy, a portion of the *hermanos lejanos'* earnings was a fortune, allowing their families to build the mansions. You could see at a glance who had relatives a world away.

Jose and Asura spent three days guiding us to sites of photographic interest around the community. Each evening, J.C. and I arrived back to our concrete icebox with lots to do to prepare for the following day. We had to download photos, review footage, and most importantly, recharge batteries. What looked like working like a dog, felt like partying like a rock star. We were having a blast! We were up at dawn, excited about getting footage in the early morning light. There was passion and purpose in our project. Our hosts were excited about our efforts and being featured in the videotape. They wanted a copy as soon as it was available.

We were sad to move on. Like all the villagers, they were shy at first, but our gracious hosts had warmed up and taken great care of us. However, we were ready for a warmer climate, and to reconnect with our pal Max.

Max took a bus from Quito and met us in the town of Guamote. He had asked us to attend a meeting of mayors from the surrounding villages. They were talking about issues pertinent to the area, including attracting tourism. I couldn't contribute much, other than to say I was there to make a videotape. They were pleased about the video and the possibility of bringing in more eco-tourists. Max had lots to contribute to the discussion in explaining the scope of his program. He talked a lot about how much his type of client wanted a personal experience rather than a guided-tour type of scenario.

We got VIP treatment including a tour of anything that could be considered an attraction. One of the distinguishing features of the region is an organized, efficient, and huge co-op system called *mingas*. The farmers work, harvest and sell together. They even have their own gigantic earth-moving equipment for building roads to the farms in outlying areas.

We had planned our trip around the co-op's weekly market day. There were different markets spread throughout the town. Carrots and potatoes would be in one place, leafy greens in another, and two livestock markets also separated— sheep and cows apart from horses and donkeys. I was shocked by the treatment of the livestock. Sheep with all four legs bound together to form a handle were literally thrown into piles— heaps of helpless animals lying in the sun. It seemed unnecessarily rough. Their cultural relationship to animals is less emotional and more practical than mine. I had ridden a horse on a farm in Ingapirca. I'd asked the farmer the horse's name. He was surprised by my question and said, "We don't baptize horses," noting a clear distinction between people and animals. Do you baptize cars? I'd like to introduce you to Baby Blue.

Relatively speaking, these sheep had a better life than livestock on industrialized farms in the U.S. Okay, so they get a little tied up in the end. Who doesn't like being tied up once in awhile? At least they got to graze on some grass and be out in the open rather than being penned up, eating genetically engineered grain pellets, punctured with antibiotics and hormones, and living in their own waste.

On our last day in Guamote, the Mayor's staff treated us to a tour of a fishery located about an hour outside of town. Tons of North American rainbow trout were being raised in gorgeous crystal blue lakes high in the mountains. I was impressed by their efficiency and organization. There was a hatchery with a progression of small tanks all the way up to large ponds, with a corresponding progression of fish from a few days old to six-pounders! I was treated to one of them for dinner — fresh from the pond and delicious.

We had discussions about the pristine mountain lakes and their hopes of developing them. Though very concerned about conservation, the locals wanted to share the beauty with visitors and generate some income. I really hope they're successful in developing their area in a way that maintains the beauty of their resources and the integrity of their community.

One of the highlights of our video tour was La Tolita. Just getting there was part of the adventure. We drove north up the coast past commercial shrimp farms and cultivated fields. In spite of the agricultural activities, it was very remote. Our interim destination was La Tola, within spitting distance of the Colombian border. La Tola was the place where travelers and transport went from bus to boat and vice versa. There were no parking facilities, so we struggled to find a safe place to house Baby Blue. Ultimately, we found someone willing to shelter Baby Blue in a fenced in area at his home before making our way to the water. Narrow canoes piled high with coconuts arrived at the dock as passengers, including us, boarded larger boats for passage upriver. La Tola was a tiny enough place already, but we were on our way to La Tolita (Little La Tola).

After a 40-minute boat ride we pulled up to a dock in La Tolita. Adjacent to the dock, stood a small shack where workers husked coconuts prior to transport. Coconuts were a major part of the village's economy. With only a couple hundred people, we were amazed at what we found. They had their own archaeological dig and museum!

I was fascinated and delighted. I would have expected them to be hunting and fishing and concentrating on putting food on the table, but here they were doing scientific research. With no full time staff, museum visits were by appointment only. Our personal guided tour didn't take long, there were only two small rooms lined with shelves. Our guide complained about how the national government had appropriated some of their specimens for a museum in Quito. We also toured a little ceramic studio where reproductions of the anthropological finds like figurines and urns were created. I was blown away by their efforts.

My amazement continued later that day, as I filmed a rehearsal of their school dance program. Every semester they put on a very sophisticated performance. The choreographer seemed to be the Hollywood cliché — flamboyant and light in the loafers. I couldn't help but wonder about his social outlets and his acceptance in this tiny little community. The musical director was pounding the rhythm on a massive base drum as the choreographer directed a group of about twenty kids who were performing elaborate dance steps to native music. I was captivated by the performance. In light of the location, I was once again, blown away.

La Tolita is an unusual example of a community doing a lot to preserve their culture through dance, archaeology, education, and nurturing the skills of their craftsmen. It was a treat to see. How had the culture of this village developed? It was like the golden age of a civilization, flourishing as its own little island.

It was time for a break from the video tour so we headed to J.C.'s coastal hometown of Atacames. Time to party! Although Atacames is not a volunteer location itself, there's an Ecotrackers satellite office which helps organize volunteers in the surrounding communities. Atacames is a beach town, resort community and the perfect spot for volunteers to relax and unwind. For over a mile along the beach, there are cabañas selling drinks, snacks, tourist trinkets and hair-braiding services. Visitors sun themselves on the beach during the day, and then move across the street to the restaurants and nightclubs later in the evening. By no means an international destination, it's a well-known party place for Ecuadorians.

J.C. was thrilled to be back in his hometown. Over the next couple of days, we had fun visiting his local haunts, friends and family. He was very proud of his participation in our project and showed off the video camera to everyone. His family welcomed me into their home and vacated a bedroom for me. They took time out of their busy lives to make me feel as welcome as a long-lost member of the family. Their home was above their family-run tailor shop. They were an industrious group, with the mom in charge of a crew of four at the shop and his brothers running another business, a juice bar cabaña on the beach.

Monstrous papayas and mangos decorated the counter and provided the ingredients for fresh fruit smoothies and ice cream sundaes. While we were in town, J.C. took some shifts at the cabaña. His role as the DJ and his presence behind the bar made the place come alive.

After night fell, the festivities shifted from the beach to the street that paralleled the beach. Each restaurant and cabaña had its own music blaring. Within twenty yards you could hear four different sound systems, all very loud and lively. We stopped at one cabaña that was particularly inviting. Swings, hanging from the ceiling, replaced barstools around the bar. Patrons swayed gently with their toes dangling in the sand. The combination of the ocean breeze, the lively music and the rocking motion had you floating away in a tropical paradise before you were even served your first drink.

Then there were the drinks! The *caipirinhia* is a drink transplanted from

Brazil, made with a sugarcane based liquor called *aguardiente* that tasted like it belonged in a gas tank. They use a mortar and pestle to mix the lime with sugar, then add *aguardiente*. Mixed with enough sugar and lime, even diesel fuel would taste good. Another drink was *la cucaracha*, the cockroach! It was a coffee liqueur with flammable, high-proof alcohol served in a coconut shell. The bartender ignited a small inferno in front of your face and you were expected to drink it while it was still on fire. That is, if you were both brave and stupid. And yes, of course, I tried one.

Later, I was having dinner in a small restaurant run by a Colombian family and listening to *Cumbia* style music, which nearly caused my eardrums to bleed. From my patio table, I watched the steady stream of vacationers cruising the strip. Young panhandlers weaved their way through the river of humanity. The street kids didn't seem to have the same kind of desperation or problems with glue-sniffing that I had seen in Managua. Ten-year-old Javier approached my table, looking for food or spare change. Even though he lived in the streets he looked very presentable. He was cheerful, friendly, and polite. I shared some of my meal with him and we began talking. I couldn't believe how charming he was, and how desirable he would have been in any home in the U.S. looking to adopt. Javier slept under a bridge. He had four or five places where he knew he would get food or where he could do chores for small amounts of money. The community seemed to have an informal network of support for Javier and the other street kids. However, basically he was on his own, fending for himself and somehow surviving. He seemed surprisingly well adjusted under the circumstances, even thriving. I wish I could have done more for the little guy. Still, when we said our goodbyes, I was left with the impression that he would be okay.

The rest and relaxation in Atacames soon came to an end. J.C. and I bid our goodbyes to his family and made our way to our next destination.

The last stop of our trip, a few blocks from the main highway, was the little town of Santo Domingo. It's home to the indigenous Los Indios Colorados, The Colored Indians (two politically incorrect names in one). Famous for their *brujos*, witch doctors or shamans, they're also known for their peculiar red hairstyles. At first glance it looked like they were wearing hats or some kind of helmet. Actually, their hair had been styled into what appeared to be bright red Frisbees. They use red pigment from the seeds of a local tree, a natural hair gel concoction, to create this hairstyle. So, when in Rome….

They wanted to baptize me. I participated in the ceremony by dressing in native garb and doing my hair up with the red pigment. On top of the red hair, they put a little white halo made from a fungus. They formed it into a doughnut and put it on top of the helmet to indicate that I was single. Oh boy, was I ready for the ladies!

We got to know our host and his family and a couple of local shamans. They took us on a fruit and vegetable tour of the surrounding area where we got pictures of a little vine snake flicking his red tongue back and forth. They promised us it wasn't venomous, so I had the courage to get up pretty close. The community was famous around the country for its shamanic tradition. People came from all over to take part in their ceremonies to get healed. I was very interested even though there was nothing ailing me. They said it would be a great to participate for a general health and spiritual tune-up.

I participated in two different ceremonies. The first was an herbal steam bath. They picked fresh leaves from the surrounding jungle and made a cauldron of boiling water with the variety of medicinal herbs. I squatted on a small stool next to the pot.

Editor's note: Squat, stool, pot? Your word selection stinks.

They placed a sheet over me, creating a sauna inside my own personal tent. I stayed inside for 15 minutes. When I emerged, I was told to lie down and rest. It was quite relaxing. I hadn't had a sauna in a long time. After a new hairstyle and a sauna, I wondered if I could get my nails done.

The other ceremony was more intensive, actually working one-on-one with a shaman. A half-hour long, it involved incantations and medicinal ceremonies in front of an altar which was covered with eye-catching statues, photos, carvings, and stones. It was basically a little temple. Seated in front of the altar, with candles burning, he asked me about my life. He spoke Spanish whenever he needed to interact with me, but used his native tongue for the incantations.

The incantations and his interactions with the icons on his altar were spellbinding. I was blown away by his intensity. He was definitely in another world. He mixed up different ingredients with each incantation. He asked me to spread some on my skin and others he'd spew into the air. He'd grab a pinch of this and a pinch of that, mix it up and chew it and then take a swig from a bottle of something and spray it into the air.

I had a couple of different emotions. One was revulsion, when he chewed up the stuff and spewed it into the air over my head and into my face. The other was the humor of seeing him take a bite of a cigarette and chew it up as part of his medicinal mixture. A part of me was reverent and fascinated, while the other part wondered, "What is this guy doing to me? He just spit a chewed up Marlboro all over me!" He had told me it was going to have positive effects on my health and my love life. Who could argue with that?

We completed the Ecotrackers video tour and returned to Quito. The entire trip took two weeks. Back at the Ecotrackers apartment, we met a stranded German traveler named Toralf who Max had taken under his wing. He had been traveling across North and South America. Starting in New York, he had made his way to Alaska before heading south to the end of the world like me— but on a bicycle!!

He was just outside of Quito when he ran into misfortune. At a specific spot on the highway in a little valley where *banditos* hang out, he was knocked off his bike. The *banditos* stole it, and took his camera, journal, and twenty rolls of film on which he had captured his trip. He had ended up in Quito looking around for somebody to help him, and Max put him up. We spent some time discussing how to get a new passport. We wanted to try to get him back on two wheels again, but he literally had five *centavos* to his name.

We were sitting in the living room having a cup of tea. He was a little banged up from the robbery, bumps and scrapes but not anything serious. Max told him about the *Mercado de Los Ladrones*, the robber's market, just outside of Quito, where thieves take their stolen merchandise to unload it. The locals know that if you have something stolen you can go there and maybe get it back. Also it was a good place to look for a new bike if he couldn't find the old one. We printed up some flyers and headed to the market. He was mostly concerned about his journal and film because everything else was replaceable. At the market we saw rows of cameras and telephones and all sorts of stuff that was probably stolen. A couple of times I tried to take a picture and was obviously not welcome. The sellers objected very strenuously to my camera and me.

Toralf's misfortune made me contemplate my good fortune. I've felt blessed, with my own force field protecting me. Misfortune was in the neighborhood, even in my face, but never tapped me on the shoulder. Within a short period of time after Toralf's incident, both Max and Juan Carlos got tapped.

While I had gone on another Ecotrackers trip out of town, Max had been on the main street with his three daughters, coming back from a soccer game. Ecuador had won, and pandemonium broke out in the streets. Everybody was celebrating. Some kids were hassling one of his daughters. Max tried to intervene; an altercation ensued. One of them pulled a knife, which ended up in Max's shoulder. He had to be taken to the hospital. His artery had been severed between his shoulder and his chest. He was spraying blood on the ceiling in the emergency room! The young doctor couldn't stop the bleeding for a long time. Max took weeks to recover from the very close call.

J.C. was in Quito, when late one night after a disco, a couple of thugs confronted him and pulled a knife. One of them swung at him, cutting him on the forehead just above his eye. Luckily, J.C. escaped with only a scratch. Like most capital cities, Quito has its share of dangerous areas. Even going the eight blocks from *Gringolandia* back to the apartment was dangerous at night. Often I would work late at a nearby Internet café. The proprietors would not let me out the door unless there was a cab waiting at the curb.

Unknowingly, I had my own brush with death on the streets of Quito. Walking down the main street between *Gringolandia* and the apartment in broad daylight I didn't think safety was an issue. A guy about my height walked along side of me, getting right in my face. I presumed he was just a pushy panhandler. He asked me for my wallet in Spanish, but I thought that he was asking for a ticket for the trolley, or spare change for a ticket. I wondered why he was being so aggressive. "Back off!" I said as I reached into my pocket for change and handed it to him.

But he stayed right in my face, pointing to my pockets, repeating, "No! I want your *billete!*" Irritated, I backed away raising my voice, "Get away from me!" He responded with a phrase that included the word *mata*. The meaning didn't register and I kept walking. I had walked a block when I stopped in shock, "OH! *Mata!* From *matar*— to kill!" He said he was going to kill me! Naïve, ignorant or perhaps both, I cheated death once again!

I was sad to be leaving Quito and all of the friends I'd made there. Still, something inside of me told me that it was time to go. The road was calling me. It was again that juxtaposition of sadness and excitement. Leaving people I'd grown to care about and looking forward to being back on the road again. It's a great feeling to know that I'll have those friends if I ever go back, and I know I can keep in touch with them by e-mail.

I'm surprised how much I enjoy being on the road alone. Some days, I was on the road non-stop for ten hours. I would get some food to set on the passenger seat, like chips, cookies and hard-boiled eggs (got to have that protein in your diet). Then I only had to stop to download and upload fluids for my vehicle and person. Otherwise, I cruised comfortably in Baby Blue, riding down the highway absorbed in my thoughts. On this particular day my thoughts were with my Dad and how proud he'd be with my explorations. It was the anniversary of his death.

We called him Good ol' Dollar Bill. A tightwad, Dad was nevertheless willing to lend us money when we were growing up — as long as we signed a note for the loan plus interest. We often joked that we should have had an ATM installed in the living room because of all the financial transactions and paperwork. At the time, I hated him for being so cheap, especially since many of my friends were given money for college. However, as I reflect on the wisdom I have garnered, I think he was a very wise man. I can only speak for myself, not my family members, when I say he instilled in me the value of a dollar. He was a dentist with a traditional family practice. His kids were all out of the house, his house was paid for, and his expenses were nil. Still, he drove around in a beat-up old white pick-up. He prided himself on the fact that it never got washed except by the rain (don't forget we're talking about Arizona).

I also remember that he wasn't much fun to hike with. I went on a hike with him when I was an adult (as a child I hadn't know any better). We hiked in the Grand Canyon from rim to rim to rim, going from one side down, up to the other, then back again. There were four older couples who were part of his hiking club, and me.

My Dad was always the drill sergeant. "Okay, 7:00 a.m., up and at 'em!" At this point in my life, I had learned to relax and enjoy myself on my vacations. I was not into waking up at the butt crack of dawn to go hiking when I could relax and enjoy a cup of tea. As we reached camp at the bottom of the canyon it began to rain. My mom and another older woman were a couple hundred yards behind the group. Some of the husbands took shelter from the rain, letting their wives straggle into camp. I thought, "What's up with this?" I went back alone to help them.

I thought that my father and these other men were insensitive louts. Now however, I can recognize the good traits he modeled for me like courage when facing the unknown and an adventurous nature. In addition, I can distinguish the less desirable traits.

The next morning we were up at the crack of dawn to hike to the top of the other side with the plan to return the next morning. It felt like a race and I wanted to relax. My mother and her friend had painful blisters on their feet. We decided to break off from the pack and take a plane back across.

The next day we flew across the canyon and got a different perspective. We had already seen the canyon from the inside. Getting to see it from above was an additional treat. While my Dad and the others were trudging back through the canyon we were thoroughly enjoying our leisure time. We were well-rested and cheerful when they came straggling out the next day. I'm sure Dad was thinking "You're a pussy, Mark," but I didn't give a shit. I had a blast and I got to see more of the canyon than he did.

As I mentioned, my Dad was an inveterate backpacker. He loved trekking around the mountains of Arizona. When he died, his wishes were to have his ashes scattered from one of his favorite spots, Spud Rock in the Rincon Mountains overlooking Tucson. Every Memorial Day weekend, my Dad would guide a group of ten to twenty of his friends to the peak. We wanted to recreate his traditional trip as a memorial event for him. All seven of us kids, plus a few of his friends, hiked up to Spud Rock to carry out his last wishes. Well, partially.

We drove up to the trailhead on Friday afternoon so we could camp there for the night and leave early in the morning. We hiked for ten hours that day, most of it uphill. We joked about how Dad got the best of us by getting us all to do the strenuous hike. From Spud Rock you can see the whole valley of Tucson. Standing there, we all took handfuls of ashes and hoisted him into the wind. Some of him anyway.

My Mom wasn't physically up for the trip, but we were able to call her from a cell phone while we were scattering the ashes. She was definitely involved in the process. My Dad's wishes were to have his ashes scattered, but my Mom's wishes were to be buried next to him. They both got their way because we only took a small portion of his ashes to scatter in his chosen spot. I guess my Mom got the last laugh. It was very fitting because he always got his way in life. In the end, my Mom finally got hers.

There I was in Ecuador on the anniversary of my Dad's death, and in my mind he was looking over my shoulder as I reached the border to Peru. I arrived at the border very late in the day and backtracked a few miles to find a hotel. The only hotel was a sad and dingy low-budget version of the anonymous Auto Hotel in El Salvador. It was a pathetic situation, but it was a bed for the night. Alone again with a stale, store-bought sandwich and watching old, poorly dubbed British porn on TV (I'd like to think he wasn't watching over me just then). Still, I know the drill sergeant would have been proud the next morning. I was up at the butt crack of dawn to get across the border into Peru.

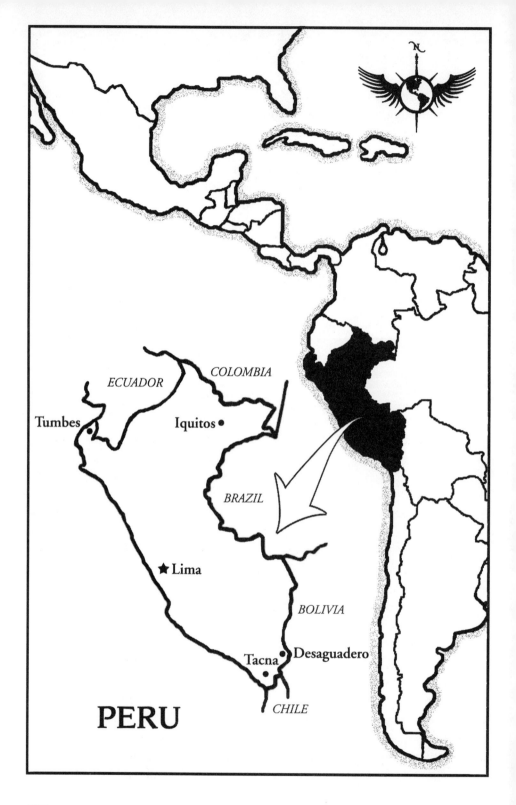

ECUADOR

COLOMBIA

Tumbes

Iquitos •

BRAZIL

★ Lima

BOLIVIA

Tacna • Desaguadero

CHILE

PERU

CHAPTER 34

It's amazing when you cross an imaginary line in the sand between two countries how much things can change. Everything from the color of the paint to the make of the cars is different. Part of it is due to the differences in businesses. Some companies will have a foothold, totally dominating the market in one country. When you go across the border, they're totally absent. For example, Inka Cola is a national favorite in Peru, but you can't buy it in Ecuador. Back in Ecuador, police drove Japanese sedans, busted up and broken down. You cross the border into Peru and they all drove brand-new SUVs.

On the Peruvian side of the border was a town called Tumbes. It took me about three-quarters of a day to get the border-crossing paperwork done, but relatively speaking it was straightforward. I got a 60-day permit for Baby Blue, the only time frame available. South of the border in Peru is a desolate stretch of desert where there are hundreds of miles of nothing but sand. The road was straight with no power poles or signs, just sand as far as the eye could see. With few other cars on the highway, the sense of isolation was dramatic.

Peru is shaped like a jagged-squarish kidney bean, with the longer side on the coast and the smaller inside curve lying in the Amazon basin. Lima (the capital, not the bean) is right in the middle of the longer curve on the coast. I ended up coming and going through it a number of times and never got to like it. A dirty gray town, Lima is one of the most difficult to navigate and the weather was always overcast. The town was a maze of confusing intersections where streets could go off at any angle. Right angle intersections are a rarity. In addition, the heavy overcast skies made orientation even worse. Also, Lima (like the rest of the country) is not known for safety and security. Even in the nicest neighborhoods, one has to be ever-watchful for banditos.

My only haven was the clubhouse of the South American Explorer's Club. As in Quito, the club welcomed adventurers from all over the world. Its library contained numerous pertinent books and a huge bank of trip reports that were made by members and used for research on the region. I spent several days researching trips to different parts of the country, interspersed with exploring the limited highlights of Lima.

The most upscale neighborhood in town was Miraflores. Located on the coast, the neighborhood was home to an extravagant mall built into a cliff overlooking the ocean. It was five stories tall with striking views and designer shops. There were a couple of American luxury hotels in the area that were out of my normal price range. However, I enjoyed the ambiance as well as the restaurants of the shopping district where I first tasted tuna-flavored ice cream. Tasted like chicken? Of the sea? No, it's not what you're thinking. Tuna is actually a fruit. In Arizona we call it prickly pear cactus fruit and it is used to make jams and iced tea when it is ripe, purple and sweet. In Peru, it is a staple in their diet and they eat it both ripe and green. In addition to finding them in supermarkets, sidewalk vendors would peel and slice them for you to eat on the street. The ice cream was a bright green color with a mild flavor.

My visit to Lima coincided with Carnivale. I soaked in the local celebrations, which included some mischievous aquatic antics. Everyone was open season for water pranks. I watched in amazement and amusement as people dumped five-gallon buckets of water out of second story windows onto unsuspecting victims. The targets' reactions ranged from amusement to extreme irritation. Like a kid, I jumped into the fray (or I should say spray). A group of teenagers on the street taught me how to use a homemade Super Soaker made from two pieces of plastic tubing. Like a plunger in a giant syringe, it blasted a gallon of water all the way across the street. We hung out in the bushes and ambushed bicycles and taxicabs as they passed by. Ten points to knock down a bicycle rider, fifteen for a passenger in a cab, and a five-point bonus if they curse at you!

After my research at the South American Explorer's Club, I decided on an Amazon jungle trip. Although the Amazon River is mostly found in Brazil, some of its origins are in Peru where the Ucayau and Maranon rivers come together. From there, it snakes its way past the city of Iquitos. All roads lead to Rome— but none to Iquitos. Surrounded by a myriad of rivers that rise and fall with the seasons, Iquitos is the largest city in the world inaccessible by road, with a population of over 400,000. Cut off from the rest of the world, it has developed its own fascinatingly distinct culture. Built up during the rubber boom of the '30s, this metropolis in the middle of the jungle is home to wrought iron buildings designed by Gustave Eiffel, of Tower fame.

Iquitos, a hub of tourist and local commercial activity, has a primarily indigenous population. Belén, a floating suburb of Iquitos, has all of its buildings constructed on floats and its streets paved with water. Because the seasonal change in the water level in the Amazon basin varies by fifty feet, Belén, and all of its structures, rise and fall. Belén has a large and diverse market with trade boats arriving from throughout the region. It featured exotic wares including food and animals, the likes of which I had never seen. One stall sold grub worms found in the bark of palm trees. The worms were the size of my thumb in both width and length. They were skewered and barbequed right next to the fried bananas! I had always thought of myself as an adventurous eater. I believed I would do almost anything to have a story to write about on my web site. Well, not quite anything. I couldn't even come close to biting into one.

Another booth served as a jungle pharmacy. Bottles of dark solutions with yellow labels lined the shelves amidst bags of herbs and bundles of phallic-shaped roots, two to three feet long, that hung from the roof. The lady "pharmacist" happily told me the different uses for her goods. She was very open about the multiple sexual dysfunctions that could be cured by her products.

Back in Iquitos, I shopped around for jungle tours that would allow me to pursue my interest in photography and frogs. I found a lodge that offered customized packages. I prepared to visit the Loving Light Lodge, located 140 km downriver, for three days and two nights. Despite a name that conjures up images of a nudist colony or church camp, Loving Light had been inspired by an Ayahuasca vision experienced by its founder. I had considered another popular place close by, the Pink Dolphin Lodge, which was named after the fresh-water dolphins that are found in the Amazon. I could live with the name Loving Light, but Pink Dolphin was just too much.

It was a five-hour motorboat trip to get to the lodge, which featured a communal dining hut and about eight or ten private sleeping huts. You had to walk along a gangway or planked boardwalk raised about ten feet above the jungle floor to get to your room. There were layers and layers of mosquito netting everywhere. You were cautioned to wear long pants and long sleeves to protect yourself from mosquitoes in the evening.

The package I chose included a variety of options. I opted out of another Ayahuasca experience (been there, barfed that) in favor of more outdoor activities, which you could mix and match based on your interests. Native guides were available to do nearly anything you wanted, including fishing for piranhas, jungle treks, and canoe tours. Some of the guests caught piranha that were prepared for our dinner. I was a man eating a man-eating fish! Tasted like chicken.

The lodge was in a clearing, surrounded completely by jungle. At night, as if controlled by opposing electrical rheostats, the sunlight would go down and the sounds of the jungle would go up. It was almost deafening. Sounds of frogs, insects and birds were constant through the night. Occasionally, an unidentifiable screech or wailing punctuated the symphony. My imagination ran wild. How close? How big? What species? What planet? It was all around me— above and below the room. Still, my curiosity was outpacing my fear of the unknown.

CHAPTER

35

I wanted to look for frogs. One of the local guides advised me that the frogs in the area are nocturnal but that the lodge offered nighttime tours through the jungle, by foot or canoe. My choice was obvious. In the darkness of the jungle, I transformed into the Frog Prince once again and had one of the most enthralling experiences of my whole trip, canoeing in the Amazon at night.

I had toured the same area by day. It's not quite a swamp. If you can imagine a rainforest where the floor is water, you'll get the idea. You're navigating your way through this labyrinth of trees and hanging vines in a canoe with a local indigenous guide. You have to put your absolute faith in him because it's his world. At times, the density of the vegetation blocked most of the light as we paddled our way into clearings glowing with bits and pieces of direct sunlight.

I was transported to another childhood wonderland. I was immersed in a totally foreign environment, like a scuba diver exploring the underwater world, but without tanks. There were fifty different varieties of plant life within arm's reach. Some trees had twenty different vines, growing up, hanging down and climbing along them. Everywhere I looked, there were fascinating multicolored insects and giant four-inch spiders. Not a place for the squeamish, but Markie the little Frog Prince was in his element.

Getting ready for the night tour was an adventure in itself. We had to bundle up with long sleeves and long pants because of the mosquitoes. On top of that, we had to fumigate ourselves with insect repellent, covering any possible entry areas. Finally, we got into the canoe and headed off into the darkness.

The darkness and danger adrenalinized my childhood wonderland experience. As we glided silently into the mysterious jungle, I was energized with emotion. I peered blindly into the dense darkness, knowing that something was out there, but not knowing what. There was an intensity in the air as we searched for wildlife. When I shined the flashlight up into the jungle, I could only see red eyes shining back at me. Were the eyes friendly? Were they going to leap toward us?

Pointing the light into the water I discovered two kinds of eyes. The crocodiles and frogs were easily distinguishable by the gap between their crimson points of light. My guide pointed to a pair of eyes about three inches apart and said, "There's one." He maneuvered the canoe alongside of it, slapped his hand quickly into the water and came out holding a three-foot crocodile by the neck! He passed it over to me to examine the scaly creature before we released it back into the darkness. Then, like a challenge from Señor Eh Scott, he looked me and said with a grin, "Your turn!" My idiot tendencies clearly established, of course I accepted.

Shortly thereafter we zeroed in on another pair of eyes. As we got closer, I realized that this one was larger. My heart raced as the guide moved us into position. He coached me on the orientation of the body and how to grab it by the neck. No room for hesitation or being tentative— it was all or nothing. I slapped my hand and grabbed the crocodile in one swift motion. What a rush! Markie the Frog Prince, was officially a crocodile hunter.

With my crocodile experience behind me, we focused our attention on much smaller pinpoints of light. Frogs jerked rhythmically through the water with each thrust of their legs. I didn't have the specialized equipment for macro photography at night, so my guide suggested we catch them and take them back to the lodge. Using the same technique I had learned for crocodiles, I caught five slimy specimens to photograph the following day.

The next morning I studied and photographed my tiny captives. Different from the predominantly land-based poison dart frogs of Panama, these aquatic-based amphibians were long, narrow, and better suited for gliding through the water. I marveled at the bright colors and intricate markings on their translucent skin. Since frogs aren't known for staying still, I had to enlist the help of local kids to corral each subject as I immersed myself in the photo session. Through my macro lens, I entered into the tiny world of the beautiful bug-eyed creatures. The excitement was intense as I waited and watched for a pose that captured the essence and energy of the frog. In spite of my focus, ten-year old little Markie was bouncing off the walls. After their reluctant stint as my tiny models, I released them back into their habitat. Go my little friends, be free!

CHAPTER 36

After my Amazon adventure, I made my way back to Lima and Baby Blue. The first thing I had to do, the thing that was staring me in the face, was to get an extension on my car permit. I had obtained the original permit in Tumbes at the northern border of Peru. Lima was two days drive south and I had two more days of driving southbound to get to the border of Chile. Problem was, with all my side trips out of Lima, my permit had expired. On the back of the permit, in very plain Spanish, was printed a warning that if my permit expired the vehicle was subject to confiscation.

I thought I could rectify my permit problem in Lima, since it was the capital of the country. I spent several days going to five different offices trying to find someone who could update my expired permit. No go! I was told repeatedly that I had to return to the northern border to rectify the situation. Come on people! Can't this be handled by phone, fax or e-mail? But no! They couldn't or wouldn't do it.

As a last resort I got a notarized letter from a police station stating that the vehicle had been in storage and not on the road. With several stamps and signatures, the letter looked very official. They're very big on stamps in Peru. Every rubber stamp was designed with a little square space in the middle for the official's initials. It was not the definitive document I needed, but I hoped it would keep Baby Blue in my possession if I were pulled over. I wasn't about to drive all the way back to Tumbes. I figured I'd take care of it at the southern border.

Vehicles in Peru have license plates on the front and the back. Being from Arizona, I only had a plate on the back. Previously, I had been pulled over by police who asked where my front plate was. I had to explain to them that where I came from we only have plates on the back. I never got a ticket for it, but I got pulled over multiple times. Not wanting to risk getting pulled over again, I made up a dummy license plate using the numbers from my Arizona plate and the black-on-white design of the Peruvian plate. With the help of a clerk and his computer at my hotel, I printed, laminated, and slapped the "plate" on the front of Baby Blue. The counterfeit plate seemed to work

I did get pulled over once at a routine checkpoint between Lima and the border. This time, *la mordida*, the bite, really was just that. I was nervous because of the expired permit and phony plate. Could I go to jail? If I did, wouldn't be ironic if I ended up making license plates? The officer saw a stack of small, individual packages of Oreo cookies on the front seat. We chatted for awhile, but I could feel that his attention was focused on the Oreos. Finally, he asked for some cookies. I could have had 60 kilos of cocaine in the back but he just wanted the cookies. I obliged and he sent me on my way. My new traveling commandment: Thou shalt always carry cookies!

I got to the southern border hoping I could just show them my notarized document and pay a fine and/or the fee for a new permit. But again it was the same story. I was met with the same Spanish word that needs no translation: No! I was told to go back to the northern border, which was now four days away. I returned to the closest town of Tacna to plead with administrators there. Still, I was getting nowhere fast and I was out of Oreos. Two days later Baby Blue had her own attorney.

MARK'S ADVENTURE ALERT

Location: Tacna, Peru

Subject: Still Sssstuck!

    I have been in this tiny town for 12 days, unsuccessfully
attempting to remedy expired paperwork for Baby Blue. There is
not much to do here nor am I free to make any plans since I
must attend to my paperwork each day. Here is what a typical
day is like on the bureaucratic battlefront:
8:30 Appointment with lawyer

9:05 Lawyer actually shows up

9:15 Lawyer attempts to call customs office at northern border
using calling card. Calls don't go through.
9:30 We walk to pay phone at the corner market with pocket
full of coins. Connection made with appropriate party. They
have received my electronic documents from the Southern border
office but are unable to open them. "Can we resend via fax?"
9:40 Southern office agrees to locate documents and fax them.
3:00 Appointment with lawyer.

3:40 Lawyer actually shows up

3:50 Northern office says no fax received. "Please have them re-faxed."
...and on ... and on … for days and days.

When the northern office finally received the documents, the matter was referred to the superintendent, who referred the matter to a lawyer to render an opinion on the case (The CASE!?! Gimme a break, it's an expired permit for a car!). Soon it should reach the Peruvian Supreme Court!

The next day was the government lawyer's birthday so he wouldn't be in the office... another day shot. "It's almost Christmas so the opinion won't be rendered until after the holiday." My lawyer decides (and I couldn't agree more) that it's time to take matters into our own hands.
On to plan B.

We head for the border with cash in hand. We get there and I can't believe my eyes! With $100 of my cash in his front pocket, he couldn't bribe my way across!

On to plan C.

I wanted to get back to Tucson for Christmas. Back in Chiclayo I had purchased a ticket to fly back to Tucson from Punta Arenas. I was able to change that flight so I could cross the border into Chile, take a taxi to Arica, Chile, fly to Santiago in central Chile, where I was able to take a flight back to Tucson. At my lawyer's suggestion I parked Baby Blue in a garage next to his office, grabbed my valuables, said goodbye to the friends I'd made in tiny little Tacna, and headed home for Christmas.

I made it back home to Tucson for Christmas with my family, but we were in for a horrific shock. On New Year's Eve Day, my sister Patty and her husband Kevin, were about to head out to lunch. Kevin, my vibrant friend and brother-in-law, 37 years old, 6'4" and strappingly handsome, suddenly grabbed the counter, gasped, "Oh Shit!" and fell to the floor. He was rushed to the hospital but never regained consciousness.

I was in a shopping mall in Tucson when I got the call from my brother, Mike. I could tell by his choking and cracking voice that something was desperately wrong. He told me that I should get to the hospital where Kevin had been taken. I dropped what I was doing. With an ominous feeling of dread, I hurried to the Tucson Medical Center.

Kevin had been sick a few weeks earlier and had been in the hospital. He had spent a few days there for observation and testing. The doctors diagnosed a congenital heart problem, hypertrophic cardiomyopathy. It was something that ran in Kevin's family, but hadn't given him problems before. His heart became enlarged causing the chambers to get smaller. This in turn caused his heart to work harder and, being a muscle, his heart grew larger, thus making the chambers even smaller, a vicious cycle. As he was discharged, the doctor assured my sister, "Your husband will not drop dead from this." But in fact, that's exactly what he did.

I arrived at the hospital to find my family sitting in a semi-private reception area. With despair etched on their faces, the silence spoke volumes. My brother escorted me down the stark hallway to the room where Kevin had been taken after efforts to resuscitate him had failed. Patty was there, still clutching his hand. The grayness in his face made it clear that he was gone.

Kevin was extraordinary in many respects. His mind had wings. If you went on a flight with him, it was exhilarating. He would take you places you'd never thought you'd go. He was a prolific writer, which I'd always aspired to be. In fact, he earned his living as a writer and could sit and churn out ten pages at a time. Because he had some issues with the University of Arizona as an institution, he took pleasure in writing term papers for students. Brilliant beyond words, Kevin was an actor, musician and songwriter. He wrote and produced a couple of productions in Tucson, including a popular one-man show.

He delighted in his part-time job at an old west theme park. Old Tucson was once a movie set for several John Wayne pictures and the TV series, The High Chaparral. Kevin portrayed the sheriff, complete with a silver star, long black coat, and big black hat. He and his cohorts staged gunfights in the streets and fell off of buildings. The crowds ate it up! With all of his charisma, he stood out as the star of the show. In fact, he was the poster boy for Old Tucson. Pictures of him in his coat, star, and hat were featured on billboards around town.

As an entertainer and starving artist, Kevin held a variety of odd jobs including cooking at local diners. However, his most important job was at home. As a speech therapist, Patty was the main breadwinner, while Kevin played the role of the doting husband. He loved cooking for her, making lunches to go and having dinner waiting when she got home.

Kevin was also partly to blame for my fascination with cactus. Working in a cactus nursery, he knew the scientific names of practically every species known to man. Okay, I'm exaggerating a little, but his ability to rattle off their scientific names, properties and habitats boggled my mind.

Kevin didn't have an ordinary funeral. Rather than a service, he had a funeral "show" held in a theater for the performing arts. Memorabilia and photos from his life lined the front of the stage. His casket was center stage. Patty asked me to be the host. I was honored to be the emcee for his final act. The awe-inspiring show consisted of Kevin's family, friends and show business buddies sharing stories— and boy were there stories! As each story was told, I marveled at another facet of his character.

My favorite was about his participation in a local theater company. On opening night, the director handed a large capsule to everyone in the cast without telling them what it was. Kevin was talking to one of the other cast members and she said, "Wow, what do you think it is?" Kevin didn't know.

He replied, "Well, it's from Steven. I trust Steven!" He popped it in his mouth and down the hatch! Turns out it was a sponge animal.

The story I shared described a family outing at the beach in Rocky Point, Mexico. In the middle of the night, Kevin had a brainstorm. I'm sure we'd been drinking, but that's not the point. The point is that only Kevin would come up with these crazy ideas. We had highway flares that we had heard would burn under water. Kevin said, "Let's go snorkeling with these flares!" We tied the flares on the end of sticks and went out in a little rubber raft into the Sea of Cortez. Putting on our masks and fins, we dove into the darkness to snorkel with the bright, cherry-red flares. Only Kevin, only Kevin.

I wrote a tribute to Kevin for my web site:

MARK'S ADVENTURE ALERT

Location: Tucson, Arizona

Subject: Tucson Theatre Veteran Shines In His Final Act

Memorial services for Kevin Vincent Teed were held at Berger Center for the Performing Arts on Saturday January 6th. It was a fitting venue for the Tucsonan whose overriding passion in life was for the performing arts. Teed's most recent credits were as producer and director of *Middle Aged White Guys*, a comedy by Jane Martin, in November of this past year. He was involved with numerous productions with the once flourishing Tucson company, the A.K.A. Theater. Cowboy Mouth by Sam Shepard, In the Boom Boom Room by David Rabe, and Salome by Oscar Wilde are to name but a few. Teed also played Sheriff Jack Silverwood at Old Tucson Studios.

> *Best of all he loved the fall*
> *The leaves yellow on the cottonwoods*
> *Leaves floating on the trout streams*
> *and above the hills*
> *The high blue windless skies*
> *...Now he will be a part of them forever.*

Ernest Hemingway Idaho 1939

Over 300 family, friends and colleagues attended the service. Many shared anecdotes and stories about Kevin's uncommon personality. "Kevin was a most generous human being, especially with the focus that he gave to others. In his life and his performance, he was unrestrained," said Kitty McKay, a fellow actor.

Teachers from Wright Elementary School shared stories about Kevin's participation in the Screen Actors Guilds' BookPAL Program: "The kids were totally awed by Kevin. They loved him very, very much. He was full of life and that is the best gift he could have given to my students, the joy of life, and that will never, never pass. Thank you for Kevin."

Lucky Hayes, President of the Arizona Branch of the Screen Actors Guild had this to say: "Kevin was one of the most down-to-earth, delightful and supportive men I've ever met. He had a way of connecting with people that was extraordinary. He had a gift for bringing books alive for children. Not everybody has this gift or the will to go into classrooms and do what he did. He brought something special to their lives."

Kevin's Favorite Toast:

The Four Foundations of Friendship:
Lying, Swearing, Stealing and Drinking.
When you lie, lie for beauty.
When you swear, swear by your friends.
When you steal, steal from the greedy.
When you drink, drink with me.

Phyliss Boyd, owner of Action Talent Agency in Tucson, cherished her professional relationship with Kevin: "Only the good die young. Somehow God seems to take them from us early. Everyone who met him liked him, I mean everyone. He was a chameleon by nature, knowing exactly what someone needed. He was a little rebel and a little bit judge. God threw away the mold after Kevin."

The service was brought to a close with a videotaped performance of Kevin as the Ringmaster in Cirque de Shakespeare. He took his final bow and said, "Goodnight." Goodnight, Kevin. And thank you. You will be missed.

This was the last addition to my web site for nearly a year. The universe that had once conspired to catapult me into my adventure had turned on me and now conspired to keep me stuck in Tucson.

My journey had been seriously derailed. Although I'd had intentions of getting back on the road within a couple of weeks, it didn't happen. During the hiatus from the road, I found myself concerned about what I was going to do with my life when I was finished with my journey. I wondered who I would be. I wondered what I would do for gainful employment. Could I turn something I was doing into a way to make a living? I didn't have to worry about finances immediately, but eventually it would be an issue.

At the request of a friend, I got involved in a business venture. My business partners were people whom I had known and felt I could trust. Initially I put a lot of time and money into the venture. I hoped to be able to get things started, and then turn over my responsibilities so that I could get back on the road.

Business wasn't the only thing keeping me in Tucson. I became romantically involved with Rebecca, a tall, exotic beauty who I'd dated previously. This time I really wanted to make it work. Her energy and enthusiasm were amazing, and we hit it off on so many levels. As much as I liked my solitary time on the road, the idea of a partner was beginning to appeal to me. We fantasized about traveling together and creating a travel videotape series. However, there was a major consideration to take into account— her seven-year-old daughter, Summer. I had thought we could home-school her on the road, but Rebecca didn't like the idea.

When I started feeling the urge to get back on the road, Rebecca didn't even have a passport. For administrative reasons it had been very difficult for her to get one. Almost a year had gone by since she professed her excitement for traveling with me and she still didn't have a passport. She was very enthusiastic on the surface, but I think what she really wanted was a stable home in the suburbs for Summer and herself. I had doubts that she would ever leave Tucson. I had been very clear from the start that a white picket fence was not in my future.

Despite the passion in our on-again-off-again relationship, something wasn't quite right. I was growing closer to Summer, while my differences with Rebecca were becoming clearer and clearer. I had become a big part of Summer's life.

I volunteered as an aide in her first grade classroom and read her bedtime stories each night. At the point when I knew things were not going to work out with her mom, Summer asked if I could take her to the father/daughter dance at her school. Picture a darling, bright-eyed and energetic little seven-year-old, with me as the closest thing to a father she's ever had. How could I turn her down?

The dance was an environment I was unfamiliar with. Still, there was something incredibly comfortable about the scene with all the dads, all their daughters, and all the love in the room. It couldn't have been a bigger contrast from the nightclubs and single scenes I was used to. There was not a dad in the place who cared what he looked like or what others thought of him. It was all about the daughters. There I was, dancing with my little girl. Only she wasn't exactly mine, as much as I would have loved her to be.

On the dance floor, Summer was a miniature of her mother, with the same headstrong behavior and body language, and completely uninterested in following my lead. She had a blast with her little buddies, posing for photos, eating cookies and drinking punch. As we were driving home after the dance she looked at me and said, "This is the happiest day of my life." Tears welled up in my eyes. I experienced the joy of the moment as well as the sadness of what lay ahead.

MARK'S ADVENTURE ALERT

Location: Tucson, Arizona

Subject: Many Layers and Levels

I am aware of the many layers and levels of my psyche that push and pull and squeeze me in different directions. I certainly am feeling the squeeze at the moment. Pulled by my desire to create something out of my life.

Pushed to simply enjoy the experience. Compelled to create a home for myself and simultaneously pulled from that home to create something on the road. All of these forces combined seem to keep me stuck under the covers.

I can't speak for the inside of anyone else's life but I am often amazed that I am able to accomplish anything in my life (much beyond getting out of bed) given the conflicting parts of my personality. Phew. I am sounding overly dramatic. Almost to the point of parody. It would be funny if it weren't so real to me. Could somebody please point all of these parts of myself in the same freakin' direction for a few moments? I look back at my journal as if someone else wrote it. Who was that person? How was he motivated to do what he did? Where is the clarity to just get up and GO? What does he really want to do right NOW? This is just another, "Why Am I Doing This?"

This is part of my ritual of getting back on the road. I'll get over it.

Many forces seemed to be keeping me in Tucson. Not until I had an experience related to both Kevin and my Dad was I inspired to get my ass in gear and back on the road. Just as at the beginning of my trip, death inspired me once more.

I was driving east on Grant Road in Tucson, feeling kind of sluggish and stuck. Two cars ahead of me, I saw a bumper sticker that read, "All those who wander are not lost – J.R.R. Tolkien." Yeah, that's right! I needed to get out of the Shire, back on my journey, and continue my adventure wandering through South America. It struck a cord inside me. Why wasn't I back on the road?

A small white pickup truck was broadcasting the message to me. In the lower right-hand corner of the rear window was a four-inch square sticker of a red frog on a black background. "Cool!" I thought, having just published a calendar of my own photos entitled "Fabulous Frogs" that featured brightly colored frogs from my trip.

With another car between us, my eyes continued to survey the vehicle from a distance. To get a better view, I jockeyed for position in the traffic and got directly behind it. To my astonishment, in each corner of the window was a sticker of a different brightly colored frog. I was startled by the coincidence. In fact, I just happened to have a stack of my calendars sitting next to me. At the next stoplight, I grabbed a calendar, jumped out of my car and hopped over to the little white truck.

"Excuse me," I said, startling the woman behind the wheel. "From the stickers on your truck, I thought you might enjoy this."

"Oh yeah, um…" she said, surprised by a stranger in the middle of traffic, "My daughter is into frogs. Wow, she'll love this!"

I quickly thanked her for the message I had gotten from her bumper sticker before I leapt back to my unattended car. At the next light she turned right, while I continued east, pleased about the encounter and getting my calendar into the hands of another frog freak. Shortly thereafter, I turned into the parking lot of a friendly merchant. I took care of my business and chatted with the owner.

"When are you getting back on the road?" she wanted to know.

"Soon I hope. I've been struggling with that lately. But I just saw this bumper sticker that gave me some hope. It said, "All those who wander are not lost," by J.R.R. Tolkien. You know, from The Lord of the Rings."

She nodded with agreement and encouragement. We said our goodbyes and as I left, I noticed a trampled movie ticket stub on the sidewalk in front of the doorway. The store was many miles from any theater. Something compelled me to pick it up. On it I read the words that had come out of my mouth not ten seconds earlier. "The Lord of the Rings. J.R.R. Tolkien" (Cue dramatic music here).

I turned back around and said to the merchant, "Look what I just found on the sidewalk!" Her eyes got big and she hummed the theme from *The Twilight Zone*.

"Any lottery numbers for me?" she asked jokingly.

"I wish…. Strange, huh?" I replied. We bid our goodbyes anew. I continued east to my home, with the ticket stub on my dashboard.

The string of coincidences continued and got more personal. To follow the string from here, the reader needs some background information. In the years prior to my father's death, he drove a small white pickup truck similar to the one with the bumper sticker. After his death, my mother sold the truck to Patty and Kevin. It became Kevin's primary vehicle. After Kevin's death, in spite of the creepiness of two previous owners passing away, I bought the truck from my sister. It was perfect for landscaping, odd jobs, and as a back-up vehicle. Mostly it sat dormant in my driveway.

As I pulled into the driveway that night, my headlights reflected on a sticker in the corner of the back window. A frog sticker! It was a highly stylized rendering of a psychedelic frog on a toadstool, obviously put there by Kevin, not Dad. I had never made a connection between the sticker on the truck and my own frog photos, but now it jumped out at me as if it were alive.

The Cosmic Coincidence Control Center was broadcasting loud and clear. It was like Bill Moyer said, "Coincidence is God's way of remaining anonymous." My father's death was the impetus to start my journey. My Dad, Kevin and J.R.R. Tolkien were all joining forces to push me back on the road. The message was clear and it had an electrifying effect on me. I pushed through my mental fog and got back on the road.

I made flight arrangements and was in the air within the week. Little did I know what I was to encounter next. I was already at an emotional low point but I had no idea how low I could go. The next section is a series of online journal entries that describes the story blow-by-blow:

MARK'S ADVENTURE ALERT

Location: Tacna, Peru

Subject: Baby Blue Highway to Heaven?

My flight into Tacna arrived after dark. The dusty little airport in this border town only receives flights from Lima and one other city. Outside the terminal building a gauntlet of taxi drivers squawked for my business. The driver I chose was willing to make many stops for an extremely low price. So low that I was embarrassed to bargain with him, even for the sport of it.

First stop, bad news. Baby Blue was not where I had left her. Then again, what could I expect after a year? Well, my expectations were good, based on a recent phone conversation. The conversation was with the lawyer I had entrusted to watch over Baby Blue in my absence. The lawyer's office was next door to the garage where I had left my truck.

Bad news gets worse! The lawyer's office was no longer there either. Oh my God!

The lawyers currently occupying the space guided me in the general direction of the new office after I declined their offer for their services. I found the new office but it was well after hours and I would have to wait until morning to get any answers.

Thoughts of finishing my trip by bus did not appeal to me. Going back home was not attractive, except for the fact that I could hide under my own covers. I could do nothing but wait until morning.

After breakfast, I walked five blocks from my hotel to the office. The legal assistant and the wife of the lawyer greeted me as if I was an old friend. But it was very awkward. I was leery of their friendliness and just wanted to know the whereabouts of my truck. They blamed the garage for the disappearance just as the garage had blamed them last night.

I had a knot in my stomach. They were pointing fingers at each other and probably in cahoots. Did they just not expect me to come back, in spite of my e-mails and phone calls?

The lawyer arrived shortly and produced a document that did little to ease my fears. Soon we drove to the police station. The proper authority was not there. The lawyer left me and the aide behind to wait for the officer to return. An hour or so later we were telling a brief version of the Baby Blue story to the commanding officer. He listened intently and said we should come back tomorrow morning. Ohhh Noooo! Not another ride on the bureaucratic merry-go-round from a year ago.

I was not up to it. I did not know who to trust. If I could trust anybody! The legal assistant's name was Carmen. She had been a guide and a friend to me during my previous stay in Tacna. I could not imagine she had any knowledge of or involvement in a plot against me. As we shared a cab back from the police station she said, "We can't waste any more time. We must find out where Baby Blue is." She wanted to consult a psychic! I went along with the idea mostly for the entertainment value.

The psychic was named Javier. In his consultation room we were totally surrounded by Christian images and memorabilia. I felt like we were living parts of a shrine. Javier seemed credible enough. He had a presence and a confidence that seemed very out of place in Peru. After some chitchat Carmen posed the question. Javier listened with his eyes closed and answered without hesitation. "Baby Blue is okay and in the hands of the owner of the garage." Simple enough.

That evening I ran into a friend I had made in an Internet café during my previous stay in Tacna. She said that I looked very calm for having lost my vehicle. She said Baby Blue was most certainly chopped up and sold for parts by now. God rest her automotive soul. I couldn't bear to think of all those wrenches and crowbars tearing her apart for black market pesos (The currency would actually be soles in Peru, not pesos, but you get the point). It was not a good day for me or my adventure.

MARK'S
ADVENTURE ALERT

Location: Tacna, Peru

Subject: A Ray of Hope

I am feeling a little more optimistic today. Yesterday, chances of recovering Baby Blue seemed slim to none. A few things happened today to give me some hope. I spent about three hours with the police this morning. My lawyer accompanied me and paved the way for me. He was very friendly with many of the officers at the station and it seemed that they respected him. A six page, no spaces, manually typed report was generated that I was asked to sign and fingerprint! I said, "Hey! I'm not on trial here!" Actually, I went along with the program. I was glad they were taking it seriously.

On the wall at the station were stats from 2002. Out of 28 vehicles stolen last year, 24 were recovered! Pretty good odds, even better considering the increased difficulty of disposing of an American car. After the interview my lawyer invited me for lunch. His first name is Jesus. His nickname is *Huevo Duro*, hard egg. For the shape of his bald head or for being a hard ass, I'm not sure. He can turn on the charm, but I would not want to be on his bad side.

My suspicions of his possible involvement were diminishing. He actually filed a report with the police and had done some investigations on his own. He has a busy practice and the respect of many people in the community. I did meet some people who did not think highly of him. But some people just don't like lawyers.

Huevo Duro seemed to genuinely empathize with my situation and felt he had let me down (I would have to agree!). He welcomed me into his home as a friend. Lunch was good. It included a casserole with hard-boiled eggs.

In the afternoon, Carmen, who had taken me to the psychic, asked if I wanted to consider a private detective to speed things up. She has a friend who would only charge gas money and a *propina* (tip), a gratuity of my choosing if there are results. Hmm. The plot thickens.

MARK'S ADVENTURE ALERT

Location: Tacna, Peru

Subject: Captain Moodswing meets Captain Beefheart

So far I have talked to the police, a lawyer, a psychic and soon a private eye! Can't say I haven't tried. The sad thing is, even when I recover Baby Blue, my original permit problem will still be waiting for me. We'll cross that bridge in due time— or cross the stream directly in my recovered vehicle. I saw the following quote online a few days ago:

"Nothing is a waste of time if you use the experience wisely."
August Rodin

I have chosen to perceive my predicament as an adventure. At least something I could have fun writing about! My mood has improved dramatically. I have not watched any TV in a few days. That's a nice switch. Between research and investigations I have been getting out for some recreational and social activity.

I had some *ceviche* and *anticuchos* for lunch today. *Ceviche* is raw fish "cooked" by the acidity of the limejuice in which it is marinated. *Anticuchos* is beefheart! A delicacy in Peru and quite tasty. More tender than I expected.

MARK'S ADVENTURE ALERT

Location: Tacna, Peru

Subject: More Adventures in the Occult

I was up and on the street by 7:30 this morning. Now that's a BIG switch for me. Had planned to meet with the police this morning and then the private investigator. The police appointment fell through because the President of Peru is passing through town. Come on, officers, get your priorities straight. Get busy on the Baby Blue case! Lacking support from the government, Carmen, my Legal Aide, wanted to consult the Occult once again. This time we consulted a leaf reader. Not tea leaves, but coca leaves. Si, cocaina! I chewed one just to make sure.

The reader was an older woman whose house was under construction. Carmen sat on a bed next to her and asked questions. The reader placed individual leaves down on a cloth to represent the subjects of the question. Then she dropped a handful of leaves on top of them and interpreted the answer. Again, good news from the other side! The owner of the garage is scared. Action from the police may not be forthcoming. She would work her mojo so that the garage owner could not sleep.

Carmen thinks we should go to the newspaper. I'm not so sure. I am only willing to go so far with matters in my own hands here in this foreign culture. Sorry Baby Blue. My own health and safety are far more important than my truck.

We still have the private investigator we can talk to.

MARK'S ADVENTURE ALERT

Location: Tacna, Peru

Subject: Summons Served in Baby Blue Case

Tacna police served a summons this morning on the wife of the prime suspect in the Baby Blue case. The suspect was employed at the garage were Baby Blue was last seen. The wife was interrogated and had to sign and fingerprint the police document.

The wife claimed the suspect is out of town visiting his brother in the town of Ica. She claimed not to know when he would return. When asked for the phone and address of the brother she said she did not know. If she does not cooperate with authorities in locating her husband, she is liable to be included in the criminal complaint.

MARK'S ADVENTURE ALERT

Location: Tacna, Peru

Subject: Rattling Cages

I spent the better part of the last two days rattling cages. Trying to get some action taken on the Baby Blue case. We contacted anyone and everyone who might have some influence short of the mayor. Come to think of it, why didn't we go to the Mayor's office?
My/our agenda today included:

USED CAR SHOPPING
For possible Baby Blue replacement

RESEARCH ON BUSES TO BOLIVIA
I'm going to be in La Paz next week, one way or another.

VISITING SUSPECT AGAIN

Accompanied by lawyer this time, not police. Found him home!

VISITING POLICE STATION
Lobbying for the suspect's arrest.

ANOTHER COCA LEAF READING
Nothing too exciting...

VISITING THE GARAGE OWNER
Asking him to put pressure on police.

VISITING ANOTHER POLICE STATION
An appointment with the top cop in town!

NEWSPAPER INTERVIEW
They are gonna do a story, due on stands Thursday morning! I
have been taking some snapshots here and there, only with my
Canon Elf. I have not been inspired to bring out my bigger,
more conspicuous equipment for security reasons.

MARK'S
ADVENTURE ALERT

Location: Tacna, Peru

Subject: Made the News Today

Locals have told me this may help my cause. My plight
becoming legitimized in print. It made page two of the local
daily newspaper; Diario Capalina, named after a nearby river.

It explains how my "modern truck" disappeared from a
downtown garage. I suppose eighteen years old qualifies as
"modern" in these parts. The garage owner, the former employee
(the suspect), and my lawyer are all mentioned in the article.

The police had already promised that the suspect would be
arrested today. That failed to happen. Another promise was
made for tomorrow at 10:00 a.m. sharp. They were very specific
this time.

They said they would bring him in and "rough him up" so that
he would talk. I didn't like hearing about that part, I just
want my truck back. But things are not that simple. I suppose
if he talks, he won't get hurt. The wheels are in motion.

MARK'S ADVENTURE ALERT

Location: Tacna, Peru

Subject: They Got Him!

He's in custody, but he's not talking. Yet.

I got a call early in the afternoon to come to the police station. I was to take part in the interrogation. Little did I know that I would be spending time alone in a room with the suspect. He asked me what I wanted from him. He asked, "What can we do?" I told him I don't want anyone to go to jail, I just want my truck. He said that I was the boss and if I wanted him to go to jail, that's what was going to happen.

He could not answer my questions about discrepancies in his story about locks and keys and a mechanic who had to help get the truck started. His story was that he had released the car to my cousin. There were big holes in his story.

Alone in the room, with him pleading about his wife and young kids, I felt like the judge, jury and executioner. I re-emphasized that I just wanted my truck back.

It was some of the strongest culture shock I had experienced! I felt for the guy. I was pretty sure he was in for some, *"interogacion scientifico."* That was the euphemism used by the police yesterday, accompanied by insidious smiles and punching motions.

MARK'S ADVENTURE ALERT

Location: Tacna, Peru

Subject: E-mail To The Editor

I was grateful to receive many letters of support and encouragement regarding the disappearance of Baby Blue. One in

particular was from someone with some personal experience with
Latin American "justice." It pertains directly to what I was
dealing with and feeling. On the street here in Tacna I was
called a "mongo norteamericano," a stupid American, by someone
who didn't think I could hear or understand. The story below
ended differently than mine, but believe me, I could relate:

Mark,

Thank you for your never-ending e-mails, they do serve to
keep me connected with the south land. Actually I am going to
be going back to Honduras for most of the month of May. Why so
long? To see my in-laws, visit with friends, see my
goddaughter, and just hang out. A friend of mine who is in the
Air Force may even come down for awhile and visit if the war
doesn't get in the way. I need to set him up with a good
Honduran wife.

Central America used to seem so exotic to me, but after a
tour in The Peace Corps and the few years that have followed
it just seems like a quirky version of reality. I sometimes
find it strange to think of a tiny town in the middle of
backwoods Honduras as the home of my son's grandparents, but
it makes more and more sense with time. A world away, yet
right next door.

Your story of the missing car sounds exactly typical. Sad to
say, but even your lawyer friend might have the car. My take on
the culture is that it is perfectly permissible to lie and
steal from anyone who has more money than the thief in
question. A quick trip to church and all guilt is absolved. You
are undoubtedly correct in your assumptions about either the
lawyer or the garage owner having your car. Hang around long
enough and after talking for days on end one of the street kids
in the area will give you the real story. It is probably too
late, but it can't hurt to hang out with the kids (little- 5-12
year olds) in the area. They usually see everything and like
talking. Might work and the price is right.

Unfortunately, probably all you will learn is who took your
vehicle. Then what? In Honduras the police always acted like
they were very helpful and tried to look professional,
however, looks can be deceiving. After my house was robbed one
time I went and made a report, the cops came, tried to take
fingerprints, took lots of pictures, etc. I told them who the
thieves were and where to find them (the building owner's
family). They said all the right things and talked all the
good talk, but they didn't know that a secretary there was my
girlfriend's cousin and I later heard how they laughed about
the stupid gringo who was so dumb that he thought there was
really film in the camera they were using, thought that they

```
could really compare fingerprints, how the dumb gringo
deserved to get robbed living in that neighborhood, etc....
Actually quite amusing if I hadn't been robbed.

   So what to do? Find out who did it. Just before you leave
(on your way out of the country) offer the right person (tough
to find, but look around) a promised hundred bucks if the
guilty party's house/car/whatever burns down mysteriously
within a month. Send payment Western Union under an assumed
name. Won't get your car back, but I felt… uh… I mean… you
will feel better and justice will be done.

Regards,   xxxxx
```

After a long day of dealing with my lawyer and the police, I returned to my hotel around 10:00 p.m. in the evening. The hotel clerk gave me a small, brown paperback book written in Spanish that someone had left for me. I was tired, so I didn't give it a lot of thought. It was from my friend Samuel, a shopkeeper from a nearby market. Since I knew him to be a devout Christian I thought it might be religious literature. I tossed it onto my nightstand and went to bed.

In the morning I got up and meditated on my bed. During my meditation, I had an eerie feeling of Kevin's presence in my bathroom. I sensed a connection with the bathroom's deep green-colored tile. I thought, "Wow, Kevin's in there." I entered into a silent dialogue with him. I started writing our conversation in my journal. He told me that I could have all of his gifts. He was a very prolific writer and I admired that. I admired the breadth of his imagination and how his mind could just take off on a flight of fancy. He said I didn't have to take any of his foibles, just the gifts. I thought to myself, "Am I just crazy? Am I talking myself into this? Is this all in my head? Am I nuts? Yes, you are crazy! You just have an overactive imagination. You're making shit up."

I put down my journal and, for some reason, picked up the little brown paperback from the nightstand and opened it up. The twenty-five year old book was about Tacna and its sister city, Tucson. The book opened up to the middle section with photos of the Old Tucson movie set where Kevin had worked. There was the sheriff with his black hat and silver star staring back at me. It would have been a photo of Kevin had he been working there twenty-five years earlier. It was the most striking, otherworldly experience I've ever had. I got goose bumps for 45 minutes. It was Kevin saying, "No, you're not crazy! I am here." It was too far-fetched to believe, and too far-fetched not to believe.

This experience seemed disconnected from what was going on in my life. It gave me a feeling of peace, but it did not solve the dilemmas I was facing. I was no closer to recovering Baby Blue than I had been two weeks earlier. It was time to move on.

MARK'S ADVENTURE ALERT

Location: Tacna, Peru

Subject: Case Closed

At least for me anyway. I will be on a bus for La Paz, Bolivia tomorrow. The suspect is in jail. Still no sign of Baby Blue.... The lawyer and his aide are confident that they can recover civil damages from the garage owner. I have signed papers for them to do so in my absence. I'm not holding my breath.

In the end it has been but a deep dive into the culture and legal system here. It was fascinating. I did manage to make a few friends. I had breakfast with my lawyer's family most mornings. They said I was more than a client to them. It seemed to be true. I finally made it out of the city for a day trip to an archeological park. Pretending to be Indiana Jones, for a moment, forgetting about my own crises.

CHAPTER
41

I was leaving town without my beloved Baby Blue. As if things weren't bad enough, some rat-faced little bastard tried to steal my camera. I was still struggling to come to terms with the aftermath of my relationship with Rebecca, and realizing that my association with my business partners was disintegrating rapidly back in the U.S.

I was waiting after dark in the Tacna bus station talking to Carmen, when I felt somebody jostling against my leg. Instinctively I pushed him away and then thought, "Oops, maybe he was just accidentally brushing against me." Since there was a bicycle next to me, I thought perhaps he was just fixing it.

I reached down to my cargo pants pocket to feel for my camera. It was still there. Then I felt around a little further, only to find a hole in the back of the pocket! That rat-faced little bastard had sliced my pocket and was struggling to get the camera out when I felt him! In the instant all this occurred to me, he backed away and disappeared into the crowd. It was a good thing for him that he got away. He was smaller than me and I probably would have channeled all of my pent-up frustrations into his face. Given the fact that he had a sharp blade in his hand, it could have been bad for both of us.

I said goodbye to Carmen and got on the bus. I had a seat on the top level in the first row directly above the driver. For the entire all-night bus ride I felt like I was hanging out over the street. It seemed like the worst seat on the bus. On the dark and winding road, the bus driver spent more time in the left lane than he did in his own. I tried to sleep, but every time I opened my eyes, I would get the shit scared out of me by headlights heading straight toward me. My head was spinning from the near theft of my camera, my relationship problems, my car problems and my business problems. I couldn't get to sleep, which unfortunately gave me more time to think.

My relationship with Rebecca was finished. I still cared about her and knew she was in a lot of pain. She was struggling and I was sure Summer was struggling too. I was not in the position to make it any easier for either of them. It left me feeling sad and frustrated.

Further, I hated being at the mercy of public transit. I hated the feeling of insecurity of having my camera, computer equipment, and personal belongings in the cargo compartment of the bus, which was opened every time the bus stopped. I hated the thought of having to buy another vehicle and all the paperwork involved. I envisioned that process as a huge bureaucratic nightmare. In addition, the new vehicle would not be customized to my needs for security and comfort like Baby Blue.

I should have gotten on a later bus so I wouldn't have arrived in Desaguadero, the border between Peru and Bolivia, at four in the morning. It's the most God-awful time to arrive anywhere. An awkward time to get a hotel and much too early to do anything else. So what did I do? I got a hotel. I found a God-forsaken little room in a miserable hotel. On an uncomfortable cardboard bed, I got a few hours of fitful sleep before wearily heading for the border.

I gave a notice to the border guards and asked them to contact my lawyer in Tacna if anybody should try to cross the border with Baby Blue. Though I didn't have a lot of hope, I thought I would try anyway. The official looked at my camera equipment. From his actions I inferred that he wanted some kind of duty or tariff. It seemed so transparent, just a way to get some cash from me. I was pissed off and tired, and I'd had so much anger and frustration, that I did something completely out of character. In broken Spanish, I blasted the guy, "This is my stuff! There's no buying or selling going on at either side of the border. I'm sick of you guys! Leave me alone!" He did.

I could have gotten in trouble, but the official seemed to take it in stride. He began to ask questions about my equipment, leading me to believe he had an interest in photography. I felt a pang of guilt that perhaps he wasn't looking for la mordida but had a genuine personal interest in the subject. We chatted for awhile before I sheepishly apologized for my outburst.

I headed out of the office and into Bolivia on foot.

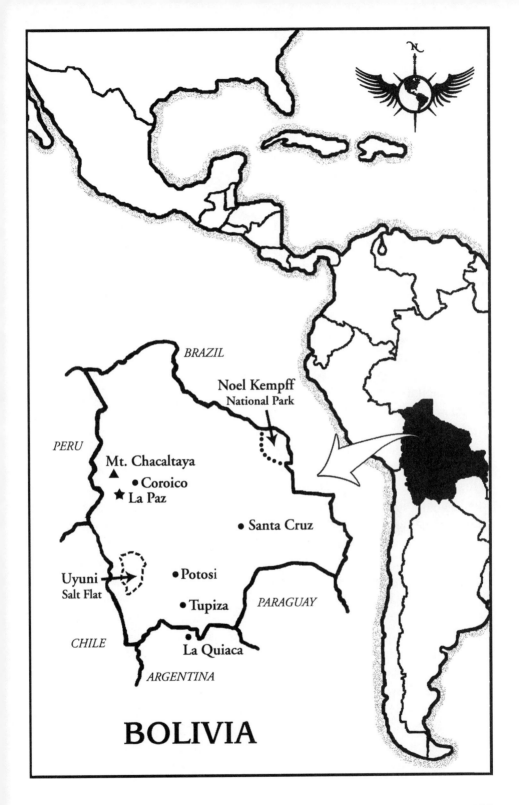

BRAZIL

Noel Kempff
National Park

PERU

Mt. Chacaltaya
● Coroico
★ La Paz

● Santa Cruz

Uyuni
Salt Flat

● Potosi

● Tupiza

PARAGUAY

CHILE

● La Quiaca

ARGENTINA

BOLIVIA

The town on the Bolivian side was so small there wasn't even a bus station, simply a dirt lot where vans would show up and local hustlers sold tickets in advance. I had been really spoiled. I missed Baby Blue and the freedom she provided me. I had to suffer through a couple of hours drive in a small van packed with seventeen Bolivians. The seats were not designed for my body size. I wanted desperately to get some sleep but people's bags and bodies were pushing at me from all sides.

Finally, the grueling ride ended in the capital city of La Paz. La Paz is the highest capital in the world at 11,800 feet. At the top of the world, I was at the bottom of my barrel and the end of my rope. I had a dull headache brought on by the altitude. I was physically and emotionally immobilized.

La Paz is like a giant bowl in the mountains, with houses built up the sides all the way to the rim. With the exception of the very bottom of the bowl, everything in the town is on a slant. Everywhere you go, you have to walk up a steep slope, which, in the thin air, is even more difficult than normal. Venturing out for any reason was a huge chore and any kind of activity exacerbated my headache. I hibernated for a couple of days.

I had gone to La Paz because I had heard that it had the largest auto market in the region. I wanted to find a reasonably priced vehicle to finish the trip. I'd been in touch with my buddy Señor Eh Scott. Since it was his slow season again, he had agreed to come out to join me touring Bolivia. Scott knew more about cars than I did, so I looked forward to his guidance in purchasing a vehicle.

I still had a few days to wait for his arrival. I decided to do some shopping and research on trucks. One morning, I walked down to the main drag through the bottom of the bowl, where I saw a couple of buildings burned out. I came to find out that there had been a riot over a tax increase less than a week prior to my arrival. People took to the streets and proclaimed, "We're not going to take it!"

Police had shot twenty-four people in the street. The center of the whole confrontation was directly across from the coffee shop where I was calmly enjoying my early morning coffee, scribbling in my journal, and wondering about freedom and democracy.

At that moment, the first bombs were about to be dropped in Iraq. I thought about how the local people in Bolivia got their way by rioting in the streets. They were successful in rolling back the tax increase. If only our democracy could work that effectively. "It's so simple," I thought, "Why can't we do that in the U.S.?" It seemed that the overwhelming majority of Americans wouldn't want us to go off and bomb another country, so why can't we just take to the streets in a demonstration telling the government not to do it? The death in the streets of Bolivia was sad, but you can't argue with the results.

My father and brother had both served in the army. My own teenage years had contained the shadow of possibility of being drafted into Vietnam. What would I have done if I had been confronted with that reality? Back then I had a gut feeling that I didn't want to go. It was not based on any in-depth political reasons to be sure, mostly self-preservation. As I've mentioned before, I have been politically unaware for most of my adult life.

Viewing my own country from the outside has definitely altered my perspective and brought about a newfound political awareness. Our own self-image differs so wildly from how we are seen from outside of our borders. We see ourselves as a charitable protector of the helpless and downtrodden. Outside our borders, we are often seen as blatantly selfish, only looking out for our own interests.

A scene from the Academy Award winning documentary, *The Fog of War* points to the ultimate futility of a war that could have been avoided with better communication. Robert McNamara, the Secretary of Defense for both Presidents Kennedy and Johnson, was speaking with Vietnam's former Foreign Minister long after the war was over. An astounding misunderstanding came to light. McNamara spoke about the encroachment of communism as the reason for the war. The Vietnamese official was very indignant, "We were fighting for our independence, you were fighting to enslave us." He continued, "We weren't pawns of the Chinese. We have been fighting the Chinese for a thousand years." They would never have become an ally of communist China as we feared. The very reasons for the war were not clearly communicated. The entire war may have been avoided with better communication.

Drawing the parallel to Iraq made me wonder why we are fighting and what the insurgents were fighting for. I thought about our soldiers over in Iraq. Volunteers! Risking their very lives! For what? Freedom and democracy? Oil? International domination?

Later on in the trip I found out about another revolt in Bolivia over the sale of natural gas. The politics seem strange in some of these countries, but the people get their way. The indigenous people in Ecuador were able to shut down the country the same way they did in Bolivia by stopping up the roads all over the country and forcing the government to sit up and pay attention.

****

La Paz is a city of some contradictions. It translates to, "the peace," but it is high-altitude and high-octane. The people are very energetic. I don't know where they get the energy with the lack of oxygen in the air but it seemed like everybody on the streets was hustling and bustling. There was micro-capitalism on an extreme level. Everybody was making a living in whatever way he or she could. Everybody had his or her own little vending box or stand. The environment was productive and energetic — everyone toting something somewhere. In other countries I saw much less energy and focus on commerce.

I was impressed how the Bolivians in La Paz have adapted to the new technology from other parts of the globe. They embraced it on their own scale. On the streets they sold knockoff DVDs and MP3s. You could buy a CD with 13 hours of music in MP3 format or recently released DVD movie knockoffs for only a buck. Compensating the artists? Well, that's certainly another discussion. Another example was the human cellular phone booth. Young people in bright fluorescent orange or green vests with cell phones chained to their wrists stood on every major corner. Timing your call with a stopwatch, they would charge you a few coins. They were doing a gangbuster business. It was fascinating how energetic and "can-do" the place was.

I met Scott at the airport. Just seeing him boosted my spirits. I had made some preliminary inquires into shopping for cars. Scott arrived in time for us to go to the auto market in the neighboring suburb of El Alto (The Heights) where the weather was even more inhospitable than in La Paz. Braving the cold and thin air, we started shopping. At the beginning of my journey I had debated between a Toyota Land Cruiser and a Toyota pick-up truck. I had chosen Baby Blue partly out of lack of experience with jeep-style vehicles. This market had an abundance of vintage Toyota Land Cruisers that came in three different body styles. We zeroed in on a white 1978 jeep-style Land Cruiser with red and blue trim. I was pleased with the idea of sporting my own country's colors.

The vehicle seemed to have been well-maintained and even had a musical horn. The short wheelbase and low gear ratio took a little getting used to. Cornering awkwardly and not able to go fast, it was not the greatest highway vehicle. However, it was a monster on the back roads. It was a trade-off, but seemed appropriate as I was looking forward to lots of back road driving in Bolivia.

Another thing about the transaction that lifted my spirits was that Jorge, the car dealer, took care of all the paperwork (including, at the price he quoted— six months of insurance). He assured me I would be able to cross into neighboring countries with no problems. What a load off of my shoulders! Things were looking up.

I wanted to do some modifications. Jorge referred me to shops in the neighborhood that could help. I wanted a luggage rack and a secure steel box welded inside for my camera and computer equipment. We got a smokin' deal on a custom-made rack and box.

The next minor challenge was coming up with a name for my new ride. Its predecessors had been Big Red and Baby Blue. The Great White Hope? No ring there. Blanco, meaning "white" in Spanish, seemed like a possibility. Blanco Bronco? Blanco Billy! That's it! It was partly a take off of the movie, Bronco Billy, partly a nod to my father, Bill, plus a mountain-climbing billy goat reference. There was only one drawback with the name. I feared I would give the vehicle a gender identification issue by assigning a masculine name but referring to her in the feminine. She'd be okay.

The next day, after we picked up Blanco Billy from the mechanic, Scott and I made our way to Mt. Chacaltaya. At over 5,345 meters tall, it is the highest developed ski area in the world, and the only one in Bolivia. As we got close to the top, we drove through snow and had to put her into four-wheel drive. She passed her first test triumphantly. It was an incredible first day out in Blanco Billy.

We crossed streams and passed fields filled with scores of grazing llamas against the backdrop of jagged snow-capped mountains. We made it! What a triumph for me too! I'd gone from the depths of depression to the top of the highest mountain in the area. I felt ecstatic. My own personal Mount Everest.

A week before, I had felt like walking death. Now Scott and I were back at it, cheating death once again. There we were at the summit staring in awe at the surrounding beauty. My Baby Blue blues were over. For the first time in months, I was mentally and physically on top of the world. Yeah!!

Why would I want to ride a bike down the world's most dangerous road? Two words. Actually, one name. Señor Eh Scott. Back to cheating death, on a grand scale this time.

In the Bay Area where we first met, we had ridden mountain bikes together in the lush green hills and mountains of Marin County. Mt. Tamalpais, Muir Woods and Stinson Beach are renowned for their incredible beauty and manicured bike trails. However, in Bolivia they have altogether different notions about mountain biking. Fanatic. Maniacal. These words don't even go far enough to describe the trails. Dropping off of six-foot boulders? For fun? I don't think so. I value the integrity of my skull and the rest of my bones. I would rather bike *on* mountains, not *off* of them.

Somehow I got seduced into the ride. He had done it again. Okay, I'm an idiot. Señor Eh Scott assured me that there would be no boulders and we would be going down a road, not a trail. Plus, it was 95% downhill!! I couldn't argue with that. However, rain, fog, mud, 3,000 foot cliffs, landslides, and a narrow one-lane dirt road with oncoming buses and trucks? Hardly sounded like a holiday bicycle outing. But, that's exactly what it was. Travelers from all parts of the globe joined us for the ride. The road drops almost 11,000 vertical feet from La Paz, high in the Andes, down to Coroico at the edge of the Amazon basin. We experienced all four seasons during the course of a single day (fear, panic, fog and velocity!).

Gravity Bolivia is the name of the company that shepherded the group down the mountain. Alistair, the proprietor and lead guide, looked like the front man for a punk rock band. He sported an exotically trimmed, bright red beard with shocks of bleach blond accents. As our early morning bus ride headed for our point of departure, the wild-eyed Aussie set the mood by telling stories of cannibals native to the region. His persona transformed from that of a punk rocker into a demanding drill sergeant. He was all business and his tone inspired confidence and purposely instilled some fear.

The top of the ride was on a paved road coming down through the Andes. Flanked by ominously beautiful slate peaks capped with white, we began our descent. Lack of traffic and the smooth road allowed gravity to do its thing. Flying downhill, the exhilaration was intense. I was ecstatic. Focusing on the road ahead, I still took in the incredible scenery flying by. I flashed on my father as my face pierced the cold mountain air. I thought of our ill-fated bike trip to Ireland and how very proud he would be of me now, having a blast on a bike in another faraway land. Tears of joy streamed horizontally across my temples and pooled in my ears. The emotional current electrified my body. The speed, the beauty and my heightened emotions created a peak experience that I will never forget.

We had yet to reach the portion of the ride known as the world's most dangerous road. At rest stops, the safety briefings and equipment checks continued as we approached the one-lane dirt segment. Years ago it had been a one-way road with the direction determined by the day of the week. Currently there is two-way traffic on the same one-lane road with blind corners and 1,000-foot drop-offs.

Traffic control at these blind corners came in the form of volunteers who sat on the roadside with red and green flags. They lived off of gratuities from drivers and bike riders, but the gratuities were not their reason for being there. They were there because they had lost family members over the edge and have since dedicated their lives to preventing more deaths. There are reportedly hundreds of casualties every year. A car here, a bus there, it adds up pretty fast (Let's skip the morbid math).

The dress code for the ride called for layers. An uphill section necessitated shedding nearly all layers. Soon thereafter, faced with clouds and rain, all twelve riders and both guides were soon thoroughly splattered with mud. Fog came and went as we pedaled through puddles and under waterfalls. The fog was a blessing at times because it obscured the nerve-racking view of the deadly drop-offs immediately to our left. Humidity took its toll on my small camera, which failed before the end of the ride.

We stopped midway to enjoy a Styrofoam box lunch consisting of local cheese, a banana and some sort of four-inch beans. We washed it down with a cup of hot coca mate (that's coca, not cocoa) made fresh with coca leaves. As if we needed more of an adrenaline rush! Coca mate is actually recommended for high-altitude acclimation. A bit late for us— we were losing altitude rapidly.

Following behind the bus was another vehicle, none other than Blanco Billy. I hired one of Alistair's guides to drive her down the road so that Scott and I could tour the lowlands and return to La Paz after looping around from another direction. Later we would find out that these plans were not feasible.

After lunch and an equipment overhaul on each and every brake system, we continued to snake our way down the mountainside. Our only delay was a landslide that had buried a portion of the road. Yes, a landslide! Landslides make the news where I come from, but in this part of the country it's aspect of everyday life. With bikes on our shoulders, we trudged through the sand to the other side. We continued on our bikes while the vehicles were delayed for another hour. We made it down to the floor of the valley but still had another hour of riding to get to our destination of Coroico. We were now cruising on a hot, dusty road and the accumulated layers of mud were getting baked onto our clothing and skin.

Our exhausted but exalted group arrived at a designated hotel where showers awaited us. I was so thoroughly covered in mud that I started my shower fully clothed, shoes and all. A late buffet lunch had been prepared for the group. After an hour or two of reveling and relaxing, we mounted our bikes on the custom-made rooftop rack and most of the group boarded the bus to make the trip in reverse. Scott and I had other plans and our own means of transport. We were thankful to be able to recuperate and enjoy the late afternoon and evening in the quaint little town of Coroico.

In spite of its size and location, Coroico has a thriving seasonal tourist trade with several small resort hotels and four excellent restaurants catering to tourists. That night we ordered lasagna and pizza baked in an outdoor, wood-burning oven. The preparation took forever, but it was worth the wait. The food was mouthwatering and the delay gave us time to get to know our waiter.

Mario was an Italian who spoke fluent Spanish, English and Italian. When he learned that I was a photographer, he brought out a sample of his art. Colorful and whimsical, but surprisingly realistic, his own peculiar form of sculpture was miniature motorcycles made from recycled cigarette lighters! He used pieces from old clocks and watches for parts that he could not create from lighters. He implored me to come to his home to photograph his entire collection, which I did. Negotiating for an exhibition in La Paz, he desperately needed a portfolio. His studio, like a kid's secret playhouse, was located in the attic of his small home. He was as charming as he was eccentric. It was good to have a friend in Coroico because our stay turned out to be longer than we had planned.

We found out that the road we had intended to take out of Coroico was in desperate shape even for four-wheel drive. The consensus was that our only option was to go back up from whence we came. That too became problematic. Another much larger landslide had stopped all traffic. It was anyone's guess when it would be cleared. I was okay with the uncertainty, but Scott was a little antsy because of his tighter schedule. But it was out of our hands.

At the same time we heard that bombs were being dropped in Iraq. We didn't know for sure because the landslide had cut off delivery of newspapers. We hoped it wasn't true. Thoughts of war were surreal in our paradise retreat. We had rooms with a view in a cozy resort hotel with a pool and Jacuzzi. Our reality was a million miles away from bombs and death.

Mario continued to introduce us to interesting locals and expatriates. One fellow I chose not to meet was a U.S. Drug Enforcement Agency (DEA) agent stationed at a compound just outside of town. The guy was ever-present in the bars late at night. If I could see auras, I'm sure his would have been very, very dark. He looked like he was dealing with some serious demons and it looked like they were getting the best of him. I would have loved to find out more about him, but my curiosity could not get past the creepy vibe I felt from afar.

The region is home to lots of *cocaleros*, growers and traffickers of coca leaves. Coca leaves are legal in Bolivia. Cocaine is not. In the street markets you can buy a quart-sized bag of coca leaves for less than a quarter from old women who are surrounded by huge trash bags full of the stuff. The DEA compound had a small airstrip used for reconnaissance missions to root out illegal growers. I still wonder how they sort out the illegal *cocaleros* from the legal. It's a shame that the U.S. government must come down on growers of something that has been an accepted part of life here for centuries. It is a dramatic example of our cultural insensitivity. The real source of the problem is the habits and behaviors of Americans in the U.S.

But back to more pertinent and practical matters of rain and landslides! We were still faced with the prospect of driving back up the most dangerous road in the world. I couldn't decide whether I preferred to be a passenger or the driver. I certainly did not want to go up on a rainy day or even when the roads were still wet. Fortunately for us, the landslide crew and the weather conspired in our favor fairly quickly. A day later the rain stopped, two days later the road was clear.

Finally, I chose to be the driver. We cautiously hugged the side of the mountain through the most dangerous section. After three hours of, "slow and steady wins the race," we made it back to La Paz alive. We cheated death once again— both ways!

Next stop, Potosí, and another episode in our saga of cheating death!

MARK'S ADVENTURE ALERT

Location: Potosí, Bolivia

Subject: Silver and Slavery

TWO FEET AWAY FROM DYNAMITE being packed into a crevice, twenty feet away when it was detonated!

My travel buddy señior Eh Scott wanted to go on a tour of the silver mines in Potosí. The idea of an underground Disney-tram-type experience didn't exactly thrill me. Then again, señior Eh Scott had yet to disappoint me with his agenda. I went along with the plan.

There was no tram and there was nothing "Disney" about it. It was the real deal. Crouching and crawling through muddy passageways to reach miners working by hand just as they did hundreds of years ago. We watched as a miner prepared a site for a stick of dynamite. He had been working several hours with a hammer and chisel. He lit the fuse and we scurried down the tiny dark corridor and around a corner. KABOOOM!

I was fully expecting the sound, but not the shock wave that penetrated my body. A giant THUMP that jolted my whole body and overloaded my nervous system. Like a carnival ride that leaves you totally drained, except the entire ride is concentrated into a fraction of a second.

But where do I begin to tell the rest of the story?

The dynamite experience pales in comparison to the estimated EIGHT MILLION WHO DIED working the mines and refineries.

The wealth, the mythology, the world history, all intertwined in the tragic story that was and still is Cerro

Rico (Rich Mountain) and Potosí, the city blessed and cursed by the mountain.

There is a painting that tells the story, at least the first part of the story. It hangs in a museum that was once the mint that made much of the currency for the entire Spanish colonial empire. It depicts Diego Huallpa, an Indian sheepherder discovering the richest source of silver the world has known. It has all of the major players in the early history of the mountain and the town, both real and mythological. The Spanish Emperor and Conquistadors, the Christian God and the officials of the Catholic Church, The Virgin Mary combined with Pachamama, the Incan Earth Goddess in the form of Cerro Rico and the mountain itself. It's all there, laid out on one canvas.

Potosí was once the largest city in all of the Americas, rivaling contemporary London and Madrid in size. But, the wealth and size of the city came with a price. The price was the lives of the indigenous and African miners forced into the service of the mine. The system of obligatory labor commanded that indigenous communities send one seventh of its work force to the mines. There were up to 13,500 miners in the mines at one time, many of them spending weeks at a time underground. The vast majority of these miners did not survive to return to their homes.

The complicity of the Catholic Church in the exploitation of the indigenous people and the clash of the two religions is a whole other story. Another interesting story is the role of coca leaves in the lives of the miners, historically and to this very day.

Today the town still seems haunted by the mountain. Visible from almost everywhere, it casts its long shadow on the town and its people.

Potosí is a stopping-off point for tourists who are on their way to the *Salar de Uyuni*, the salt flats of Uyuni. The high altitude and low temperatures make Potosí a harsh place. However, there are many attractions for the hardy tourist: the silver mines, a plethora of historic churches, a former mint turned into a fascinating museum and numerous jeep tours of the salt flats. We made arrangements to hire a guide in the town of Uyuni on the edge of the wilderness area. Here's our story!

MARK'S ADVENTURE ALERT

Location: Salar de Uyuni, Bolivia

Subject: Bolivian Safari

No lions or giraffes but plenty of llamas and flamingos. The far southwest corner of Bolivia is home to some of the most bizarre and extreme landscapes in the world. By far the world's largest salt flat and some other very interesting geology make it an unforgettable place to visit. The harsh and inhospitable environment also make the visit hard to forget. Bitter cold and blistering sun made comfort a sparse commodity on the four-day adventure. In the desolate little town of Uyuni, we contracted a guide to take us through the desert and across the salt flats. A trip without guidance is nearly impossible and certainly foolhardy. A local family froze to death a few years ago when their vehicle broke down and they attempted to walk to shelter. Much of the trip is across huge expanses of flat desert or salt with no roads, only tracks and distant landmarks for reference. Sixty gallons of gas on the roof, an extra spare tire, four days worth groceries and we were ready to go. Services along the way were practically non-existent, so we were prepared to be self-sufficient for the whole trip. All of the guides working in the area look out for each other and are called upon in case of an emergency or some kind of jam.

The first day was spent almost entirely in transit. We passed a railroad graveyard with what looked like the first trains ever built. At lunch we met what had to be the most affectionate animal I have ever come across. A llama! It was after lunch, not FOR lunch. I have written previously about llama for lunch but this was most certainly someone's pet. It approached me and began nuzzling its head into my chest, begging to be petted. If I coulda, I woulda taken it home with me.

Llamas are pretty much the cows of this part of the world. Many residents earn their keep by raising them. I'm sure the locals must wonder about visitors and their fascination with their cows.

The second day was a bitch. Our guide, Ray, assured us that we needed to get up at 2:45 AM in order to get to the geysers by sunrise. Blanco Billy has no heater. In addition, the doors and other junctions leaked so much air that there was a definite wind chill factor inside the vehicle! I have never been that cold for that long in all of my life. Ray did most of the driving; I was wrapped in a sleeping bag and still shivering for three solid hours. The kicker was arriving at the "geysers" to find, basically, bubbling puddles of mud. For this I froze since 2:45 AM?? Ray! What were you thinking? A minor consolation was being served breakfast in the nearby hot springs. Flamingos stalked the icy waters of the lake next to me. When I think of flamingos, I think of Florida and balmy weather. Ice and flamingos don't seem to go together, but the birds seemed to be thriving.

The second night was spent in a primitive "lodge." The lifestyle of the people at the small settlement (you couldn't quite call it a town) was certainly not enviable. Bleak is the word that comes to mind. A cold desert with freezing wind and nothing else around for miles. Unbelievably bleak.

The glowing warm light in the hallway of the lodge was very deceiving. It was cold. The radiator was frozen in the morning. You would have thought that I would have thought, or Ray would have thought, "Hey, Anti-freeze!" Aside from that oversight and waking us up for the "geysers," Ray actually turned out to be much more than just a guide. He was a good mechanic, a good driver and a halfway decent cook. With a flaming torch under the frozen radiator, Ray got us back on the road without much delay.

The second day we visited a couple of different lakes, each strikingly beautiful with its own exotic color. The different colors were from different minerals in the water, or microorganisms, depending on which source you believe.

By the end of the third day it was like, "Oh, yawn. Another incredibly gorgeous, distinctly colored lake, dotted with flamingos and flanked by snow-capped peaks? Isn't there anything else to see around here?" The fourth and final day there was much more to see. It was another early riser, but this time it was more than worth the effort. Ray wanted us to see the sunrise over the salt flats.

So at Ray's request we got up very, very early the night before to get there in time for the sunrise. This time we weren't disappointed. It was really bizarre. Why? Well, the salt goes on for miles, and it looks like you're standing on ice or snow. Then the sun comes up and the way the light hits the flats you feel like you're standing on water. It's just trippy, there's no other way to say it.

Another thing that made it so bizarre is that you could see the Isla Pescado, or Fish Island. The "island" rises out of the middle of the salt flat, adding to that weird feeling of standing on water. Surrounded by hundreds of miles of salt, Isla Pescado has its own peculiar and very hardy little ecosystem.

The most striking part of the biology there are the gigantic cactus, some purported to be 1200 years old. As you know, I'm a freakin' cactus freak. These things were like the saguaro from my hometown of Tucson, but the needles were thicker and longer and not as pointy. So instead of the needles being an inch to an inch-and-a-half long and sharp as a tack, these were about 4" long and more like a dull toothpick. So you could actually touch them. It felt like this big cushion around the cactus. I was in my little cactus heaven, romping around this island— even though I was up all night and I had the runs, I was tromping all over and taking pictures of these cacti that I would show to the Tucson Cactus and Succulent Society when I got home. I was ecstatic.

After our Bolivian safari, we spent a night recuperating in Uyuni. The next day we headed off to Tupiza. Little did we know we would find ourselves driving only by the light of the moon!

Early into our journey to Tupiza the electrical system went out in Blanco Billy. Fuses had been burning out and we were now out of spares. We were two hours into a seven-hour trip with no services along the way. We decided to carry on rather than turn back. The engine would run with a faulty electrical system but the starter would not. We could always push-start if need be. What we had not counted on was a detour that added a couple of hours, forcing us to finish the drive after dark. Much of the trip was on a narrow, winding mountain road. We only recognized our dilemma as the sun began to set, "Holy fuse box Batman! No lights!"

Fortunately, as darkness began to fall, we descended from the mountains onto the floor of the valley. Still, we had another ninety minute drive until we arrived in Tupiza. Again, fortunately, even though it wasn't full, the moon began to shine brightly enough so that we could continue cautiously into the night. Scott and I both had our eyes glued to the road as we drove along in the dark watching for pedestrians and potholes. We weren't too concerned about other vehicles. We hoped that there weren't other people as crazy as us driving around with no headlights. We survived a couple of very dark spots where the mountain had cast its shadow across the road. Finally, we pulled into Tupiza, having cheated death once again!

Tupiza is a small town surrounded by walls of picturesque red rock spires. We found a great mechanic who fixed Blanco Billy up. I would come back to use him again many weeks later on my way out of Bolivia.

The tourist thing to do in Tupiza is horseback riding. You can tour some of the old haunts of Butch Cassidy and the Sundance Kid. On the drive into Tupiza, we passed through the town of San Vincente where they are said to have been buried after their final shootout. The Hollywood depiction of the duo's demise varies from the Bolivian reality. Under assumed names, Butch and Sundance had immigrated to South America to escape law enforcement in the States. They attempted to start over as legitimate ranchers in Argentina, not far across the Bolivian border from Tupiza. Whether it was boredom or poverty, ranching just didn't do it for 'em. They were soon up to their old tricks, and were suspected of robbing banks in both Argentina and Chile. Their last heist was the payroll of a major mining company in Tupiza. They had fled to San Vincente where they made their last stand in a shootout with only four Bolivian military patrolmen, not the entire militia as per the movie. With no hope of escape, Butch apparently killed his wounded partner before killing himself (cue revised theme song).

Raindrops keep falling on my head.

I'm just about to shoot my best partner in the head.

Fill him full of lead, making sure he's dead....

It seemed appropriate that we take a horseback tour. I was Butch and Scott was Sundance. I was assigned the biggest, strongest, fastest horse. I wasn't the most experienced rider, just the biggest. I had been assigned the biggest horse once before. In high school, some of my buddies worked at a polo field in Tucson. We ditched school one day to do some horseback riding. My pals thought it would be really funny to put the most inexperienced rider (that would be me), on the most highly spirited horse with the highest backbone. When we emerged onto the open field our horses took off like bolts of lightning!

Riding bareback, I was bouncing out of control on top of my horse. Soon I lost control completely, falling off and under one of the other horses. I landed squarely on my face. I had to go to the doctor and got busted for ditching school. Luckily, I didn't have any serious injuries, except my pride.

Since then, I've had positive experiences on horseback, but there in Tupiza, I was still nervous atop the massive beast. The six-hour tour turned out to be quite breathtaking, over mountains, through riverbeds, all the while surrounded by awesome views of red rock spires and exotic cactus. As we were coming back into town, barking dogs spooked the horses. Mine took off like a shot. "Oh, no! Not again!" Memories of my high school mishap flashed back, but this time, I was not on a grassy polo field. The horse galloped for about five minutes full out, and I could do nothing but hang on. "I'm going to smash my skull!" I thought. This time, I had a saddle to cling to. I held on rigidly for a few moments, and then my fear gave way to exhilaration. What a ride! We made it safely back to the stables, you guessed it, having cheated death once again.

MARK'S ADVENTURE ALERT

Location: Sucre, Bolivia

Subject: The Most Dino Tracks

I have experienced a lot of "biggests," "mosts" and "highests" lately. La Paz, the world's highest capital. Potosí, the highest city. The self-proclaimed highest Internet café. The world's most dangerous road. The biggest salt flats. The world's largest source of silver.

And now, the largest known collection of dinosaur footprints, estimated at 5000 from 150 different types of dinos! Included are huge prints from a Brontosaurus. Also, a long trail of tracks (over a half a kilometer long) of a baby T-rex that was affectionately named Johnny Walker by the researchers.

A cement company doing excavation discovered the footprints in 1994. The fossilized prints are on a huge vertical wall. But the dinos didn't climb the wall.

Some 65 million years ago they had been tromping around in the mud. The mud hardened, the continents shifted (this is my abbreviated version of the history of the planet), the Andes jutted into the sky and the once horizontal mudflats became vertical. Sounds amazing and it is.

The bestest part (another superlative) of the whole experience (if you're in third grade) is getting to ride in the Dino-Truck when you go on the Dino-Tour.

All good things must come to an end. We had a blast, but Scott had to get back to running his company in Berkeley. He took a bus from Tupiza to catch his flight out of Santa Cruz. I was disappointed to see him go. Scott had been a lifesaver. He had pulled me out of my funk and got me back on the road. Muchisimas gracias, Señor Eh Scott!

Another of my traveling commandments that I break quite frequently is: Thou shalt not pick up hitchhikers. On my out of Tupiza, I saw him flailing his arms somewhat desperately and pathetically. He was with a girl and I sensed a sad, romantic separation about to happen. I pulled over and picked up Pancho, a middle-aged Latino with a Fu Man Chu mustache. There were actually tears in his eyes as he climbed into Blanco Billy.

He told me he wanted to go to the town of Sucre. Within five minutes, he had told me his entire sorrowful love story. His girlfriend in Tupiza had family ties which kept her there. He traveled 20-hours each way by bus to be with her on weekends (I did the math, 48-40= a very short weekend)! Later, I realized that Pancho liked the girl a lot more than she liked him.

Since he wore his heart on his sleeve, I opened up and told him my recent romantic history. Instantaneous male bonding! His ultimate destination was Santa Cruz, same as mine, but his timeframe was much more urgent. Somehow he convinced me to make the 18-hour drive straight through so he would make it on time to teach class on Monday morning.

As a pharmacy professor at a college in Santa Cruz, one might expect him to be a respectable and upstanding fellow. However, that was not the case. Friends called him *El Chemico Loco*, the crazy chemist. He was a bit of a scumbag, but a very loveable one. It turns out we were exactly the same age and had a lot of things in common. We had been exposed to the same pop music growing up and as I drove, he sang songs from the '80s, in his broken English and terrible accent. "Chunchine on my cholder meks me happy…." He knew all the songs.

I had a collection of about ten bootleg cassette tapes that I had purchased on the road. Cassette vendors were common throughout Latin America, selling copies of mostly Latin albums. Their selection of English titles was sparse— mostly greatest hits and compilation cassettes from the '80s. "Hotel California" can be found on just about every one.

The quality is usually low, either recorded a bit too slow or too fast, making Mick Jagger sound like Willie Nelson and Bruce Springsteen sound like one of the three chipmunks. Add Pancho's less-than-stellar voice to that mix and it was as sure recipe for comedy. I tried to sing along, but mostly just laughed.

In between singing, I coached Pancho on his English. He was rusty, but still had a command of English expletives. We both took great delight in finding new ways to fit the word "fuck" (or some derivative thereof) into every sentence. You'd be amazed at what two guys can come up with during an 18-hour drive. "Where's the fucking gas station? Fuck man, look dat fuckin' big cactus." Hey fucker, give me fucking crackers please? He was great entertainment for the ride.

We stopped off for lunch a couple of fuckin' hours (oops, got carried away), a couple of hours later in the town of Sucre. There were a lot of Sunday activities going on and the streets were blocked off around the town square. We got some more cassettes to listen to along the way. Pancho bought the soundtrack from Clint Eastwood's The Good, the Bad and the Ugly. The film was one of the spaghetti westerns (American westerns made in Italy) that launched Eastwood's career. In case you are not familiar with the soundtrack, it is very intense, Wild West mood music complete with gunshot effects. It was a strangely fitting choice as we pulled out of Sucre listening to the tape.

As the music became more intense, the paved road became a dusty dirt road. Bumpty bump, bumpty bump. The rhythm of Blanco Billy and the music added to the cowboy feeling— riding on horseback through the Wild West. Surrounded by bluish-purple mountains and huge cactus, we stared out across the arid landscape, riding the same roads as Butch and Sundance before us. The music transported us to another time and space.

The mountains were like ones you would find in Sedona, Arizona with a slightly different hue. They looked like the rocks you grew in a child's Magic Rocks kit. The cactus were even more massive than the saguaros found in southern Arizona. Not quite as tall as the saguaro, they are much thicker in the trunk. It was like an oak tree that branched off very low into multiple arms, often forty to fifty rising into the sky.

We stopped for dinner in a small town. The restaurant was next to a butcher shop with a huge variety of meat and animal parts hanging from hooks. It certainly looked like we were going to be getting fresh stuff. Even though we finished our meal after 11:00 p.m., we hit the road and continued into the night.

On either end of most Bolivian towns, you must pass a checkpoint where a little guard station registers your driver's license number and license plates, and charges you a small fee of roughly 35 cents. As we were heading out of town, I was picking up speed, doing about 40 miles an hour. I saw something that looked like a checkpoint, and thought we might have to stop. However, there were no lights. I slowed down to try to figure out what I needed to do. All of a sudden, KA-BOOM, CRASH, BANG! I slammed on the brakes.

Invisible in the darkness, a heavy iron chain had been strung across the road. Fortunately, my foot was already on the brake and I was slowing down or it could have been a lot worse. I was lucky that my windshield was made of safety glass. The chain had hit Blanco Billy's grill, bounced up and smacked the middle of the windshield. The impact of each individual link of the heavy chain left its own separate mark with a spider web of cracks radiating out from each. It looked like a spray of bullet holes from an AK-47. The chain was attached to a pole in a heavy cement foundation. Or had been, until we showed up.

The police came running out of the darkened checkpoint to see what had happened. As they untangled the chain from my windshield wipers, I complained about the lack of signs and lights. "It's been this way for many years and this is the first time this has happened," they replied. Not much consolation. Fortunately, my pal Pancho yelled at them loud enough so that they didn't come after me for damages or breaking any laws.

Visibility through the middle of the windshield was gone. I rolled up a couple of sweatshirts to sit on so I could see over the "bullet holes" and we carried on into the night. We still had about eight hours to go, and I drove most of the way. As we drove into Santa Cruz, I had to wake Pancho up to ask directions through the city to his house.

I had been up for twenty-four hours straight. We were arriving in Santa Cruz just in time for Pancho to get to his class. We got to his neighborhood and found a place to park in a public garage. He took me to his apartment so I could get some sleep. I couldn't believe it! It was a one-room apartment, and I don't mean one bedroom. I mean one room, 10 x 10 with a bed along one wall and a place to hang his clothes. No closet, no bathroom, a desk and a few shelves. The bathroom down the hall was shared with probably six or eight other apartments. As I was lying there on the bed I thought, "Oh my God, this poor guy! He's a professor, a pharmacist, and this is the best standard of living he can enjoy?" I was shocked.

He had pictures of his twenty-something son on the wall, who was in college, an ex-wife, and a couple of ex-girlfriends. He was also into photography. That's one of the reasons we enjoyed our time together. He picked my brain as we shot pictures along our drive and he made me promise I would get him some photography equipment from the U.S.

Pancho got cleaned up and went to school. I drifted off to sleep, feeling awkward and uncomfortable in someone else's bed. But I was so tired I could have slept on the sidewalk.

When Pancho returned from work late that afternoon, he made arrangements for some other accommodations for me. His best buddy (besides me, his new best buddy) lived and worked nearby. Alberto, a veterinarian, had a storefront shop a half a block down the street. The front room doubled as the reception area for his veterinary practice and a shop selling pet and agricultural supplies. Beyond the main room was a treatment room with three surgical tables and all the tools of the trade.

Through another doorway, I was surprised to find an outdoor courtyard and a covered walkway that led to a very ample living space for Alberto and his nephew, Miguel, who ran the shop. Pancho's nickname for Alberto was *Caballo*, Spanish for horse. Though they were the best of friends, one cannot imagine an odder couple. Their personalities were polar opposites, which fueled the fire of friendship that burned brightly between them. They harassed and harangued each other endlessly. *Caballo* was the consummate and cordial professional. Friendly and warm, he was a prince of a guy. He was early to bed, early to rise. He minded his shop conscientiously and was a responsible citizen. Then you have *El Chemico Loco*, out carousing all night then heading straight to teach class. Butch and Sundance they were not; more like Felix and Oscar.

Pancho had an extra folded metal frame bed. We marched down the street to Caballo's place with it over our heads. With the help of my new temporary housemates, I was set up to share a bedroom with Miguel. I was not accustomed to the lack of privacy, but I was really enjoying my new accommodations. Caballo had a domestic employee who fixed meals and did laundry. I chipped in to cover her expenses and life was good— for about a week anyway. One night I came home late from partying with Pancho and had trouble getting my key to work. My pounding on the iron security door to get help disturbed the slumber and orderly routine that Caballo was used to. I knew my welcome was wearing thin. Fortunately there was a hotel directly across the street. I salvaged our friendship and got a room overlooking the street and the shop. I was fond of Caballo and very appreciative of the hospitality he had shown. It was a good compromise, close but not too close.

There were a number of establishments on the street that ran the gamut between a boarding house and a hotel. Pancho's place was on the boarding house end of the spectrum. My new place was on the hotel end, but with some curious distinctions from most hotels. I stepped up to a deluxe room that included such luxuries as a window, ceiling fan, and get ready for this, a private bath! You see, most of the rooms had none of the aforementioned amenities. But don't worry about the other guests because in the middle of the hallway was a sink and a urinal. No, not a door to the bathroom but an actual sink and urinal were affixed to the wall in the hallway!

After his classes, Pancho would meet me at the hotel for our nightly adventures. He drove a beat-up old bucket of bolts, a battered blue Toyota sedan with all four tires in such bad shape you would not trust any one of them as a spare. In the trunk was an actual spare, but it was flat. Sharing trunk space with the useless tire was a contraption that looked like it could be a small, homemade nuclear device. It was a large, rusted yellow tank complete with a variety of coils and cables. In reality, it was the tank for the natural gas that powered the car. At first I wondered how a busted-up old car in this third-world country could possibly have this advanced ecological technology. Then I learned about the massive reserve of natural gas, one of the largest in the world, lying deep under Bolivian soil.

I watched with fascination the first time I saw Pancho get a fill-up. The contraption that dispensed the gas was only part of my interest. In Santa Cruz, they have what I would call "Hooters" gas stations. Teenaged women in bikinis pumping gas! Pancho was all over it. Not every station had them, but Pancho certainly knew which did.

Over the course of a couple of weeks, Pancho had no less than three flat tires. Out of necessity, he had become quite proficient at changing them. He was on a first-name basis with the attendant who patched the inner tubes. However, one inner tube in the car never failed. It was a small scooter tire inner tube that he used as a seat cushion. *Caballo* teased him mercilessly about his makeshift hemorrhoid helper.

Pancho gave me a good introduction to Santa Cruz. The city is laid out in a series of five concentric rings. Each ring is bordered by one of the five ring roads. Inside the first ring is the downtown area and the town square. By the outer fifth ring you are at the outskirts of the city. Navigation of the streets in between the rings is not easy but the ring roads lend some helpful orientation.

The city is not picturesque by any means. There are a few historic buildings inside the first ring, but mostly there are just unsightly concrete structures. However, the sociable and modern culture compensated for the lack of esthetics. Distinct from La Paz and the rest of Bolivia, Santa Cruz is decidedly more modern and Hispanic than indigenous. People made eye contact with me easily and were accepting of me as a foreigner. The vibe was not overtly friendly but still very open. There were attractive women everywhere! If I were to get lucky anywhere in Bolivia, this would be the place.

A two-week performing arts festival that started shortly after my arrival truly reflected the modern culture. What a treat it was! Every night events were held in auditoriums, movie theaters, playhouses, school gymnasiums and even in the streets, many free of charge. Most were dramatic plays— a number of comedies and experimental pieces. The performers were usually accessible after the shows. I got to meet a number of them. It felt very cosmopolitan and at the same time, very small town.

With my informal host Pancho, I attended an event almost every night. Even if an event was sold out, Pancho could always manage to schmooze our way in. He would speak to the manager claiming that I was a North American journalist. I went along with it. It was sorta true.

Editor's note: Would a journalist use the word "sorta?"
Author's note: My sorta journalist would.

The performance groups were from all over South America though mostly from Argentina and Colombia. A group of street performers from Colombia did an elaborate musical production on six-foot stilts, complete with some very flashy pyrotechnics! Another dramatically striking piece was performed by a troupe from Argentina. Like theater in the round, it was set up in a gymnasium with the audience on three sides. The play dealt with themes of racism and war as it related to indigenous cultures. There was wailing, beheadings and lots of blood. The props were not sophisticated but still effective. Though I couldn't grasp all of the details, I was emotionally riveted.

The town square was the focus of all of the festivities and where Pancho went to cruise for chicks. Before or after shows we walked the perimeter of the square checking out the people as they passed. Pancho was like a shark on the hunt, never stopping, as if to keep water flowing through his gills. "Chill out Pancho!" I said, "Have a seat on a bench and let the parade come to you." But no, he had to keep moving. Yes, this is the same Pancho, hopelessly hung up on his long-distance sweetheart. Welcome to Latin America.

One evening on the square, while waiting for Pancho to show up for an event, I saw a woman sitting on a bench in jeans and a loose-fitting V-neck top. She was clean-cut and attractive, looking a little out of place among the Bohemian craft vendors and struggling food and drink concessionaires. I didn't want to miss the opportunity. Taking a deep breath, I walked over to the bench, and plopped down a few feet away from her. "Hola," I said, as I smiled with a little nod. A very shy smile came back my way. Contact! In that instant a connection was made. Somehow I knew I was in.

Diana, a dark-skinned *Latina* with broad cheekbones and a head full of bushy black curls, was waiting for her girlfriend. They were headed out for a night on the town. She was shy, but enthusiastic about the four of us meeting for a drink after the show. I met Pancho at the front of the theater and told him about the date I had fixed up for him. He was thrilled. I was cautiously optimistic that they would be waiting for us after the show. At the end of the performance we walked out of the theater and bingo, there they were. Pancho was disappointed by his impromptu date, but wasn't complaining. She had four limbs and a pulse — good enough for Pancho. In contrast to Diana's personality, her friend was surly and obnoxious. I was puzzled that they would be friends since they were so different. From here on out I'll refer to her as The Bitch. A little harsh perhaps, but well deserved, as you will come to find out.

The four of us walked to the Pancho-mobile while discussing our options for the evening. We grabbed some beers in a market along the way and proceeded to go for a drive. Secluded in the back seat, Diana and I were growing closer by the minute. In the front seat, the only thing growing was animosity. It was light banter at first, with a sarcastic undercurrent which quickly deteriorated into unbridled viciousness. I could see their relationship was going nowhere fast, but I was not concerned in the least. I was paying all of my attention to Diana. We were getting along famously, feeling very comfortable with each other and not able to keep our hands to ourselves. In spite of the lack of connection, to put it mildly, Pancho was still angling to get The Bitch back to his apartment. Pancho dropped Diana and me off at my hotel and continued down the block to his place.

Up in my room, the rapport between Diana and me blossomed into full-blown passion. Alone in the dark, we were having a blast under the covers, as though we were long-time lovers. Abruptly, the ring of her cell phone distracted her. I hoped she would ignore it, but she didn't (Damn!). A look of concern appeared on her face. It was The Bitch. Then my phone rang. It was Pancho! Something had gone very wrong between them. The Bitch was on her way to my hotel. Pancho was warning me to watch out for her, saying that she had tried to put a powdered drug into his beer. I got off the phone with Pancho just as Diana finished her call. The Bitch had claimed that Pancho had tried to drug her! This was way too much drama for me, particularly in the middle of the fun I was having with my new sweetheart.

The Bitch came up to the room cursing Pancho's name and promising to exact revenge. I didn't know what to think. Neither of their stories made any sense. I just wanted to get back to the action under the covers. Diana calmed her friend down and we came up with a plan. The Bitch would sleep on the bedspread on the floor, while Diana and I got back to business. I was concerned about the security of my things but thought that everything would be okay. She was on one side of the bed and all of my valuables were on the other. My romantic connection aside, I knew better than to fall asleep with two relative strangers in my room. Before long Diana and I reconnected, as if the interruption had never occurred — back into our own private world.

Everything had gone so well from the moment we met, I felt like I hit a romantic grand slam. In spite of the unusual situation, the darkness of the room allowed us to create a cocoon of privacy. The scene was almost cinematic; for the next couple of hours I was Romeo and she was Juliet. Eventually our cocoon gave way to reality. Since Diana had to work early the next morning, I walked them down to the street and said goodnight. I was feeling large and in charge. My time with Diana had left me physically euphoric.

I floated up the stairs and back to my room. As soon as I flipped on the light, my blissful bubble burst. My belongings had been disturbed. The pockets of my backpack were unzipped and their contents hanging out. Oh my God! The slimy bitch had slithered under the bed while we were occupied on top of it and rifled through my stuff. I quickly discovered that she had found my wallet in my pants pocket and removed the cash. I sprinted downstairs but to no avail. There was a cab down the street heading away from the hotel with the two girls and my cash in the backseat.

I trudged back up the stairs to my room shaking my head. I inventoried my belongings more carefully, but did not find anything else missing. She had only taken about $200 in cash. It would have been much worse had she taken something difficult or impossible to replace like my passport or my laptop, laden with photos and journals.

A huge question gnawed at me. Had Diana been a party to the theft? The events of the evening had seemed so spontaneous that I doubted it had been planned.

I'd like to think that The Bitch took advantage of the moment without Diana's participation or knowledge. I'll never know. Oh well, it didn't break the bank. I had enjoyed every moment with Diana and ended up with an exciting story to tell.

MARK'S ADVENTURE ALERT

Location: Santa Cruz, Bolivia

Subject: A Real Adventure, Third World Dental Care

I fit in better now. A lot of folks around here are missing a few front teeth. I will probably start making more friends!

I broke my tooth chewing on a hard roll at breakfast. Actually, it was not my tooth but a porcelain crown or cap. I had the first crown done when I was in high school because the tooth I was born with was a spiky little peg lateral. In case you didn't know, I was a dentist in my previous life.

Very early in my dental career a buddy of mine did some cosmetic dentistry on me. I had gaps between all of my front teeth. He bonded my teeth to close the spaces (thanks again, Dr. Joe!). It changed my smile and my career.

It made me feel better about my smile. I started doing the procedure on my own patients. I discovered I had a natural talent for the esthetics of teeth. I never looked back. It became the focus of my career for the next 17 years. But I digress. Here in Santa Cruz, I shopped around for a dentist to see if I would be comfortable getting my tooth fixed here. I was pleasantly surprised with Dr. Inez. It can be a nightmare doing treatment on another dentist. But she was flexible and open-minded enough to listen to my input.

Her one-chair office was outfitted with Brazilian equipment. It was modern and comfortably clean. I wanted to have another crown made AND do a cosmetic procedure on the gums above the tooth. When the crown was re-done last time, about 20 years ago, I was not familiar with cosmetic contouring of the gum tissue. You can change the appearance of a tooth, that is, make it appear taller by raising the gum line. Late in my career I was very proficient with this procedure. I even taught the technique to other dentists. But could I do it on myself?? I wanted to try.

I explained my desires to Dr. Inez and she was willing to go for it! So the adventure began. We hopped in her car and drove to the dental supply store across town. I was able to find and purchase the specific blades that I was familiar with. Back at the dental office I spent the entire afternoon in the treatment chair.

To some this will sound a little twisted, but it was really fun! I told her about selling my practice and hitting the

road. She said, "I hate my job! I wanna quit and travel too!"
That made me wonder if I had chosen the right dentist. But I
think it is universal. All dentists harbor secret dreams of
hanging up the drill for the last time and getting the heck
out. Even if you love it, there are aspects that are just hard
to cope with full-time. I ended up not being able to do the
gum procedure on myself. Picture me trying to do precise
incisions on myself, looking in the mirror, trying to peer
around my own fingers and lips! It was ridiculous to even try.
I ended up coaching her through the procedure. She did a great
job! I also had fun teaching her some tricks for making
temporary crowns. She was very appreciative.

All in all, the dental adventure turned out very nicely.
The lab-processed acrylic crown was ready the next morning. A
day or two later my gums were good as new and my smile looked
better than it did before the crown broke! Can't ask for much
more than that.

My baby sister Patty would be joining me in Santa Cruz for a wilderness adventure— an expedition into the largest, and by far, the most remote national park in Bolivia. Unlike traveling with my pal Señor Eh Scott, who aggressively took part in and almost took over navigation, Patty was counting on me for our itinerary. I would be the instigator, taking the lead role and total responsibility for all forms of cheating death. Patty would take over my familiar role as the dimwit who goes along with anything and accepts any dare. Since Patty is smarter and more mature than her big bro Mark, she knows better than to accept any dubious dares. However, she was not smart enough to avoid the trip altogether.

Patty and I had grown very close since Kevin's death and were looking forward to our time together. She had spent many years camping and backpacking with Kevin. Though she has an independent and adventurous spirit, more often than not, she was the voice of reason as Kevin led the charge into the unknown.

Before we went on our jungle jaunt, I had an urban adventure in mind. I wanted to show her the Santa Cruz I had come to know and I also wanted to explore the world of the Mennonites. The agricultural shopping district where Pancho and Caballo lived had a curious little sub-district, the home of a Mennonite marketplace. The Mennonites only come to the big city to buy their agricultural supplies before returning to their farming communities. They had found religious freedom in Bolivia. Creating their own kind of utopia, they have formed a completely separate, but peaceful co-existence defined by their faith and language. The religious sect is a distant cousin of the Quakers found in the eastern U.S., with many similar Quakerly quirks.

I was fascinated by this culture within a culture. The tall, light-skinned folk were in sharp contrast to the Latino and indigenous Bolivians. For practical purposes, their clothing is a uniform. Women wear bonnets and dark, mid-calf dresses while men donned denim overalls and big straw cowboy hats. Before I knew anything about them, I saw a group on the sidewalk. I was startled by how out of place they looked.

I was so curious about these folks that I made plans to immerse myself in their world by moving into their neighborhood, with Patty as my willing accomplice. Upon her arrival in Santa Cruz, we checked into their hotel. It was a small step up in quality from the hotel across from Caballo's shop. Our room overlooked a café, which was at least 80% Mennonite clientele, although run by local Latinos. Patty and I chatted with the Latino staff who confirmed how shy and isolated the Mennonites are. They just placed their orders and paid, rarely even saying hello or goodbye.

Though we physically entered their world, we did not gain entry into the mind of the Mennonites. Even though we shared their living space, we were no closer to knowing them. Though not rude or unfriendly, they kept very much to themselves, leery of our presence and especially our cameras.

While living in the Mennonite neighborhood we continued to socialize with Pancho and Caballo in the evenings. They were both eager to spend time with Patty. To them, she was an exotic rarity— a fair-skinned, green-eyed beauty. I found it amusing that Pancho tried so diligently to be respectful and courteous to Patty. I was curious how he might have treated her if she wasn't my sister.

Pancho decided to join us for our wilderness adventure. We did some shopping in the neighborhood to prepare for our departure. Pancho and Caballo did their best to help us, but we were not able to prepare adequately for the unknown that lay ahead. *Cue foreboding music.*

MARK'S
ADVENTURE ALERT

Location: Noel Kempff National Park, Bolivia

Subject: What Doesn't Kill You...

"The most isolated, pristine and spectacular National Park in the country and one of the most remote wilderness regions in all of South America. The Huanchaca Plateau, rising 500 meters from the floor of the surrounding rainforest was the inspiration for Sir Arthur Conan Doyle's novel **The Lost World.***"*
— Noel Kempff National Park Brochure

Those were my inspirations for wanting to visit Noel Kempff National Park. "Rustic accommodations and basic meals." That's what the park brochure promised. The perfect little eco-lodge from which to emerge each day to snap a few award-winning wildlife photos... so I thought.

The reality was not so kind. "The majority of visitors to the park arrive by chartered airplane" should have been a big clue. But no, we decided driving there would be an adventure. It was beyond adventure, bordering on nightmare. Nietzsche said, "What doesn't kill you makes you stronger." I don't think he mentions that it may also make you really, really irritated.

The expedition party (although "party" is certainly a misnomer) consisted of me, my sister Patty and Pancho, my Bolivian pal. Once inside the park, we were joined by our mandatory park guide, Juan. He was a friendly fellow and an excellent guide, but he did not have the latest data on situations in the park. He was not really to blame for the fact that the compound for lodging visitors was locked up and deserted.

This meant that we would have to survive on a bag of rice, some beef jerky and a hunk of salty cheese that smelled like a dirty sock. It was indeed a disheartening realization after all we had gone through to get there.

Fifteen hours on a deteriorated dirt road, partially overtaken by jungle. The jungle has an amazing life force. In a matter of months it can practically reclaim a road. The space gets strangled from all directions. There were sprouts coming up from the ground, branches growing in from both sides and shoots descending down, seemingly from the sky. In Mexico, atop the pyramids at Chichén Itzá, you can see other pyramids and what was once an entire city, completely overtaken by the creeping green.

Stuck in the mud for three hours we became aware of another life force. Insects! And it did not take three hours for them to make their presence known. In fact, if you stood still for 30 seconds you would have a swarm of bees, wasps, butterflies and assorted other critters orbiting your head and periodically touching down for landing.

Picture if you will, the sun beating down on a hot and muggy day. Struggling to raise Blanco Billy (my Land Cruiser) out of the mud enough to create a path of logs under the tires. The more you sweat, the more insects you attract. Bees are crawling under your clothes and in your ears! Getting stung seven or eight times. Emergency road service is nothing short of fantasy, given our location and lack of means of communication.

The kicker is seeing the path AROUND the mudhole big enough for a semi! Pancho was driving and had failed to notice the blatantly obvious detour. This was probably the reason he was working so silently and diligently in spite of the heat and the bugs. I, on the other hand, had to take a break every two or three minutes to run away and escape my own personal swarm.

At the rate of progress we were making, we may very well have been there an additional three hours had it not been for a couple of park rangers happening along in a pick-up truck. They were able to yank us out of with a towrope in fairly short order.

At the abandoned compound we resorted to breaking and entering to get bedding materials and drinking water out of a storage room. We got into the kitchen to encounter a thriving ecosystem. It included ants, roaches, moths and couple of very large frogs. The jungle again, asserting its territorial rights.

Given our food supply and preparation facilities, it was unanimous that our scheduled five-day stay would be shortened to two. At least this would allow us to experience two highlights of the park, La Meseta and El Encanto. La Meseta is the plateau and El Encanto is a spectacular waterfall that spills off of the plateau. We hiked to the base of it for a refreshing swim. The following day we hiked to the top of the mesa from the other side.

Driving toward El Encanto, a fallen tree presented another challenge for Blanco Billy. It required a few more hours of labor but fortunately it was in a cooler area with fewer insects. We had to dig a hole in the road in order to drive under the tree.

Many times I had to ask myself, "What have I gotten my baby sister into??" She was pushed close to her limit a time or two, but all-in-all, she was a remarkably good sport. On the way out of the park, at the ranger station, she discovered a small infestation of ticks on her body. Somehow I was spared their onslaught. In the relative comfort and cleanliness of the ranger station we were able to deal with the situation. Had she discovered the ticks deep in the jungle, she said she might have really lost it.

And there was no love lost between Patty and macho Pancho by the end of the trip. Pancho is a good friend and had the best of intentions, but his Bolivian machismo wore thin with independent Patty. I am, however, happy to report that she is still on speaking terms with me. All part of the family fun and adventure.

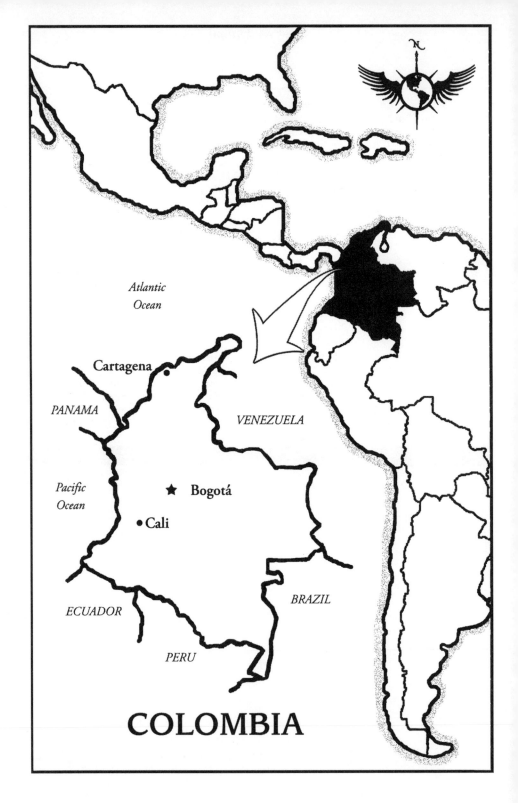

COLOMBIA

After emerging from the jungle, Patty still had time left on her holiday schedule. We took a leisurely drive back from Santa Cruz to La Paz, stopping off in a couple of cities along the way. The last few days were spent sightseeing in La Paz. The photo opportunities and points of interest seemed never ending. Eventually, we went to the airport, but boarded different planes.

I had originally planned to avoid Colombia. The dangers of driving through the country as an American were impressed upon me by numerous sources. However, I had also heard from some seasoned travelers that if you go by air and remained within selected cities, the trip was safe and well worth the effort.

I had made friends with Sandra, a Colombian woman living in Panama City, who had extended me an invitation to visit her family in Bogotá. Coincidentally, Sandra was back home visiting her family in Bogotá. It seemed like the right time to take Sandra up on her offer. I got a special deal on the Colombian Airline, Avianca, into Bogotá with free stopovers in two other Colombian cities of my choice. I chose Cali and Cartagena based on what I had heard from friends.

Bogotá was not at all what I had expected it to be. It is certainly not how Colombia is represented by the American news media. It is a huge city with a burgeoning middle class. There were far fewer armed guards than in other Latin American capitals. The populace is educated, even somewhat sophisticated. On Sunday mornings in Bogotá, many of the major thoroughfares are closed to motorized traffic and reserved for walkers, joggers, and bikers. Not exactly what I expected from a country supposedly overrun by gun-toting rebels.

Sandra's family home in Bogotá was small but comfortable. I was treated to the best bed in the house despite my protest and offer to sleep on the couch. Her family wouldn't hear of it. The first evening I was immersed directly into the social fabric of the neighborhood. Invited to a police academy graduation party, I was warmly welcomed into the festivities complete with streamers, balloons, cake and plenty of beer. I sensed close ties between the neighbors and friends and was pleased to be included in the merriment.

I enjoyed a couple of days in Bogotá, sightseeing with Sandra, her mother and her 10-year-old sister. I was their excuse to get out and go to restaurants they enjoyed. However, Sandra had to get back to work. She had a flight back to Panama City and I had a flight to Cali. A small city in Central Colombia, Cali is nestled in dark green hills surrounded by a predominantly sugarcane agricultural region. The town has many historic neighborhoods with monuments overlooking the city that attract national tourism.

Early in the evening, I was walking along the main restaurant row when I saw a burst of flame shoot up into the sky. It was from the middle of an intersection about a half a block away. The source of the flame was the mouth of a street performer. I chatted with Luis, the young entertainer, between his short shows. Camera in hand, I attempted to capture the perfect shot, with the flame at its peak, over 20-feet into the sky. After each fiery blast and a few quick juggling feats, the light would turn green and Luis would remain in the street collecting coins and kudos, standing tall between lanes of passing cars.

There is no big secret to the technique: A cigarette lighter, a deep breath, a mouthful of gasoline, and certainly some guts the first time you do it. I speak from some experience. I learned to eat fire many years ago at the International Jugglers Association Annual Convention in New York. Believe me, the first time is a bitch! However, I was a fire-eater, as compared with Luis, a fire-breather. The drama of fire-eating is more subtle, watching someone thrust a flaming torch into their mouth without disfiguring themselves. Nonetheless, it was a basis of rapport between us. I asked him if he worried about the toxicity of the gasoline. I had used high-proof alcohol, which is still a poison, but one that people willingly ingest. He said that he drank lots of milk. I encouraged him to bring a bottle of water to rinse his mouth after each blast to minimize the absorption into his system. He appreciated my concern. With a pregnant girlfriend at home, he wanted to stay healthy to provide for his new family.

After his shows, Luis took me to some of his favorite haunts and told me about life in his crazy country. He told me a parable about God creating a country blessed with natural resources beyond any other. Rivers, mountains, minerals, gems and two different oceans! But God cursed the people by not giving them respect for human life, so that they wantonly kill each other with little or no provocation. That was how Luis described his country. Sad, but true.

I met another performing artist in Cali whose temperament and life situation could not have been more different than that of Luis. Diego approached me instead of the reverse, speaking English with only a slight accent. Originally from Cali, he had spent over 15 years in Washington D.C. as a concert pianist. Though he was living back home again, he obviously missed aspects of his life in the U.S. He was no longer actively playing the piano, but instead pursued another passion for painting. He invited me to his nearby apartment, which doubled as his art studio. He stored his paintings at his mother's home, and many of them adorned the walls of her large flat. He invited me there for dinner so that I could see his work.

His mother was gracious and sweet, and seemed delighted to have company to entertain. I met Diego's brother at the home but he didn't join us for dinner. He quickly disappeared to another part of the house. I sensed that something was not quite right about his brother and their relationship. A day or two later it would all make sense.

Diego didn't have a piano, but wanted me to hear him play. He made arrangements for us to visit the municipal opera hall, the home of a monstrous grand piano. He had played the last concert of his career there, to a sold-out house. He was totally exasperated that, despite his prior arrangements, we were denied access the first time we went. He cursed his own people and culture for their lack of follow-through on absolutely everything in the country.

We had better luck the next day. Though the palatial hall had seen better days, it was still a sight to behold. Four levels of balconies were crafted with intricate woodwork. A workman helped push the massive grand piano from a locked storage compartment onto the stage and then departed. Alone with Diego in the cavernous hall, I was treated to my own private concert. After a few minutes of clearing the cobwebs, his fingers were flying across the keyboard. The sound thundered out of the piano and filled the hall. I stood a few feet away with my jaw hanging down to my chest. It was like being next to the amplifiers at a rock show. The music penetrated my whole body. I requested "Flight of the Bumblebee." Instead, he played an original composition with an equivalent tempo and intensity. I was stunned by the performance. I had never experienced talent such as this at such close range.

A few days later Diego invited me to visit the family ranch about 40 minutes outside of Cali. He made arrangements with a friend who owned a car to drive us to the ranch. Consistent with Diego's negative notions about his countrymen (country-woman in this case) she cancelled at the last minute. From his mother's home we sought other transportation arrangements. That's when I found out that his brother, in the not so distant past, had been kidnapped from the ranch and held for ransom! Though he was released without physical harm, he had not been the same since. I politely bowed out of that little excursion.

Okay, so we have met Luis and Diego. You are probably thinking, Mark, what about the women? Yes, the women of Cali were beautiful, but not as approachable as I had imagined they would be. Many of them seemed very formal in their manner, slightly aloof towards me as an outsider, but still gorgeous. The typical beauty in Cali had jet-black hair with a pale complexion and a slender figure with disproportionately large breasts. I asked a cab driver if the beautiful breasts were genetic, or if there was something in the water. "It's the *chontaduro!*" he said with a big belly laugh, referring to the starchy fruit of the local palm trees.

One woman in Cali captured my heart momentarily. Tisa worked at the front desk of my hotel. Though only in her early twenties, she had the composure and professionalism of a concierge at a five-star hotel. She was making arrangements for me to visit another hotel to use their swimming pool. The hotels had an agreement for sharing facilities. She focused on the details of my visit so meticulously and personally that it felt like an angel was taking care of me. Was she flirting with me, or just doing her job? Either way, I was amazed and delighted.

Over the next few days, I chatted with her whenever I could, always hoping she would be on duty whenever I passed the front desk. She was in school, working at the hotel, and taking additional courses in hotel management through her employer. I wanted to spend some time with her away from the hotel, but her schedule was not easy to rearrange. I finally got together with her and some of her friends after work. One of her gang from the hotel had a car and we visited a couple of clubs. It was a weeknight and not much was happening, so we didn't stay out late. After that we talked on the phone frequently, me in my room and her at the front desk.

Though I had a flight to Cartagena, I really wanted to get to know Tisa better. Her sweetness had mesmerized me. I asked if she would come with me to Cartagena. On such short notice, she had too many commitments. A cab was on its way to pick me up for the airport. I didn't want to leave without her. "It's okay," she said. "Don't miss your flight! Call or e-mail me when you get there." We had never so much as held hands, yet I felt an amazingly strong pull towards her. I got on the plane to Cartagena, in spite of my feelings. As strong as they were, those feelings were soon to be completely overshadowed.

Cartagena is an international resort destination and port town with a rich history. On the coast of the Caribbean, it has a legacy of explorers, pirates, silver and gold. The historic Colonial city is surrounded by 20-foot thick walls. I found a reasonably priced hotel on the beach in a row of other high-rise hotels. Late in the day, I wandered barefoot along the beach as the sun set in the haze over the ocean.

After dinner in a café near the beach, I met Enrique, a 30-something dark-skinned black man with a friendly, round face. He had a cane and a permanent limp from an injury to his ankle. There was a lively personality trapped in a body that couldn't quite keep up. Walking along the promenade, he would break a sweat and have to take a breather every forty or fifty yards.

He worked as a tour guide selling various packages and tours along the beach. After chatting for awhile in the warm night air, he had a casual proposal for me. He offered to be my guide and guard for the evening in exchange for a couple of drinks along the way, plus a tip of my choosing at the end of the night. I accepted his proposal. I would get more than I had bargained for.

After visiting a few clubs along the beach, we caught a cab to a nightclub district a few miles away. It was predominantly a local crowd but I was not the only tourist. At the second club we visited, Enrique knew several of the staff. It made for friendly and easy introductions. The music was a combination of techno and salsa with Shakira thrown in fairly regularly. She is, after all, *una Colombiana*! We made the rounds, chatting with several different groups of partiers.

Then, all at once, everything shifted. It didn't stop; just swerved to the left. That's when Enrique introduced me to Yolanda. Her gorgeous smile drew me in. For the next two hours, eye contact between us was continuous. I felt an energy from her that just lit me up, turned me on, and more than anything else, made me smile from ear to ear! When she smiled, I smiled. It was totally out of my control.

Yolanda is about 5'6" with a slender but curvy figure. Her waist was not much bigger than a number two pencil. Her medium-length brown hair was about as dark as her complexion. Her friends called her, *"La Negrita"* (the little black one) because of her skin.

Enrique faded into the background like any good buddy would do. He checked in with us once in awhile, but mostly grinned at me from a distance, knowing I was doing just fine without him. Enrique was enjoying himself with his pals. After a number of stolen kisses on the dance floor, Yolanda and I exchanged numbers and made plans to get together the next night.

Outside the club we kissed goodnight as her cackling friends waited for her in their car. Enrique hailed a cab for our ride back to the beach. He said he fully expected to be the best man when we got married. "There was definitely something happening between you two," he said in Spanish. If it happened, it would be the second introduction he had made that led to a wedding.

The next night we had a romantic dinner inside the walled colonial city. There were blocks of restaurants and outdoor cafés, many with live music. After dinner we rode in an antique open-air, horse-drawn buggy. The walled city was impeccably restored like a theme park except it was real. We clicked along historic cobblestone streets not much wider than the buggy itself. The colonial architecture was stunning, though I wasn't paying much attention to anything outside of the buggy. We were carried out and around the perimeter of the thick walls and down along the beach toward my hotel. After the ride, we danced at some clubs near the hotel. We made it to the balcony of my room, seventeen stories above the beach. From one side of the balcony we could see the twinkling lights of other high-rise hotels with the walled city off in the distance. I got photos of Yolanda with the glittering backdrop behind and below her. It became obvious that I was going to have a guest for the night.

We wouldn't leave each other's sight for the next forty hours. The next day we went on a boat tour. We stopped to buy her a swimsuit on the way to the dock. She had never been on such a tour, nor visited any of the islands off the coast. It was a treat for both of us. But, then again, we would have enjoyed a tour of a soap factory as long as we were together. The sun, the sand and the water were all the more paradisiacal under the circumstances. Several people on the tour asked if we were on our honeymoon. It felt like it.

With our arms around each other, everything felt right and there was no need for words. Still, we talked a great deal. She spoke of the village of Monteria in the mountains, where, on a small ranch, she was raised by her grandparents. Her mother had died when she was very young. She had a good relationship with her father, although he did not play the major role in her upbringing after her mother passed away.

The boat tour lasted the whole day and we were delivered back to my hotel shortly before dark. We were secluded in the room until my flight early the next afternoon. She had a little experience with computers but had never done any e-mail. On the way to the airport, we stopped at an Internet café where I taught her how to do e-mail and we set up an account for her on Yahoo! I thought if we could e-mail, there might be a chance we could see each other again. There in the Internet café, her eyes lit up as we exchanged our very first online messages, even though we were only six inches apart.

Our goodbye at the airport did not seem sad so much as abrupt. We didn't really have time to think about being sad. It was a powerful whirlwind that ended as quickly as it started. Soon, I was on the plane and she was in a cab. My head was still spinning and I thought, "What the heck just happened to me?" It certainly felt like something I wanted to feel on a permanent basis. We had talked only briefly about the possibility of more time together. It was most definitely on my mind. Had I had been driving, I certainly would have extended my stay.

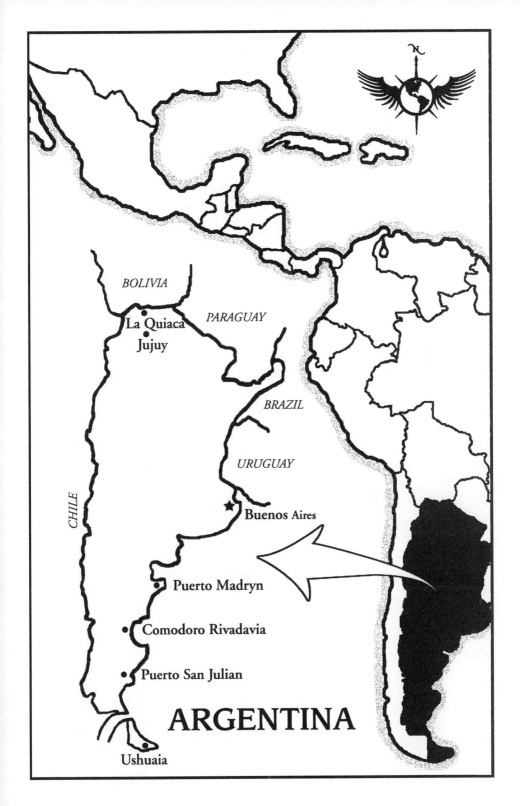

BOLIVIA

La Quiaca

Jujuy

PARAGUAY

BRAZIL

URUGUAY

CHILE

Buenos Aires

Puerto Madryn

Comodoro Rivadavia

Puerto San Julian

ARGENTINA

Ushuaia

I had the next leg of my journey well defined in my mind. I wanted to go directly from La Paz to Buenos Aires. Though my direction was clear, my head was not. In the past I had always looked forward to my solitude on the road. Even when I was saying goodbye to people I had grown to care about, a part of me always looked forward to some personal peace and quiet. I had enjoyed my time with Scott, Pancho, Patty and last, and certainly not least, Yolanda. I was due for some alone time and felt I should be looking forward to it. However, this time I was dreading it as never before.

Over the course of a few days, I said my goodbyes to a few friends, handled maintenance and repairs on Blanco Billy, and said farewell to La Paz. I had many miles of bumpy dirt road to get to the border of Bolivia, and a total of eight long days to Buenos Aires. Knowing exactly how bumpy from previous experience only added to the feeling of dread.

I was surprised by an urge to get the trip over with. To do what I had set out to do and be done with it. Without a clue as to what I would do afterwards, I wanted it behind me. That made no sense to me because I had been having an absolute blast with my recent companions. I was looking forward to visiting my friend Joel, my co-pilot back in Costa Rica, who now lived in Buenos Aires. After that, I would be back on the lonely road again from Buenos Aires to Tierra Del Fuego. I imagined that segment to be even longer and lonelier.

In Bolivia, the bumps and dust were as bad as I expected them to be, perhaps worse. It seemed to take a toll on Blanco Billy as well. Certain stretches of road were a washboard surface of proportions hard to exaggerate. You could either go less than 20 miles per hour to try and avoid being thrown out of your seat, or do better than 45 and try to ride along the tops of the bumps. If you did the latter, tires were only touching ground 25% of the time— far less than ideal for negotiating curves and drop-offs. Vibration hardly describes the concentrated, violent shaking. I feared that car parts would be flying in all directions, and then they actually did. Three different hood-latches came loose and the hood flew up in my face and fractured the windshield. I had just replaced the windshield from the chain incident, and now this! The cracks were not in a visually significant area so I carried on with the scar. Then, to top it off, the muffler fell off. For several hundred miles it rode in the backseat as a passenger (it was well-mannered and didn't seem to mind the noise).

When I wasn't straining to hang on to the steering wheel, my mind did some traveling of its own. Thinking of Yolanda back in Cartagena, I fantasized quite freely (no, not that, I had both hands on the wheel). What if she had joined me on the plane? I could be sneaking her across borders hidden in the back of Blanco Billy. The secret agent aspect of the fantasy was a bit excessive since she had a passport and could cross most borders easily and legally.

Soon the fantasy girlfriend I had written about in the mountains of Costa Rica merged with Yolanda in the never-never land of my head. All of the exotic locales of my trip and a myriad of experiences were getting jumbled around like a box of crackers. Havana, Cartagena, mountains, jungles, tropical islands and the wild and wonderful cast of characters I had met along the way were combining into the plot. They all settled into their places in the novel I had begun way back in Costa Rica. The creative process occurred of its own volition over a couple of days. I just watched as the crackers magically and delightfully settled into a dense mass in the bottom third of the box. It took my mind off of being alone.

I made it back to the town of Tupiza, where I had taken the Butch and Sundance horseback ride with Scott. Close to the border of Argentina, I was still a long way from getting across. Blanco Billy needed attention, so I went back to the mechanic who had taken good care of me previously. In addition to the laundry-list of problems, part of the suspension had cracked. A replacement part was not available, so the mechanic had to modify a part by cutting and welding it to make it fit.

Blanco Billy was back in one piece by mid-afternoon of my third day in Tupiza. I wanted to hit the road, but I would arrive at the border late in the day, once again violating one of my traveling commandments. A young man working at the hotel had worked previously as a *tramitadore* at the border. He volunteered to ride with me to the border, help me with my papers, then take the bus back to Tupiza in exchange for lunch, return bus fare and a tip. It worked like a charm. I had some company and was across the border before dark.

I broke another traveling commandment: Thou shalt not drive after dark. The border town of La Quiaca was tiny, with little redeeming social value. The Argentine highway was smooth as glass. It was paradise, a driving dream after all of the bumps in Bolivia. Shortly after midnight, I arrived safely in the city of Jujuy.

MARK'S
ADVENTURE ALERT

Location: Jujuy, Argentina

Subject: Hoo Hoooey

"The first condition of understanding a foreign country is to smell it."

T.S. Elliot

I smelled burning rubber my first morning in Argentina. Piles of tires burning in the street. I approached the scene with trepidation. I wanted to get up close for some photos. What was this all about? It wasn't violent. It seemed like a casual gathering. Almost friendly.

I got some photos. No one paid much attention to me. I relaxed a little bit and started asking questions. I talked to the fire tender. He had a truck full of old tires. When one of the three blazes got low, he would toss another on the fire. I watched the apparent leader of the group get interview by Channel 2, the local TV station.

It was about Argentina's current financial crisis. Everyone is broke. The protest was organized by a local political group trying to get their message heard. The fires were in the middle of an intersection. Police had closed the streets on all four sides, about a block away on each side. It seemed to be business as usual, nobody getting too excited.

On the way back to my hotel I made a new friend, Sylvana. She was sitting in front of her shop enjoying the morning sun and a cup of mate. With a bright green iguana on her shoulder she was obviously not shy nor avoiding attention. Moments later I met her sister Valerie and her sister's five-year-old daughter. Very soon I felt like I was immersed into daily life on the streets of Jujuy, being introduced to all of their friends and customers as if I was part of the family.

Valerie was only slightly more businesslike than Sylvana. She seemed to be the managing partner, if you could call her that. An enjoyable lifestyle seemed to take precedence over maximizing profit. It was very refreshing. Valerie and I spent time talking about poetry and publishing. She is a published author of three books of poetry and a teacher at a nearby college. The two sisters, the daughter and a cousin took me out to lunch and on a tour of Jujuy. It was delightful. I was part of the family after just a few hours. It was a quick dunk into a very warm and friendly culture. And great way to start my adventures in Argentina.

But back to the title of this entry.…I think the main reason I stopped in this town in the first place was because of the name. I had met people in Bolivia who were from Jujuy. I just loved the sound of the name. But how could you take yourself seriously if you are from here? "Hi. My name is Mark, I'm from HOO HOOOEY." I really love to say it. And I say it with the enthusiasm of an optimistic owl: WHOO WHOOOEEY!!

Perhaps I've spent a little too much time alone on the road.

MARK'S
ADVENTURE ALERT

Location: Buenos Aires, Argentina

Subject: Long Way From Bolivia

From Bolivia to Buenos Aires. Now there's some contrast for ya. From least developed to most sophisticated. From a bumpy dirt road to Avenida Nueve de Julio, the widest street in the world— eighteen lanes! Smooth pavement. Lane lines. Drivers who actually use their high beams courteously. Civilization, what a pleasure! One thing did seem out of character for the Argentine drivers: they are ruthless about tailgating and passing. I was startled on several occasions, doing 50 miles an hour, looking up in my rear-view mirror, and seeing someone staring back at me, so close I could count nose hairs, literally inches between bumpers.

I was in awe of another highway scene that unfolded before my eyes. On a two-lane highway four tiny compact cars were bunched up tightly behind a semi. I was #5 hanging back in amazement and for my safety. All four were rapidly bobbing and weaving into the oncoming lane looking for their opportunity to pass. They were so close together and darting so quickly it looked like a video game come to life! When the chance arrived, all four went for it at once, two of them effectively drag racing head to head in the oncoming lane.

It took two more days on the highway from Jujuy to get to Buenos Aires. It was every thing I had heard. The Paris of South America. Having never been to Paris I would personally call it a cross between San Francisco and New York City. It's huge. It's beautiful. It stays up all night. You can't buy a bad meal there.

In some ways my time in Buenos Aires did not seem like part of my trip. An open-ended stay in a downtown luxury apartment does not quite qualify as adventure. However, there was the adventure into the culture of *los Porteños*, the residents of Buenos Aires. I took some private Spanish classes. But wait! I can hear the *Porteños* correcting me already. They don't speak Spanish, they speak *Castellano* (Castillian). Of course it is Spanish, but it is very different than the rest of Latin America. It took awhile for my ear to catch on. They use a "zh" sound like in Dr. Zhivago, in just about every sentence. "Yo me llamo," becomes, "Zho me zhamo." Zheesh! It changes the texture of the language completely. I thought I was hearing Portuguese or Italian when I first arrived. To add to the challenge, different forms of grammar are used as well.

MARK'S ADVENTURE ALERT

Location: Buenos Aires, Argentina

Subject: Living Large

It doesn't take much to live large here. Since the currency was devalued, just having dollars enables you to have a nice standard of living. You get three times more bang for your buck than you did in 2001. And they do know how to live here. With a long European tradition of dining out and great ingredients (especially if beef is your thing) you simply can't go wrong in restaurants here. I am used to cheap food in Latin America, but not 5-star cuisine. My $10 dinner last night included an excellent cut of beef, wine, dessert, style, service, and ambiance. Makes you wish you were hungry enough to do it all over again. (I think I'm starting to get the binge and purge rationale.)

The residents here (they call themselves *Porteños*) love their cafés. In some neighborhoods there is one on every corner. Elegant little places that are busy all day long. Then there are the massive ones with huge banks of pastries on display. Your beverage is always served backed by a small glass of soda water plus a croissant or sample-sized pastry. Starbucks has not arrived in Buenos Aires yet. Perhaps for good reason. Why would you grab a cup to go when you could linger and enjoy? Starbucks coffee to go? Not on your life! McDonald's has adapted successfully to the *Porteños* way of life. McCafés seem to do the trick here. And then there is McDelivery. Big Mac, fries, and a Coke to your door for $2.50. On the phone they ask what denomination of peso you will be using and your change is ready in an envelope when they bring your meal. But McDonald's isn't the only one to deliver. In Recoleta, my adopted neighborhood, everyone delivers! Cafés, restaurants, groceries, even the local version of Sam's Club and Costco. Doggie-Day-Care even picks up and delivers. Exercise and a social life for your pooch, five hours each day for 80 cents!

Joel, my pal and host here, earns California dollars as a Bay area accountant, but spends money and three-quarters of his time here. He's got it dialed in. He earns big-city bucks but only spends a pittance here in pesos. For what he pays for his luxury apartment here, he could not afford a hovel in San Francisco. He does his work online and returns to the States only for tax deadlines. This lifestyle is not for everyone, but it has its advantages. He has a surrogate mother figure in the form of a warm and caring maid. Twice a week she cooks and cleans for him. He never needs to leave the house except for fun and Spanish lessons. And his new Venezuelan girlfriend may see to it that he never returns to any semblance of his former life in the States. I wish him well and appreciate the hospitality!

I am happy to have contributed to Joel's technology for living here. I brought an Internet based phone system (VoIP) with me that I will be donating to his cause. I got it for myself to see if it would work for me on the road. But it is so perfect for his situation that I am going to leave it with him. It's simply a regular phone connected to small box that's connected to the Internet. With it you can call anywhere in the States or Canada for free ($25 monthly fee). But the best part is that people in the States can call you as if you were in the States! You choose your own area code. Think about that for a moment! Joel's clients in San Francisco can call a local phone number and reach him as if he were down the street—when, unbeknownst to the caller, he is several thousand miles away, <u>living large!!</u>

MARK'S
ADVENTURE ALERT

Location: Buenos Aires, Argentina

Subject: Crying For Argentina

I had some time to wander the streets and read up on the history of Buenos Aires. Like any big city is has its down side. Intertwined with its financial floundering is some history that is much, much sadder. And the remnants of this chapter are very creepy. As you sit in a café you can't help but wonder who could possibly be sitting on your right and conversely (and perversely) who could be sitting on your left.

I am referring to Argentina's Dirty War of the late '70s. It was the, "ethnic cleansing" of the reigning regime. It was political rather than ethnic, but you get the point. Between 20,000 and 30,000 people were "disappeared." Many were tortured; many were drugged and dumped from airplanes into the sea while still alive. Pregnant mothers were abducted and murdered after giving birth. The babies were then adopted by the perpetrators. Think about the consequences of an 18-year-old discovering his diabolical family history.

Some of the architects of the cleansing campaign were convicted then later PARDONED! All of the underlings who carried out the deadly details were never tried based on the fact that they were only following orders. To this day, the murderers walk the same streets of Buenos Aires as the families of their victims!! Perhaps on my right, maybe on my left.…

I am staying at the apartment of a friend in the Recoleta District in Buenos Aires. It is the ritziest neighborhood in town. It is also the home of the ritziest cemetery in all of Argentina. This is very important to Argentineans. I have a little cemetery fetish. I like to wander around and take pictures. Argentineans on the other hand, are full-scale perverted about them. The eternal home of your corpse is much more important than where you rest your weary bones in life. Recoleta Cemetery is a necropolis with maps and addresses. The streets are lined with miniature cathedrals. The sculptures decorating the crypts are immense and all of museum quality. You can peer into windows of crypt/cathedrals to see the coffins of the country's forefathers and wealthy elite.

The only specific site I wanted to visit was that of Eva

"Evita" Peron. This leads us to that part of her history that was not covered in the Broadway Musical— her afterlife adventures. You see, she did quite a bit of traveling after her death. An opposing political party eventually took power and did not want her gravesite becoming a shrine. They took the body into hiding. She was then kidnapped by her supporters and housed discretely in various attics throughout the city. She was later shipped secretly overseas and buried in Rome.

Eventually she made another trans-Atlantic journey back to Buenos Aires and was finally laid to rest in Ritzy Recoleta, much to the chagrin of the wealthy elite and her political enemies. In life Evita rallied for the poor and very hard against the rich. They were not in the least bit fond of her and it was the ultimate insult for her to be resting among their ancestors.

I delved much deeper into the Dirty War, only to be left with more questions than answers. Imagine living in Argentina at that time. A white Ford Falcon pulls up containing two guys in dark suits and dark glasses. The secret police hit men. Someone was about to disappear. They picked up people who were anti-government such as student dissidents, uncooperative journalists, or anyone opposed to the current régime. They would never be seen again. To this day, the victims are called *los desaparecidos*, the "disappeareds." An estimated 30,000 people were tortured and murdered. How could the sophisticated and educated citizens of Argentina let this happen? How could those, "just following orders," actually follow those orders?

If you remove the distinctions of citizenship and national borders, it's not that much different than what is happening now in Guantanamo Bay. Citizens of other nations are "disappeared" indefinitely without trial, kept 90-miles offshore. Their rights under the Geneva Convention, not to mention basic civil and human rights, are being trampled. At first I thought the comparison was a stretch, but the more I learned, the more valid it seemed.

The Argentine perspective on U.S. politics was striking. The U.S. is perceived as a bully big brother who may be capable of loving, but could also beat the crap out of you. To them, becoming crapless seemed like the more likely scenario. President Bush is viewed in their mainstream media as a religious nut job. I spoke to educated people who compared Bush to Hitler without a hint of sarcasm. From outside of the U.S., a preemptive attack does not look much different than terrorism.

The perspective I gained from being outside of the country for so long opened my eyes and gave me a newfound political awareness. I hate to think about how oblivious I was before I started my journey. Yet, I value my country more than I ever did in spite of the troubles I now perceive.

After Buenos Aires, I became a man on fire, devouring everything I could find about the politics and the history of my country. I watched numerous documentaries and learned the details behind the headlines I had only scanned in the past. The Trials of Henry Kissinger was perhaps the most eye opening. I was shocked by Kissinger's role in Indonesia. Using American weapons, the Indonesians slaughtered tens of thousands of East Timorese. Kissinger and President Ford were in a meeting with President Sahuarto the day before the slaughter began. In a transcript from the meeting, Kissinger stated, "It is important that whatever you do succeeds quickly. We would be able to influence the reaction in America if whatever happens, happens after we return."

His behind-the-scenes actions in the illegal bombing of Cambodia were equally disturbing. The destruction in the wake of the bombing left a void in power that allowed the rise of Pol Pot, the dictator responsible for the death of millions of Cambodians. Closer to home in South America, Kissinger's role in Chile led to a coup of democratically elected President Allende. Augusto Pinochet, the U.S.-backed dictator, replaced Allende with his brutal regime which lasted 15 years and included the slaughter of over 3,000 citizens. More recently, President Bush tried to appoint Kissinger as the head of the 9/11 Commission (I smell a rat!) until public outcry and demand for disclosure derailed the idea.

A book I mentioned previously, Confessions of an Economic Hitman by John Perkins, helped to tie together everything I had seen and learned on my way through Latin America by clarifying the economics behind U.S. foreign policy. The pattern was all too clear in so many different countries. First, there was economic intervention. If that wasn't successful then came covert operations (the CIA). Finally, if those failed, military action ensued (Panama and Iraq recently). Though not so clear to the American public, Latin Americans know that our actions are not about justice or democracy but the best interest of the, "corporatocracy."

Recently, I heard Jennifer Harbury, an attorney and human-rights activist, speak about the disappearance, torture and death of her husband in Guatemala. A Guatemalan, he made the "mistake" of being on the wrong side of the political fence. For years it was her obsession to find out what had happened to her husband. Her hunger strikes in D.C. eventually led to the release of information from the State Department and the U.S. Embassy in Guatemala. She did extensive research in Guatemala and other parts of Latin America. She interviewed survivors of the camp where her husband had been to learn about CIA involvement in Latin American torture chambers. Her findings made it clear to me that the techniques at

Abu Ghraib are not isolated. According to survivors of the camps, the hood and postures in the iconic Abu Ghraib photos were part of the protocol back then.

Within the context of the Patriot Act, Homeland Securities Act and the government eavesdropping without a warrant, it is not difficult to see how anyone who disagrees with the current regime could be deemed a traitor and a terrorist. The Pentagon's database, created ostensibly for homeland security, contains 260 peace activists. It is not a stretch to envision an environmental activist being deemed an eco-terrorist and thereby being designated as an enemy combatant liable to be legally "disappeared" under the terms of the Patriot Act.

At first I didn't know what to do with my newfound knowledge. Over the course of my trip, I had gone from apathy to activism, and began to write and speak about what I had learned. As much as I might have wanted to, I couldn't go back to sleep. In spite of everything, I still value my U.S. citizenship. I believe that our Constitution and Bill of Rights are the best things we have going for us and must be honored and protected. Currently, our government is not representing the best interests of its people. We are steadily descending into a fascist state. If the public does not wake up, there will come a time when it will be too late.

With Joel having so much fun with his Venezuelan sweetheart, I couldn't help but think about Yolanda and our time together in Cartagena. We had been in regular contact by e-mail and VoIP phone. Gradually, a plan began to emerge. I thought about flying back for another visit. Yolanda invited me to visit her hometown village of Monteria. It was appealing but I didn't know how safe I would be there. Cheap vacation packages were available from Buenos Aires to the San Andreas Islands, a popular vacation destination in the Caribbean for Latin Americans. Under the Colombian flag, the islands are actually closer to Panama geographically and far removed from mainland troubles.

However, the romantic adventure theme from my novel outline finally won out. Life imitating art. She could fly to Buenos Aires and we could hit the road south together. "And what exactly are you waiting for?" asked my host Joel with wholehearted encouragement.

So flight arrangements were made and I met her at Ezeiza International Airport a few days later. It had been a couple of months since we had seen each other and I was a bit apprehensive about whether the magic from Cartagena would still be alive between us. She got off of the overnight flight looking sheepish and shy, seemingly as nervous as I was. She was dressed in jeans and tennis shoes and wearing no make-up after spending the night on board. She struck me as much younger than I had remembered. I had a momentary twinge that I was robbing the cradle. After a nap at a hotel in Joel's neighborhood, things warmed up between us. There was room for her at Joel's apartment, but the privacy of a hotel seemed appropriate for our reunion. (Dim the lights, cue romantic music.)

The next two weeks were a pure delight. Yolanda and Joel's girlfriend Dairen hit it off like sisters. They were, in a way, practically neighbors in their respective hometowns, separated by a couple hundred miles, and of course, the border between Colombia and Venezuela. Their relationship was something friendly and familiar in this faraway place. They spent hours together in the kitchen and out shopping. I found a perfect balance, plenty of time with Yolanda, yet enough quiet time for my reading and writing. We did lots of sightseeing. I had already gotten to know the city fairly well and it was fun to see the highlights again through her eyes.

Despite all of the fun we were having, we still needed to make plans for our departure to Tierra del Fuego. I bought a guidebook in Spanish so Yolanda could participate in the plans and decisions along the way. We hit the road for our first destination, Puerto Madryn on the Valdez Peninsula and then had an unscheduled stop shortly thereafter.

MARK'S ADVENTURE ALERT

Location: Puerto Madryn, Argentina

Subject: Sex on the Beach

It's springtime here in South America. Love is in the air. Looks more like domestic abuse, but that's how they do it here. Male elephant seals are four to five times bigger than their female counterparts. It seems the biggest and most brutal bull gets all the cute chicks. One bull elephant seal can have a harem of up to 40 females! About 1100 km south of Buenos Aires is Peninsula Valdez, a nature reserve known for its whale-watching tourism. Timing was not right for me to see the whales.

But as timing would have it, I did get to see penguins and elephant seals during their mating season. And elephant seal sex is indeed a spectacle! If I were on the jury I would certainly not describe what I saw as consensual. It looked more like one partner was going to be killed in the process. A body slam from someone 5 times your size could not possibly be fun. I like it a little rough sometimes, but ZHEESH, this was brutal! The biological urge to find the best partner has got to be pretty strong for 30 to 40 females to get that kind of treatment and still keep coming around. After enough cringing for the tiny female seal, it was time to head down the beach to watch the penguins procreate. Penguin daddies like to take charge too, but they are only slightly larger than their mates so their aggression did not seem to be life threatening for anyone involved. Just nature taking its course.

MARK'S ADVENTURE ALERT

Location: Comodoro Rivadavia, Argentina

Subject: Stranded in Comodoro

I spent a week waiting in Comodoro for a box. And it was certainly not in Argentina's most picturesque community. No, no, far from it. I was stuck in Podunk-Industrial-Wasteland, East-BumFuck-Oversized-Truck-Stop, Might-as-well-be-called-Armpit-Argentina.

My humble apologies to all of the friendly residents of Comodoro Rivadavia who treated me so kindly, even on Thanksgiving. They were certainly sweet and helpful people, but they haven't a clue about the wretchedness of their own little town. Okay, I am exaggerating a bit, it's just that I had so much time to ponder these overstatements... if it weren't for my laptop and the small selection of DVD rentals available here my embellishments would have been even greater.

And how did I end up here for a week? And what was in the box? I had some work done on Blanco Billy (my Toyota Land Cruiser) at my last stop in Puerto Madryn. Some much needed bodywork and some work on the engine. It was still running a little rough afterward. The mechanic claimed I still needed a new distributor cap, a part not available in that small town.

In the next big city, that was my assignment, to find a distributor cap— then everything would be tip-top. So he thought. The problem was not the distributor cap but rather a broken seal on the head gasket. It was causing the roughness, and eventually some more serious symptoms.

I sputtered into Comodoro Rivadavia on Thursday evening. My new mechanic diagnosed the problem and said it would be ready in two days... until he realized it was Friday. Then he informed me that no one works weekends in Argentina. "But Monday you'll be ready to go!!" Monday came, but I didn't go. No replacement gaskets in town. One would have to come from Buenos Aires. Tuesday I would learn that there are none in Buenos Aires. One will have to be *hecho en casa*, custom-made for Blanco Billy. How long? Coupla days?

I conferred with some stateside sources. A custom-made job would be a bit iffy and certainly not as secure as factory made. Factory-made parts are readily available in the states and not expensive. FedEx? Coupla days? I conferred with my

```
local guy (whose name, I now realize, I never learned.) He
agreed that factory made was a much better option. FEDEX DON'T
FAIL ME NOW! I'd had some bad luck with DHL while trying to
procure some much-needed computer equipment. It got stuck in
customs and no one could tell me where it was. Una pesadilla,
(a nightmare, one of my many new words learned watching
subtitled DVDs, this word from the movie, Vanilla Sky— more
about that later.)
    My prized package was scheduled to arrive Friday evening at
the latest, entitling me to one more delightful weekend in
cozy Comodoro. Oh well, relax and grab a couple more DVDs and
learn some more new vocabulary. BUT NO! FedEx comes through
Thursday afternoon! Yee Haa! (Thanksgiving, and yes, I am
thankful! Thankful that Thanksgiving isn't observed here by
anyone other than me!) My no-name mechanic comes through too!!
Ready to go Friday, midday! YESSSS!! So long Comodoro... it's
been swell but... GOTTA GO!!!
```

Well, that light-hearted journal entry told only part of the Comodoro story, the tip of the iceberg as it were. Now I am going to tell you the underwater portion, the part not visible but lurking ominously below. The part that was too raw to even make it into my private journal. You may have noticed the lack of any reference to Yolanda in the previous Adventure Alerts. I had not gone public about my sweetheart traveling companion. I did not write about what was going on between us, nor inside the dark depths of my psyche. Much too intense and personal then, the passage of time has made it easier to talk about. Bronco Billy had broken down and so had our relationship.

Our hotel room in Comodoro had no windows and no TV. It was disturbing to wake up and not know whether it was midnight or 7:00 a.m., in a place of physical and psychological limbo. Dark indeed, we started calling our room *La Cueva*, The Cave. Yolanda earned the title *La Reina de la Cueva*, The Queen of the Cave. Although the nicknames were in jest on one level, the darkness that had crept into our relationship was real.

Tension had been building between us ever since we had hit the road from Buenos Aires. Our first moments together in Cartagena had been the closest thing I had ever come to love at first sight. Now I felt like I was a miserable and cruel bastard stringing her along selfishly, strictly for my own gratification. What had happened between then and now?

Buenos Aires had been a continuation of the Cartagena honeymoon. I was treating her like my princess and all was glorious. The royal treatment continued as we began our journey south and ventured out of the big city. She rode like royalty in the passenger seat of Blanco Billy, never lifting a finger as I took care of all of her needs. At stops for gas and snacks I handled absolutely everything, from auto maintenance and goodies for the road, to reviewing maps and the guidebook.

It really hit me after one such stop a week or so into the trip. We pulled out of a rest area where I had bought sandwiches, drinks and snacks. It was past lunchtime and I was famished after driving since early morning. Our lunch was in a bag on Yolanda's lap. Driving down the highway, I asked if I could have my sandwich. In response to my request, or I should say, ignoring my request, she reached into the bag, got her sandwich, unwrapped it and ate it. I was incredulous, thinking, "How did I get into this?" There are two of us on this trip, one of them working a lot harder than the other. Was she oblivious to my needs while I was spending all of my energy catering to hers? Could she possibly not notice? Or did she just not care? Did my doting on her from the beginning cause this? Was this her personality? Was it a male/female dynamic from her culture? My trip had gone from all about me to all about her, and she seemed to expect it and not appreciate it in the least. She certainly didn't express any appreciation.

After all day on the road, when we arrived at a hotel, Yolanda would not voluntarily help to check in or unload. Instead, she would plop down on the bed to watch her *novelas* on TV. *Novelas* are the equivalent of daytime soaps in the U.S., but air during evening primetime in much of Latin America. After a long day of driving, it was the last thing I wanted to do. She was not the least bit interested in exploring a new town or socializing at a restaurant. Her typical request was pizza delivered to the room. Our differences were becoming blatantly obvious.

In hindsight, and in her defense, there were personal and environmental factors affecting her that I took for granted. In spite of having a passport, she had never been out of her country, or even very far from Cartagena and Monteria. It had been the first plane ride of her life. She had never experienced weather this cold before and was not accustomed to the different rhythm of the sun. Living so close to the equator, sunrise and sunset happen almost the same time every day, year in and year out. The further south we got, the more the daylight increased each day. One's internal clock takes a whack on the side of the face, cracking the crystal and leaving a buzzing noise inside. The buzzing energized me, but had the opposite effect on Yolanda. Additionally, my on-the-road lifestyle, which I had consciously chosen and become accustomed to, is certainly not for everyone. Her life had been turned upside down and inside out.

Then there was the sex. Generally speaking, if the sex is good enough, a guy is willing to put up with, or overlook, just about anything. Generalizations about other guys aside, I had been having an incredible time in bed, making bowing down to the princess worthwhile.

This was certainly the case during our honeymoon period. She was as romantically and sexually playful as a little fairy. Her smile hypnotized and swept me away to other worlds. However, after many weeks, I realized that the fairy only took flight when she was drinking. She just could not get there without it. Her Catholic conscience told her that something was wrong with all of our sexy fun. Neither of us wanted to be drinking all of the time. I sadly came to grips with the fact that my love at first sight had not been with her, but her tipsy alter ego. I had fallen in love with a part of her that only appeared under the influence of alcohol.

With that realization, I reckoned that there had to be a better way to gain access to that fun-loving part of her without drinking. This was a bigger challenge than I had anticipated. Try as I might, the concept of having the same kind of fun without the alcohol did not even register for her. I hit a wall trying to communicate the concept in Spanish and get past her cultural and religious belief system.

With the passage of time and the pressure cooker of the confined quarters of Blanco Billy and small hotel rooms, we began to get on each other's nerves as our sexual connection began to lose its luster. The boredom of Comodoro and the difficulty of our relationship was a painful combination. The dark cave of our room was a metaphor for our relationship. I had reached a dark place in my heart, coming face-to-face with aspects of myself that were not so pretty.

During the period of darkness and disconnection in Comodoro, my mind wandered ahead to the end of the journey. I was confused and just wasn't excited about the completion of my mission. About to accomplish a huge goal with a gorgeous girl at my side, and I am still whining and despondent? The question, "Why am I doing this?" was leading to a new question, "What comes next?" I had ideas about driving back and going all the way north to Alaska. I also thought about driving Blanco Billy into the ocean for dramatic effect.

But these were only ideas; nothing had taken hold inside of me for my post-trip life. All I could see or feel was black, the darkness of nothing, trapped in my own personal cave. My former identity as dentist no longer existed. Who was I? An adventurer? My adventure was almost over. A boyfriend? That seemed shaky at best. Something happened late one night inside The Cave that brought it all to a head.

The only light inside The Cave was the electronic glow of my laptop's screen as we watched porno DVDs rented from a local shop. Quite coy at first, I wasn't sure whether they were new to her or she was feigning innocence. One of the non-porno DVDs we rented was Vanilla Sky with Tom Cruise, Penelope Cruz and Cameron

Diaz. The movie, an intense psychological drama with multi-layered realities, makes you wonder what is really going on. I had seen it before, so for Yolanda's convenience, we watched it in Spanish with English subtitles. I wasn't paying much attention to the language. I was relating to the Tom Cruise character in a way that scared me to death.

Yolanda fell asleep midway, but I was wide-awake, my eyes open (in fact *Abre Los Ojos*, Open Your Eyes, was the title of the original Mexican version). I restarted the movie in English. I watched in horror, thinking that I was the callous, self-centered, eventually psychotic character played by Cruise. I felt like I was suffering my own psychotic episode. I was relating very closely to his egocentric treatment of girlfriends and others in his life. It was as if I were Ebenezer Scrooge in <u>A Christmas Carol</u> and the movie was my ghost of Christmas future revealing what life would become if I continued in my uncaring ways.

My head had certainly not been in a clear and upbeat place before the movie. The experience pushed me down further into my own dark labyrinth. What were my real intentions with Yolanda? Was she just a plaything that I would tire of and toss aside? Was she just a bit of research for my writing? The movie made me question myself and I wasn't liking the answers.

What had happened to the Mark that was part of the ecstatic, loving couple? That light had dimmed and was in danger of being extinguished completely. Were we headed for a total meltdown? Our relationship, our trip, the final leg of my adventure, could any of it be salvaged? I was uncertain.

It was sometime after 3:00 a.m. Yolanda slept soundly as I tossed and turned anxiously in a painful state of disconnection. It seemed like an eternity as I sweated in agitation. I felt myself sinking with each passing moment. Something inside of me, something distinct from the darkness that was drowning me, told me to reach out and connect with her.

She was sleeping with her back toward me. I reached over to grasp her shoulder, like it was a life preserver. She turned toward me in confusion and concern for me. We embraced as I broke down in tears. Her tears were not far behind. I apologized profusely, babbling as our lips and tears intermingled, but the words didn't really matter. In the wee hours of the morning, we had reconnected.

I reflected on the notion that at any moment there is the possibility to begin again, completely anew. This instant, perhaps more than most, certainly qualified as "any moment." I knew I could not take her for granted nor let her fall into the category of a thing or possession. However, I knew I had to start taking care of myself and communicating my needs to her. What a relief! I knew there were challenges and work ahead, but at least it was out on the table. A meltdown had been averted. My honeymoon fantasy was giving way to something more genuine—real life.

The next day, as our reconnection process continued on many levels, the long-awaited head gasket finally arrived from Tucson via FedEx. Like magic, we were released from our Comodoro detention. We came out of The Cave and into the light.

We had escaped from Comodoro. Driving out of the town and only five minutes down the coast, we were in another world. The highway weaved its way between green pastures dotted with sheep and rocky crags overlooking the expanse of the chilly Atlantic. Waves crashed on the rocks below, creating a white spray that contrasted with the intense, deep blue-green water. The dirty, industrial gray and our seven-day detention were behind us. The sun, the water and the new breakthrough in our relationship had created a brand new world for us. We were both physically and mentally elated to be on the road again.

Puerto Julian was only 260 miles from Comodoro, but the differences between them could not be more dramatic. It was tiny, almost a village rather than a town. From a truck stop on the highway, only one main road led straight to the beach. There were only a few side streets off the main road and a handful of businesses near the water. That was it.

My pen cast a long shadow across the page of my journal notebook as the clock passed 8:00 p.m. The closer we traveled towards the South Pole, the longer the days became. Sitting in the restaurant of our new hotel after hours, I was alone, but not lonely. I was right where I needed to be. Yolanda was upstairs in our hotel room in front of the TV, exactly where she wanted to be. Some private time away from each other, something we had not had since Buenos Aires, made all the difference in the quality of our time together.

Penguins and dolphins were the draw for tourists who visited the picturesque beach town. I had heard about their distinctive black-and-white dolphins and wanted to check them out. However, it was off-season and the hotels and restaurants were practically deserted. Serene and spooky, Puerto Julian felt like a ghost town, though the ocean made it feel very alive.

The only tour company operating needed a minimum of six passengers for a boat tour. It was uncertain whether we would get out to see the penguins and dolphins since other tourists were noticeably absent. We could have paid the equivalent of six passengers for a private tour, but decided to hold out for more tourists. After our depressing stint in Comodoro it was paradise. We could deal with a couple of days at the beach. We got a call the next day saying there would be a tour early the following morning. It was worth the wait.

MARK'S ADVENTURE ALERT

Location: Puerto San Julian, Argentina

Subject: Stalking Flamingos and Killer Dolphins

5:30 AM. I'm alive and awake! I would even go so far as to say alert. Often you will find me smack in the middle of a good night's sleep at this hour. But there is something about the light here that excites me. It energizes me. In this part of the world and at this time of the year you get more than your fair share of sunlight. As I continue south the days will be even more exaggerated. For as long as I can remember, I have always resisted going to bed. I have always liked staying up late, as if I were going to miss out on something by going to sleep. But there is another part of me that wishes I could get up and get going at the crack of dawn. Obviously these two habits do not go hand in hand. But the sunlight here naturally pushes your body in that direction. More light, more living! Feels awesome for now. I imagine that my need for rest will catch up with me. Perhaps if I lived here full time I'd just catch up in the winter when the lighting is reversed?

Back to our title, I am up early and I wanna get some photos of the flamingos I saw along the road yesterday. I head out of my hotel and up the highway that led me to this tiny seaside community. I am barely out of town when I come to the first lake. Actually it is more of a large pond and was by no means pristine. Signs of civilization are all around it, even in it. Lots of power lines and partially submerged cement structures. But there on the edge, partially obscured by some brush, is small group the long-legged freaks. Flamingos, looking quite comfortable surrounded by urban waste. These flamingos are beefier than their purely pink counterparts I had photographed in Bolivia. They had only twinges of pink feathers along with black and white, which equals gray from a distance.

I pull over and cautiously approach the lake, taking photos through the brush. Not knowing when they will get spooked and be gone, I snap photos continuously as I look for a good vantage point. The brush obscures their view of me and allows me to get very close. But my view is obscured also. I have to find a way to get around or through the brush without frightening them. My attempts yesterday taught me that they were very wary of human attention. I have to be very sly. A tree had fallen through the brush and into the lake. If I can get over a fence, through the brush and out onto the fallen tree I will be in perfect position.

Gently over the fence, slowly through the brush, I make it to the tree. I ponder my situation and the downside potential. If I emerge from the brush balancing on the fallen tree, the flamingos will likely see me and, even worse, I could fall in the lake with my camera. The depth? I couldn't really tell, but it was enough that for practical purposes my camera would be a goner. But the upside? Exotic creatures in the early morning glow... gotta go for it! Baby steps. Baby steps. Edging my way into place, trying not to think about the depth of the water beneath me... Holy shit! I'm in position. I raise my camera and CLICK! One shot and they are off to the far side of the lake. But I got the shot!

The next day or so would prove to be a continuation of a photographer's fantasy. A few hours later I was on a tour boat in search of penguins and a particular brand of exotic dolphin. Brand of dolphin? Can you tell I have a science background? Commerson's Dolphin. *Cephalorhynchus commersonii* to be even more specific. They are tiny critters by dolphin standards, only 4-5 feet in length. But they are colored like a miniature killer whale, in stark black and white. It was a good day for dolphin watching. We were very fortunate to see and interact with several groups. They were usually in groups of 4 or 5. Sometimes in pairs. They would swim playfully underneath the boat darting out on either side to blow water and air into the faces of the delighted tourists. What a thrill. They were so playful and lightning fast, like birds underwater— and sometimes above! They were a challenge when it came to taking photos because they were so very quick and unpredictable. They would often leap out of the water, but you never knew quite when or where. I came sooo close to capturing one fully airborne— just a fraction of a second too late.

In between dolphin sightings we stopped at a beach where there was a penguin nesting ground. Magellanic penguins to be exact, also referred to as Donkey penguins for the braying sound they make. We encountered large numbers of them. I must say that the penguins were a bit of a let down after the dolphins, though they did share the same fashion sense in tasteful black and white.

On the highway southbound the next morning I was treated to yet another gift from Mother Nature. Guanaco are llama-type (how is that for scientific?) animals that roam the plains in this part of the Argentina. They are significantly larger than llama and much more athletic. I was thrilled to watch them bound over chest-high fences with the greatest of ease. They are a frequent site along the highway. I stopped to get a shot of a group of three of them. Unlike others I had focused on, these three seemed very interested in me. They scampered to the top of small hill nearby and waited. They looked at me and whistled. Something between a whistle and a screech. I whistled back. I approached a few steps, they retreated the same distance. I backed up, they advanced. They had very defined boundaries, but they were teasing me! Flirting with me! I was Eddie Murphy in Dr. Doolittle. I was in the zone. I thought I had died and gone to photographer's heaven.

Chile/Argentina Border

CHILE   ARGENTINA

Falkland
Islands

Straights of
Magellan

Punta
Delgado

Rio Grande

Tolhuin

Ushuaia

Beagle Channel

TIERRA
DEL FUEGO

(ANTARCTICA)

For two days we motored down the coast with our goal in our sights. Finally we reached Punta Delgada where we would cross by ferry to Tierra del Fuego! The highway ended at a cement ramp on the beach, where a ferry the size of an ocean liner dropped off and picked up cars, buses and trucks. Driving Blanco Billy onto the boat was a dramatic moment, leaving the continent behind. On the other side, we finally set foot on the island of Tierra del Fuego, the land of fire.

What looks like the last bit of the continent on most maps is actually an island split off from the mainland by the Straits of Magellan. The border between Chile and Argentina engages in some irrational behavior in the region and does some incomprehensible zigzagging at the tip of the continent, through Tierra del Fuego and beyond. The city of Ushuaia is in Argentina on the southern edge of the island, bordered to the south by the Beagle Canal. The Chilean border and another smaller island are on the other side of the canal (Confused? Yeah, me too. You do the map.) After the zig through the Beagle Canal, the border does a final zag out into international waters. When it gets to Antarctica (Personally I'd turn around and go home) the border is disputed by Chile and Argentina (while not critical to the story, I thought that one of you might find all this fascinating). The important point is that I needed to pass through the tip of the first zigzag in Chile, to get to Ushuaia back in Argentina, where I would consider myself triumphant. I feel triumphant finally finishing this paragraph.

Halfway through Tierra Del Fuego, we pulled into the town of Rio Grande and stalled at a major intersection. Mechanical issues had been cropping up, forcing us to push-start Blanco Billy for the past couple days. I decided to seek help (mechanical, not mental). I left Yolanda and Blanco Billy in the intersection and ran across to a used car dealership on the corner (for a referral to a mechanic, not another car). Within moments, a small army of guys from the dealership were push-starting me in the direction of a mechanic. The hotel we had been looking for happened to be across the street from the recommended shop. The friendly mechanic chatted with me about his role in the war in the Falklands Islands. The war was fought over territory known to Argentineans as the Malvinas Islands. They lost the war, but romantically they have not given up the fight, still claiming the islands as theirs. We also talked about his son who lived in Minnesota. I was confident that I was in good hands. Everything would be fine in the morning and he would do some follow-up on the recent replacement of the head gasket.

The car was ready by the time I got up in the morning. The garage had charged the battery, repaired the faulty alternator and re-torqued the cylinder head bolts — all for less than twenty bucks. Gotta love those Latin American mechanics!

MARK'S ADVENTURE ALERT

Location: Tierra del Fuego, Argentina

Subject: Mark and the Mechanics

The world of oil filters and air filters. The Auto Parts Store! It was foreign territory to me. When I was preparing for my initial departure over four years ago, I listened in awe as the manager explained why his heartfelt recommendation of an air filter for my motor differed from that of the auto manufacturer. Something about blah blah blah if I recall correctly. This was his world. Nuts and bolts. Belts and brake shoes. Fluids and flanges. What is a flange anyway? Do cars even have them?

It made my brain fog over (and still does) just thinking about cataloguing the hundreds and hundreds of gizmos and doodads for the hundreds and hundreds of different makes and models. I had been worried that I was biting off more than I could chew, embarking on this automotive adventure by myself.

History has proven that the answer would be "no." However, it certainly provided some trials for me. But the mobility and freedom that it provided me more than made up for the challenges. It also introduced me to a world I would not have known, the world of the Latin American auto mechanic.

I have come to expect getting shaken down by the occasional cop or border official now and then. But never by Latin American auto mechanics. As a group I have found them to be the extremely forthright and friendly. In fact, some of my favorite people along the way were mechanics. Many of them salt-of-the-earth kind of guys, some of them real characters who I enjoyed immensely.

> The problems I had to repair certainly would have bankrupted
> me in the U.S. for two reasons. As a traveler they gotcha over
> a barrel, they know it and exploit it. Many people assume they
> will be taken advantage of by mechanics and dentists. When your
> car is broken down, or your mouth, it's impractical, even
> downright difficult to get a second opinion. And would you
> understand the second one any better? South of the border it
> never seemed to occur to them to take advantage of me. Reason
> number two, is the parts! Down here they will weld it back
> together or just make a new one right there on the spot.
>
> Having an old car break down once in while is normal and
> expected. Repeat with me the automotive mantra: "It's all part
> of the adventure." But two and three times a week gets really
> old, really fast. A little louder now, with more feeling:
> "It's all part of the adventure! IT'S ALL PART OF THE
> ADVENTURE!"

Not far out of Rio Grande, another automotive-related opportunity to stop and smell the roses was forced upon us. It was in the tiny town of Tolhuin, known for its seasonal trout fishing. While not an actual breakdown this time, we experienced a significant threat. It was just prior to the last segment of highway before Ushuaia. There were signs posted with serious warnings about the lack of services ahead. Last chance before Ushuaia. No pavement and no services from here to the end of the world. Do not pass go, do not collect $200!

Blanco Billy was leaning severely to one side. I looked underneath her and noticed that the repaired suspension was fractured again. The collapse made the right side of the back bumper a full eight inches lower than the left. It had to be taken care of before we could continue. There would be many more options for mechanics in Ushuaia than there were in this teensy town. Had it been paved, I might have been tempted to go for it. But with a bumpy dirt road ahead there was no way. We had to remember the automotive mantra, "It's all part of the adventure…."

There was only one gas station in town. After a quick look underneath, the attendant was emphatic that he could not help us. Our only hope, he said, was the *gomeria* about a block down the street. What is a *gomeria*, you ask? It is a shop that specializes in tires. Typically in Argentina and much of Latin America, gas stations don't do tires. It's a, "we don't do windows" sort of thing. You must go to a *gomeria* to even have air added to your tires.

Goma means rubber in Spanish. Hence the name: *gomeria*. Hence the new name I assigned to our attendant — Gomer! His real name was Lucio, but Gomer just seemed to fit. After a few minutes underneath Blanco Billy, Gomer slid out nodding his head slowly. He could do it, he said, but not before the end of the day. We would need a place to stay and Gomer said he could help us. He sent us into town to the local bakery/café and told us to ask for Mateo. Mateo worked behind the counter and also owned a vacation rental cabin. We enjoyed a cup of hot chocolate surrounded by the smell of cinnamon rolls while Mateo finished what he was doing. It wasn't long before he threw his white apron on the counter and the three of us were strolling down the street, downhill towards Lake Tolhuin.

It was about four blocks to the little log cabin. It was a two-bedroom place with enough beds for eight. The living area had a large fireplace and a small TV. The kitchen was fully furnished with utensils and basic condiments. It was more than we needed, and the price was much more than we had been paying for hotel rooms. Mateo could see that we were undecided. He told us to hang out as long as we needed to make up our minds. He said we could find him back at the bakery. He left us the keys without even asking our names.

We decided to splurge and take it for the night. I liked the fireplace and the proximity to the pristine mountain lake, plus the TV put a smile on Yolanda's face. That is, until she turned it on. There were only two stations and both had pitiful reception so it was easy to coax her out for a walk along the lake.

We were on a romantic roll, our hands and hearts connected as we strolled. The early afternoon sun peeked out from behind the clouds. Pine trees surrounded us, lending their fragrant contribution to the fresh mountain air. Back in the cabin by mid-afternoon, we lit a fire in the fireplace. Then we started a fire in the bedroom, so to speak. We had the rest of the day to ourselves and took advantage of it. We got wild and crazy without partying beforehand. There was a new level of intimacy we had not shared before. Intimacy without alcohol, what a concept! It was another breakthrough for us, and a very memorable afternoon.

We decided to venture out into the town for some dinner. Our options were limited to two or three places. We chose the pizza and sandwich pub where we found a couple of locals shooting pool and one young family enjoying dinner out. And this was the busiest place in town! Everyone seemed peaceful and content. Our faces too, must have been glowing with contentment after our private time together. In addition to that, we were filled with the anticipation of reaching our goal within 24 hours.

We slept soundly that night until 7:30 a.m., when there came a rambunctious banging on our front door. It was Gomer; Blanco Billy was ready. Gomer wanted to be paid, and also wanted a ride back to the *gomeria*. Bleary-eyed, I threw on jeans and a coat and headed out with Gomer. He said he had worked most of the night and complained of all of the problems that had come up. He wanted more money then he had quoted. It was the first time this had happened with all of the mechanics I had encountered. Part of me wanted to argue, but it was too early in the morning to even talk. At the shop he invited me inside for some *mate* and *media lunas*. *Media luna*, half moon, refers to a pastry known elsewhere as a croissant. *Mate* requires a little explanation as well, but no translation. *Mate* is maté.

Mate is the national hot beverage of Argentina. Gas stations have hot water dispensers for the express purpose of making it. You see people on the streets, in parks, just about everywhere carrying their hot water thermos bottle and their special round *mate* mug complete with a silver straw.

Editor's note: You said it needs no translation then you gave one.

Author's note: I couldn't help myself. It's different from coca mate and even more different than the Australian version.

First you fill the mug with the green herb that is *mate*. We are not talking a tea bag here, you fill the whole mug over the brim with the dry herb and then pour your hot water in. After a minute or two, you start sucking on your special silver straw with a built-in strainer on the bottom. A couple of sucks later, all the liquid is gone. Since you still have a mug full of green muck, you pour in some more hot water and pass it along to your pal (your mate, if you're Australian), or even a perfect stranger in some cases. For example, at the border crossing between Argentina and Chile, I was invited into a circle of five bureaucrats behind a counter passing a mate mug around. I was a little leery of sharing spit with a bunch of government workers. Since I needed my papers processed, I didn't want to be rude, so I joined in and took my turn.

At the *gomeria*, sharing with just Gomer was no biggie. When it was my turn, I added sugar to cut the bitter taste. You get a coffee-like buzz from the stuff though allegedly the drink had no caffeine, but rather matteine, said to have many health benefits. It felt like caffeine to me.

Gomer had a fire burning inside of an old oil drum to warm the disheveled little office. He wanted to hear some of the details of my trip. We chatted between pours of *mate* and Gomer told me about his motorcycle tour of South America á la The Motorcycle Diaries about Che Guevara. He had a large calendar featuring a topless women on motorcycles adorning the wall. My attention to the topless beauty led to a discussion of his dreams. His goal was to one day convert the *gomeria* into a strip club. The plan didn't seem to fit into the social structure of the small, family-oriented community. "Truckers!" he said confidently, "plenty of customers passing through."

Gomer offered to fix *asado*, a traditional Argentine barbeque, for lunch. I declined. We were just hours from the end of the world. I could feel it and I could not wait. I headed back to Yolanda at the cabin and we departed mid-morning.

After four years, I was on the final stretch of my journey, with Yolanda at my side. Blanco Billy weaved through the winding roads of a vast mountain range. The roads were lined with blossoming wildflowers and the views of the surrounding area were magnificent. The spring air provided a feeling of youth and enthusiasm as we came down from the mountains, drove through countryside and entered the tourist section of the small town of Ushuaia. At that point, it had seemed like just another stop on our journey, searching for a hotel room in high season. The accomplishment of my goal had not yet hit me. After several stops, we found a hotel toward the end of the tourist strip. Yolanda relaxed in the room, while I took a walk on the outskirts of town. Hiking along the waterfront, the enormity of the moment finally struck me.

MARK'S ADVENTURE ALERT

Location: Ushuaia, Argentina

Subject: I Freakin' Made It!!

Speaking directly into my digital audio recorder, I captured the raw emotions of the moment. Here is the transcription (minus a few expletives):

Hello. Ushuaia! The freakin' end of the world! Whooo! Feeling incredible.

Incredibly alive! I had written recently about perhaps it feeling a bit anti-climactic or even being depressing. And in fact I feel more alive than I remember feeling in a long time. I don't think it's just reaching the goal. I think it might be some personal growth and the energy of all the light, maybe I'm just sleep deprived. It's freakin' gorgeous.

> *It's incredible. It's 9:00 p.m. and almost broad daylight. I'm standing next to the Argentine Naval Base surveying the waterfront area. Snowcapped peaks! Almost surrounded by snowcapped peaks. In fact I am surrounded. There's water, there's a channel, and I think I'm looking across the Beagle Channel at some islands. I'll have to look at a map. I'm standing on the edge! Wow! I'm standing on the edge overlooking the water. The whole of both of the Americas are behind me.*
>
> *Endings and new beginnings.*
>
> Then I shut off my recorder and continued walking along the waterfront. Almost immediately I came to this giant slogan emblazoned on the cement, the words nearly echoing my last recorded words. "El Fin del Mundo, El Principio del Todo" "The End of the World, the Beginning of Everything." Pretty cool.
>
> In my mind I was flopping back and forth between my accomplishment and what will be next for me. I was thinking about what I've done and what I will do when it hits me. This moment! The one in between "have done" and "will do!" That's what I am feeling. Being alive right now. A metaphor for every moment of my life. Celebrating life for its own sake.
>
> I feel somehow I have come full circle since I departed over four years ago... in some ways not much has changed. The Kate Bush quote that inspired me back then still seems to apply. "Feels like something good is gonna happen." That's the feeling, but the words are not exactly accurate. More like "Something good IS happening. RIGHT NOW."
>
> Sounds crazy but ... this moment is being born!

I was not the same guy who had pulled out of his driveway in Tucson four years ago. Would anyone recognize me when I returned? I felt like I had broken the bonds to my own cultural identity and gained a new global perspective. The U.S. will always be my home, but my relationship to it had changed. My exposure to foreign cultures helped me recognize my own identity, as well as the bond that connects us all. The journey had opened up my eyes and my heart. I got to see and feel both the good and the bad of different cultures. In so doing, I gained a perspective of my own culture and its ups and downs. I am learning not to judge any of it.

We celebrated in our hotel room that evening with a bottle of champagne. Our hotel was on the main tourist street that paralleled the waterfront. From a small window in the corner of our room, we had a view over some rooftops toward the scenic docks of Ushuaia Bay. The strange ambient lighting enhanced the beauty and lent a mysterious mood and a palpable energy to the scene.

One bottle did not last long. Though it was close to midnight, the deceptive sunlight had elevated our energy levels, so the night remained young. Yolanda had picked up on the electricity of the accomplished goal and was just as excited. I was dispatched to retrieve more champagne. I returned from my mission to the liquor store with two more bottles!

Yolanda was in rare form that night. We had a blast taking digital pictures in the room and out the window— which I hoped would jog her memory the next day. She is less than two-thirds my size, but drank more than two-thirds of the champagne. You don't need to do the math to figure out that she was feeling more of the effects than I was (and you can guess the aftermath).

As the doting nursemaid, I held her hair back out of her face as her body indicated that she'd had enough. I cleaned her up and tucked her into bed with a smile and a kiss. There was no doubt she was done for the evening, but I remained awake and alert. I was on a roll, buzzed on more than just the champagne. The remaining twilight called out to me. I could not resist a walk through the quiet city streets along the waterfront.

The crisp, salty air cooled my cheeks and filled my lungs. My earlier revelation with my digital recorder had sunk in and solidified in my gut. Call it my adventure epiphany. Adventures behind me, adventures ahead of me, and the most authentic and real adventure welling up in my chest. The adventure of being alive in the moment.

My perennial question, "Why am I doing this?" had been obliterated and rendered obsolete. What would be my next adventure? Who knows? Who cares? It absolutely does not matter. The adventure of a lifetime lay behind me... and the possibilities of a budding new relationship ahead of me .... Both were wonderful as well as wonderfully irrelevant to what I was experiencing right then as I strolled along.

The end of the world, the beginning of everything! Every completion is another beginning, happening again and again in every moment! Powerfully and profoundly simple, I felt it in my bones. The future and past connect through the only thing that is real— being alive in the moment! Yes, it's true— I'm gonna die, but right now, I'm Alive!

The End

...and the Beginning

Mark McMahon

Have fun visiting some of the author's online resources:

LiveYourAdventure.com

PortableProfessional.com

FrogFreak.com

Mark-eting.com